THE AGE OF THE CRUSADES
The Near East from the eleventh century to 1517

A History of the Near East
General Editor: Professor P. M. Holt

* The Prophet and the Age of the Caliphates: the Islamic Near East from the sixth to the eleventh century
  Hugh Kennedy

* The Age of the Crusades: the Near East from the eleventh century to 1517
  P. M. Holt

The Rise of the Ottoman Empire 1300–1574
  C. Kafadar

The Decline of the Ottoman Empire 1574–1792
  R. C. Repp

* The Making of the Modern Near East 1792–1923
  M. E. Yapp

* The Near East since the First World War
  M. E. Yapp

* Medieval Persia 1040–1797
  David Morgan

* *Already published*

The Age of the Crusades

The Near East from the eleventh century to 1517

P. M. Holt

Longman
London and New York

Longman Group UK Limited
Longman House, Burnt Mill, Harlow
Essex CM20 2JE, England
and Associated Companies throughout the world

Published in the United States of America
by Longman Inc., New York

First published 1986
Sixth impression 1993

British Library Cataloguing in Publication Data

Hot, P.M.
The age of the crusades: the Near East from the eleventh century to 1517.
– (A History of the Near East)
1. Crusades 2. Islamic Empire – History –
750–1258 3. Islamic Empire – History –
1258–1517
I. Title II. Series
956′.01 DS38.6

ISBN 0-582-49302-1 ppr
ISBN 0 582 49303 X csd

Library of Congress Cataloguing in Publication Data

Holt P.M. (Peter Malcolm)
The Age of the Crusades.
(A History of the Near East)
Bibliography: p.
Includes index
1. Islamic Empire – History. I. Title II. Series
DS38.3.H65 1986 909′.097671 84-27801
ISBN 0-582-49303-x
ISBN 0-49302-1 (pbk.)

Set in 10/12pt VIP Bembo

Produced by Longman Singapore Publishers (Pte) Ltd.
Printed in Singapore

Contents

List of Genealogical Tables

List of Maps

Foreword

This volume is intended to offer the student and the general reader an account of the political history of the eastern Mediterranean lands from the eve of the First Crusade in the late eleventh century to the Ottoman conquest of Syria and Egypt in 1516–17. Although much has been written on some aspects of this period, notably the Crusades, for which European sources are abundant, others have been left in obscurity; there is, for example, no comprehensive modern treatment in English of the Mamluk sultanate, although this was the great power of the eastern Mediterranean for two hundred years and more. It is still true today that any general survey of developments in these centuries must be uneven in its treatment, sometimes because of an actual lack of primary source-materials, and often because of the irregular progress of research and publication in various parts of the field. My hope is, nevertheless, that this book will serve as an introduction to a fascinating period, relevant in one respect to the history of medieval Europe, whose rulers shared many of the political and administrative problems of their Muslim counterparts, in another to that of the modern Near East, whose peoples are the heirs of the region's past.

My thanks are particularly due to my former colleague, Professor V. L. Ménage, for his advice on the forms of Mamluk names. For anomalies and errors in this as in other matters, the responsibility is mine.

P. M. HOLT
Kirtlington
November 1984

Acknowledgements

We are indebted to Franz Steiner Verlag GmbH, Wiesbaden, for an extract from al-Ṣafadī, *al-Wāfī bi'l-wafayāt,* VI, ed. S. Dedering (Wiesbaden 1972), pp. 182–4; and an extract from P.M. Holt (trans.), *The memoirs of a Syrian prince* (Wiesbaden 1983), pp. 16–17. Also to the Editorial Board of the School of Oriental and African Studies, University of London, for permission to quote from 'Some observations on the 'Abbāsid of caliphate of Cairo', *BSOAS* XLVII/3, 1984, pp. 501–7.

We have been unable to trace the copyright holder in *Kitāb al-sulūk li–ma'rifat duwal al–mulūk* (Cairo 1970) and *Kitāb al–mawā'iẓ wa'l-i'tibār bi–dhikr al–khiṭaṭ wa'l'āthār* (Beirut) and would appreciate any information that would enable us to do so.

Note: Names, Titles and Dates

NAMES AND TITLES

There was an elaborate system of nomenclature among the medieval Arabic-speaking peoples. In full, each individual's name consisted of four elements:

1. The personal name (Arabic, *ism*). This was most commonly Arabic, e.g. Aḥmad, Fāṭima, or Qur'anic, e.g. Ibrāhīm, Maryam, but many warriors and rulers bore Turkish or Mongol names, e.g. Aktay (meaning "White colt"), Salāmish for the Mongolian Sülemish.
2. The formal name (*kunya*), sometimes inaccurately called the patronymic. Originally this was a courteous way of indicating or addressing a person without using the *ism*. These names are of the form Abū —— and Umm ——, i.e. "Father of ——", "Mother of ——". It might indicate actual parenthood, e.g. the Prophet's *kunya* was Abu'l-Qāsim from the name of his son al-Qāsim. In this period the *kunya* is usually metaphorical, e.g. Abu'l-Futūḥ, "The Father of Victories", i.e. "The Victorious".
3. The patronymic proper (*nasab*) indicating the individual's father or extended pedigree. This takes the form ibn —— or bint ——, i.e. "son of ——", "daughter of ——", abbreviated b. or bt. The abbreviation B. —— stands for Banū —— , literally "Sons of ——" indicating a tribe or clan. The ancestry is always shown in the male line. Since the fathers of Mamluks were almost always unknown, Mamluks had the conventional *nasab* ibn ʿAbdallāhi, i.e. "the son of ʿAbdallāh".
4. The generic epithet (*nisba*) indicating a group (religious, ethnic or otherwise) to which the individual belonged, e.g. al-Yahūdī (the Jew), al-Miṣrī (the Egyptian), al-Kurdī (the Kurd), al-Ṣāliḥī (the

Mamluk of al-Ṣāliḥ). The *nisba* was an adjective ending in -ī (masc.) or -iyya (fem.) and several might be appended to a name.

A ruler, a member of a ruling group or a dignitary might have a title or honorific (*laqab*) prefixed to his name. Apart from titles of office (e.g. *al-sulṭān*, *al-wazīr*), there are in this period two types of *laqab* which are of an honorific nature:

1. Of the form al-Malik ("the King") followed by an adjective, e.g. Nūr al-Dīn's *laqab* of al-Malik al-ʿĀdil ("the Just King"). *Laqabs* of this type were borne by all male members of the Ayyubid clan, whether or not they were actual rulers. Under the Mamluk sultanate, a *laqab* was usually borne only by a reigning sultan.
2. Of the form —— al-Dīn, i.e. "—— of the Faith", or usually for a reigning sultan —— al-Dunyā wa'l-Dīn, i.e. "—— of the World and the Faith". "Saladin" is the Frankish corruption of the *laqab* Ṣalāḥ al-Dīn, "the Goodness of the Faith". During the Mamluk sultanate, all Mamluks bore honorifics of this type, and by the end of the period Sayf al-Dīn, "the Sword of the Faith" was the one almost invariably used.

A ruler's style was usually augmented in inscriptions and elsewhere by a number of other titles which express his supposed qualities, powers and functions. Territorial and ethnic designations, where they occur, are complimentary or propagandist rather than descriptive, e.g. al-Ṣāliḥ Ayyūb (637–47/1240–9) who ruled over Egypt and part of Syria is styled "the sultan of the Arabs and the Persians, the king of Hind, Sind and the Yemen, the king of Ṣanʿā', Zabīd and Aden".

In accordance with the above analysis, the name and style of Saladin are as follows: (honorific 1) Al-Malik al-Nāṣir; (honorific 2) Ṣalāḥ al-Dunyā wa'l-Dīn; (*Kunya*) Abu'l-Muẓaffar; (*Ism*) Yūsuf; (*Nasab*) b. Ayyūb b. Shādhī; (*Nisba*) al-Kurdī.

The part of the name which is conventionally used by modern writers is quite arbitrary. Ayyubid rulers (apart from Saladin) are known by part of their first honorifics, e.g. al-Kāmil for al-Malik al-Kāmil, al-Ṣāliḥ for al-Malik al-Ṣāliḥ, and Mamluk sultans by their personal names, e.g. Baybars, Barkuk. Arabic authors of this period are usually referred to by a patronymic, e.g. the historians Ibn al-Athīr, Ibn Taghrībirdī, but the *nisba* is also commonly used, e.g. al-Maqrīzī, and sometimes the *kunya*, e.g. Abu'l-Fidā'.

DATES

The Muslim era opens with the *Hijra* (conventionally spelt Hegira), i.e. the Flight or Emigration of the Prophet from Mecca to Medina in AD 622. Muslim years are therefore indicated by the abbreviation AH (*Anno Hegirae*). The Muslim year consists of twelve lunar months and is therefore approximately eleven days shorter than the solar year of the Western (Julian or Gregorian) calendar. To find the Western (AD) equivalent to Muslim (AH) dates and vice versa, conversion tables are necessary. A useful compendium is G. S. P. Freeman-Grenville, *The Muslim and Christian calendars*, London 1963. It should be noted that the Muslim day begins at sunset and thus straddles part of two Western days.

In the Notes and Bibliography, where place names and/or dates are enclosed in brackets, this signifies that this information is not given on the title page of the related work.

Introduction: The Lands and their Peoples

The area of which the history will be surveyed in subsequent chapters consists of three main regions: in the north, Anatolia (substantially the modern Turkish Republic); in the centre, geographical Syria or the western Fertile Crescent comprising the modern states of Syria, Lebanon, Jordan and Israel; in the south, the Nile valley, now divided between Egypt and the Sudan. Each of these regions has its distinctive geographical characteristics, which have influenced both its own history and the relations of the regions with one another.

The greater part of Anatolia is a peninsula. To the north is the Black Sea with a narrow outlet by the Bosporus, the Sea of Marmara and the Dardanelles to the Aegean Sea on the west – a channel then as now of great strategic importance. The Mediterranean proper lies to the south of the peninsula. To its east lie the great mountain-ranges of the Armenian massif in which rise the headwaters of three major rivers, the Araxes (Turkish, Aras), flowing eastwards into the Caspian Sea, and the Tigris (Arabic, Dijla) and Euphrates (Arabic, al-Furāt) setting their course ultimately south-eastwards to the Persian (or Arabian) Gulf through the modern state of Iraq. South of the upper valleys of the Euphrates and Araxes lies Lake Van. From this highland knot two mountain-systems run westwards along the northern and southern coasts of Anatolia respectively. The northern range or Pontic Mountains leaves only a narrow coastal plain with few harbours. Among the ancient cities of the coast is Trebizond (Turkish, Trabzon), where a Byzantine state maintained its independent existence from the thirteenth to the fifteenth century. The southern mountain-system, known generically as the Taurus, is more complex and in parts higher than the Pontic Mountains. The main range extends westwards to reach the sea beyond the Gulf of Antalya at the south-western corner of the peninsula. The southern coastal plain is also generally narrow but there is one important exception – the plain of Cilicia lying between the Taurus and the Gulf of Alexandretta (Arabic, Iskandarūn), with Adana as its chief city. Here and in the surrounding mountains was the medieval kingdom of Lesser Armenia. The Amanus range, a branch of the Taurus, separates Cilicia from geographical Syria and the northern cities of Aleppo and Antioch, the latter now part of the Turkish Republic.

The country lying between the Pontic and Taurus ranges is a high plateau, drained on the west by rivers running down into the Aegean. Their valleys are among the most fertile parts of the peninsula, and have been the sites of important cities since Classical times, when western Anatolia was colonized by the Greeks. Some of the ancient harbours have been silted up, but Smyrna (Turkish, Izmir) was in the Middle Ages, as it still is, a great port, which served the Byzantines and Turks in their turn. Other historic cities lie on or near the passage from the Black Sea to the Aegean, above all Byzantine Constantinople or Turkish Istanbul, the guardian of the straits on the European shore. Nicaea (Turkish, Iznik) and Bursa, early capitals of the Seljukids and Ottomans, lie inland on the Asian side.

Geographical Syria, although a mountainous region like Anatolia, is essentially different in its configuration. Basically it consists of two parallel highland ranges, running north and south and divided by a rift-valley. The northern sector of the rift-valley forms the bed of the River Orontes (Arabic, al-ʿĀṣī), which after running north for most of its course turns sharply westwards past Antioch to enter the Mediterranean at the port known to the Crusaders as St Simeon and to the Arabs as al-Suwaydiyya. The River Leontes (Arabic, al-Liṭānī) and the Jordan, both running southwards, occupy the central sector of the rift-valley, which continues beyond the Dead Sea as the dry depression of the Wādi'l-ʿaraba until as the Gulf of ʿAqaba it merges into the Red Sea. The western highland range includes Jabal Anṣāriyya in the north, Mount Lebanon in the centre and the Palestinian hills in the south. The plain of the Biqāʿ with Baʿlabakk as its chief town lies between the Lebanon range on the west and Anti-Lebanon on the east. The coastal plain is usually narrow, and has since ancient times been the site of important ports. Among these in the period of the Crusades were Tripoli, Beirut, Acre and Jaffa. A break in the western highlands giving access from the coast to the interior is the plain of Esdraelon and its continuation, the valley of Jezreel, in northern Palestine. Of strategic importance from biblical times, this was the site of the critical battle of ʿAyn Jālūt between the Mamluks and the Mongols (658/1260). The eastern highland range is for the most part lower and more broken than the western, and forms the rim of the Syrian Desert, which extends to the Euphrates. On the fringe of the desert lies the great southern city of Damascus in an oasis watered by the River Baradā, which flows down from the Anti-Lebanon range to lose itself in the sands.

The desert and mountains of the Sinai peninsula separate the western Fertile Crescent from the Nile valley, where since ancient times human life has been able to subsist, and civilization to flourish, within the range of the annual inundation. The most extensive area of cultivation is, and has always been, the Delta, lying between the two branches of the Nile which fork below Cairo and reach the sea at Damietta in the east and Rosetta in the west respectively. Between Cairo and the First Cataract above Aswān is the long, narrow, inhabited stretch of Upper Egypt. Chief among the towns on the Nile banks at this period was Qūṣ, whence a route ran across the eastern desert to the Red Sea coast. The First Cataract formed until modern times a natural frontier on the south of Egypt as the deserts did on the east and west. Above it in the upper valley of the Nile was the land of the Nubians, a different people from the Egyptians with (at this time) a different language and religion. Beyond the Nubians and their neighbours in the eastern desert, the nomadic Beja, were the legendary tribes of the unexplored heart of Africa.

Travel or transport over any considerable distance in Egypt was by the Nile, but elsewhere a network of land-routes linked the principal towns and ports. From Baghdad, which until it fell to the Mongols in 656/1258 was the main emporium of the eastern Fertile Crescent, travellers and goods went by river to al-Raqqa on the Euphrates and thence to Aleppo, the chief town of northern Syria, to Antioch and the Mediterranean ports of St Simeon and Latakia (Arabic, al-Lādhiqiyya). Aleppo was also the northern terminus of the great spinal route of Syria, which ran northwards from Damascus through Ḥimṣ (conventionally spelt Homs) and Ḥamāh. Damascus was the assembly-point for pilgrims going south to the Holy Cities of Mecca and Medina in the Ḥijāz. Two important branches from the Aleppo–Damascus route passed through breaks in the western highlands. The shorter linked Ḥimṣ with the coast at Tripoli. The longer crossed the upper Jordan above Lake Tiberias at Jisr Banāt Yaʿqūb (i.e. the Bridge of Jacob's Daughters, "Jacob's Ford" to the Crusaders), and passed through Galilee to the Palestinian coastal plain. Then from Gaza it traversed the Sinai peninsula to the Delta.

The routes of the northern arc of the Fertile Crescent were linked with those of Anatolia, but they constituted a distinct system formed by geography and the historical fact of Byzantine rule. The main Anatolian routes radiated from the north-western corner of the peninsula, the nearest part to Constantinople across the Bosporus. Chief among them was the military road to the south-eastern Byzantine territories, which had been a threatened area since the Arab conquests of the first/seventh century. This route ran from Nicaea up into the central plateau at Dorylaeum (Turkish, Eskishehir). Thence one branch went south-eastwards to Philomelium (Akshehir) and Iconium (Konya), through the Cilician Gates, the pass across the Taurus, to the plain of Cilicia. This was the route taken by the First Crusade in 1097. Another route made its way across the centre of the plateau with branches to Cilicia, Caesarea (Kayseri), Sebasteia (Sivas) and the towns of the upper Euphrates and Araxes. Finally, the north-west of Anatolia was connected with the southern coast by a route passing through Cotyaeum (Kütahya) to the port of Attaleia (Antalya).

The society of the Islamic lands of the eastern Mediterranean was a symbiosis of three sub-societies: the nomads, the cultivators and the townspeople. Nomadic Arabs had played an important part in the initial spread of Islam; they had provided the warriors for the conquering armies and the garrisons for the conquered provinces. Through intermarriage with the indigenous peoples of the Muslim empire they were an agent in the arabization of much of the Near and Middle East. There were, however, tribal Arabs who had never left, or had gone back to, the nomadic life of their pre-Islamic ancestors. These were to be found in the original homeland, the Arabian peninsula and its northern continuation, the steppe (usually called the Syrian Desert) between the arms of the Fertile Crescent. Other nomad Arabs had migrated to the desert fringes of the Nile valley. In the fourth/tenth and fifth/eleventh centuries, when the ʿAbbasid caliphate was weak, Arab tribal chiefs succeeded in establishing territorial principalities centred in one or other of the towns of the Fertile Crescent. A notable Arab dynasty of this kind was that of the Hamdanids, who ruled in Mosul and Aleppo (see below, p. 13). Even later, a large tribe strategically placed was a factor of importance in the politics of the region. Thus Āl Faḍl, a division of the tribe of Rabīʿa, nomads of the Syrian Desert, were alternately coaxed and coerced by the Ayyubids and Mamluks, who bestowed on the head of their paramount clan the title of *amīr al-ʿArab*, i.e. chief of the [nomad] Arabs. An important function of the Arab tribesmen in the Mamluk period from the later seventh/thirteenth century was the service of the *barīd*, the royal mail carried by post-horses, which provided a communication and intelligence network throughout the sultan's dominions. The Arab tribesmen in Egypt were favoured by the Fatimid caliphs between the fourth/tenth and sixth/twelfth centuries, and they played an important part at court and in politics. Shāwar and Ḍirghām, rivals for the office of *wazīr* in the reign of the Caliph al-ʿĀḍid (555–67/1160–71), were both Arabs. Under the Ayyubids, the Arabs of Egypt lost their ascendancy and their ultimate downfall as a politically significant element occurred under the Mamluks. The Sultan al-Muʿizz Aybeg suppressed a serious tribal revolt in 651/1253, and a long period of repression, migration and sedentarization followed.

As well as the Arabs, there were two other ethnic groups who lived as nomads in the eastern Mediterranean lands. The Berbers were chiefly to be found in North Africa west of the Nile valley, but part of one important tribe, Hawwāra, which shared in the Fatimid conquest of Egypt, was settled in the Buḥayra, the semi-desert province west of the Rosetta branch. Late in the eighth/fourteenth century, some of these Hawwāra were transferred to Upper Egypt, which they frequently dominated until the time of Muḥammad ʿAlī Pasha in the early nineteenth century. The second group, nomadic Turkish tribesmen, usually called Turcomans, accompanied the Seljukids on their advance westwards in the fifth/eleventh century. Some found territory and grazing for their flocks and herds in the Syrian Desert, but the majority flooded into Anatolia when the Byzantine frontier defences broke down after the battle of Manzikert in 463/1071 – the start of a process by which Christian and hellenized Anatolia was transformed into the Muslim Turkish homeland.

Although the cultivators settled in the villages presumably formed the majority of the population in the eastern Mediterranean lands, their history is even more fragmentary and obscure than that of the nomads, who from time to time disturbed the social and political order. In Syria and Egypt the peasantry were for the most part Muslim and Arabic-speaking; in Anatolia by the end of the period, Muslim and Turkish-speaking. Speech and religion, however, give uncertain indications of the ethnic origins of the cultivators – how far they were descended from the Arab, Berber and Turcoman immigrants, how far from the former inhabitants of the region. Nor is it easy to assess economic and social changes in their condition in these centuries, although it may be said with certainty that the migrations of the steppe peoples of Central Asia, the Seljuk Turks in the fifth/eleventh century and the Mongols in the seventh/thirteenth, by causing movements of refugees disturbed both rural and urban society outside the territories they actually raided and occupied. Another factor in the deteriorization in the condition of the cultivators in this period was the *iqṭāʿ*, i.e. the grant to officers of land-tax to be levied directly from the peasantry, a consequence of the militarization of government.

The history of the eastern Mediterranean lands in this period is, as far as we know it, largely a history of the town-dwellers. Although the original conquering armies of Islam were recruited chiefly from the nomad Arab tribesmen, they were commanded, and the campaigns were planned, by an urban mercantile aristocracy, Quraysh of Mecca; and the towns became and remained the centres of Islam. Their origins were diverse. There were the three Holy Cities – Mecca, Medina and Jerusalem; the garrison cantonments of the Arab conquerors such as al-Fusṭāṭ, in Egypt, which had grown into great towns; the palaces and governmental complexes founded by particular dynasties, such as the Fatimid capital, Cairo, which had undergone a similar transformation; finally there were the ancient cities which entered on a new epoch with Islam, such as Damascus and Aleppo. In these and the other cities and towns there were three essential institutions, symbolizing respectively their religious, administrative and commercial significance: the Friday mosque (*jāmiʿ*) for the weekly observance of congregational prayer at which the ruler's name was recited in the sermon (*khuṭba*); the official quarter, which in great cities such as Cairo, Damascus and Aleppo was centred in the citadel; and the market (*sūq*), subdivided according to the crafts practised and commodities sold. The various quarters of the town were inhabited by separate communities, distinguished by their occupations, their ethnic origins or their religions. The whole was protected by a city wall.

The tripartite subdivision of the population into nomads, cultivators and townspeople was politically less significant than another grouping. On the one hand, there were the rulers and warriors, the military in the widest sense; on the other, the subject population. The militarization of society and government in the eastern Mediterranean lands was already far advanced by the late fifth/eleventh century, and was virtually complete 300 years later. The coming of the Seljuks initiated a new phase in which the rulers and warriors were principally of Turkish origin, either free-born Turks such as the Seljukid ruling clan and the Turcoman tribesmen, or Turks recruited as slaves (Arabic sing., *mamlūk*) outside Muslim territory, then converted, trained and emancipated to fight or to govern. The apogee of this system came with the establishment of the Mamluk sultanate in Egypt and Syria in the mid-seventh/thirteenth century. Another wave of central Asian conquerors, the Mongols, failed to overthrow the Mamluk sultanate and occupy these western territories. The one notable exception to the general Turkish military and political ascendancy in this period was the rule of the Kurdish Ayyubids, who were, however, in all but their ethnic origin a successor-dynasty to the Seljukids. At the end of the period during the ninth/fifteenth century, Circassian Mamluk sultans maintained the traditions of the previous Turkish Mamluks until they were overthrown by the Ottoman Turks.

As members of the community of Islam, the *Umma*, the rulers and warriors were theoretically equal in status under the Holy Law (*Sharīʿa*) with the other Muslims, their subjects. In practice, of course, this was not so: wealth, privilege and naked power overrode and often negated the ideal equality and brotherhood of all believers. The rulers were nevertheless deferential to the *Sharīʿa* and its experts, the scholars (*ʿulamāʾ*) and jurists (*fuqahāʾ*). In return, the *ʿulamāʾ* legitimated the rulers' frequently usurped authority: instances of overt opposition by an individual jurist are rare, by the *ʿulamāʾ* as a body virtually unknown. There is a familiar genre of anecdotes told for instance of Nūr al-Dīn, Saladin and al-Ẓāhir Baybars, which illustrate the formal submission of the ruler to the Holy Law – he appears before the judge (*qāḍī*) to answer a complaint made by a subject, wins the case and magnanimously compensates his opponent. The two royal virtues of piety and generosity are thus pleasingly exemplified.

Although the profession of Islam might be of little avail to an ordinary Muslim against a ruler or warrior, it was of great importance in defining his legal and social status by placing him on the more favourable side of the great division between believers and *dhimmīs*. The latter were the adherents of the tolerated religions – in this period and these lands, the Christians, Jews and Samaritans. In Egypt the great majority of Christians belonged to the Coptic Church, which had as its head the patriarch of Alexandria, and which was also established in Nubia and Ethiopia. The Orthodox (Melkite) Church had lost its formerly dominant position in Egypt on the ending of Byzantine rule by the Arab conquest, but in Syria it continued to be the chief Christian denomination. A smaller group, the Maronites, originally viewed as heretical by other oriental Christians, had by the time of the Crusades found refuge in Mount Lebanon, and from the late twelfth century entered into union with Rome. In Byzantine Anatolia the Orthodox Church was, of course, the state religion, although the Armenians had their own Church, regarded by the Orthodox as heretical. The Muslim rulers were uninterested in the niceties of Christian theology, and did not discriminate among the various churches.

The *dhimmīs* formed a protected minority, living under certain legal disabilities which might or might not be enforced, such as sumptuary regulations. They played a large part in the civil service of Muslim rulers. This was notably true of the Copts, who retained from pre-Islamic times a monopoly of the financial administration of Egypt. *Dhimmīs* were, however, debarred from a military career and from holding the great offices of state. Actual persecution was rare and sporadic. One serious episode in Cairo in 721/1321 followed a number of fires. The Christians were accused of arson and fell victims to mob violence, which the Sultan al-Nāṣir Muḥammad was unable to restrain. After this outburst, the persecution died down as quickly as it had begun.

It was thus to an area of considerable geographical diversity, divided among a number of rulers, and inhabited by peoples who differed in ethnic origins, speech and religion, that the Crusaders came at the end of the eleventh century. Their conquests and the establishment of the four Frankish states of Outremer – feudal Europe "beyond the sea" – was a factor, perhaps the essential catalyst, in bringing about the gradual political unification of two-thirds of the area. Muslim Syria was first brought under one ruler, then Egypt was integrated with it, and the Frankish states were reconquered, so that by the end of the thirteenth century all these territories were under the centralized government of the Mamluk sultanate. Meanwhile Seljukid Anatolia had been brought under Mongol domination. Among the Turkish successor-principalities there was one, still of recent origin at the end of the fourteenth century, the *beylik* of ʿOsmān Gazi, which was to grow into the Ottoman empire and to succeed the Mamluk sultanate as the greatest power in the Near East.

CHAPTER ONE

The Near East on the Eve of the First Crusade

When the Crusaders entered Syria in the autumn of 1097, there were two claimants to the headship of the *Umma*, the universal Muslim community. One was the ʿAbbasid caliph of Baghdad, al-Mustaẓhir; the other was al-Āmir, the Fatimid caliph of Cairo. The reason for this schism in the *Umma* lay far back in its history. The ʿAbbasid caliph was recognized by the majority group of Muslims, the Sunnīs, as the legitimate heir of the earliest successors of the Prophet, the Caliphs Abū Bakr, ʿUmar, ʿUthmān and ʿAlī. The ʿAbbasid dynasty, descendants of the Prophet's uncle al-ʿAbbās, had acquired the caliphate in a revolution which in 132/750 had overthrown the previous ruling family, the Umayyads. The founder of the Umayyad caliphate, Muʿāwiya (a remote cousin of the Prophet), had himself risen to power in 41/661 at the expense of ʿAlī.

ʿAlī was both a first cousin of the Prophet and the husband of his daughter, Fāṭima, by whom he had two sons, al-Ḥasan and al-Ḥusayn. The partisans of ʿAlī (in Arabic, Shīʿat ʿAlī), known generally as the Shīʿa or Shīʿīs, survived the downfall and murder of their leader, and in ensuing generations were transformed from an Arab political faction to a group widespread throughout the Muslim world, holding religious and political doctrines which were in some important respects different from and incompatible with those of the Sunnīs. They came to hold that ʿAlī and his descendants had an indefeasible divine right to be the *imāms*, the heads of the *Umma*, of which they were the infallible guides. To them the Umayyads and the ʿAbbasids alike were usurpers. The Shīʿa, however, differed among themselves in tracing the line of succession to the imamate among ʿAlī's posterity. One group, which developed as an esoteric, eschatological and subversive movement in the third/ninth century, was led by the alleged descendants of a great-great-great-grandson of ʿAlī named Ismāʿīl b. Jaʿfar al-Ṣādiq. This group, the Ismāʿīlīs, scored an outstanding success in 297/909, when they established their *imām* as the head of a territorial state in what is now Tunisia. So began the Fatimid caliphate, taking its name from the ancestress of the dynasty. Under al-Muʿizz, the fourth Fatimid caliph, Egypt was conquered in 358/969. Four years later the seat of the caliphate was transferred to the new capital of the Fatimids, Cairo.

By the late fifth/eleventh century neither the Fatimid caliph nor his ʿAbbasid rival held the reality of power. The ʿAbbasid caliphate had maintained effective supremacy over most of the Islamic lands for about 100 years from its establishment, but already in 138/756 a process of fragmentation had begun when an Umayyad prince, escaping from the destruction of his family by the ʿAbbasids, made himself the independent ruler of Muslim Spain. Autonomous rulers and dynasties subsequently proliferated elsewhere, preserving only the form of subordination to their ʿAbbasid suzerain. As their territorial possessions shrank, the caliphs themselves passed under the control of military chiefs who dominated the court and the administration. The earliest of these were the commanders of the caliphs' own guards; then in 334/945 Baghdad and the person of the caliph fell into the hands of a family originating from Daylam in north-western Persia, the Buwayhids or Buyids. The predicament of the Sunnī caliph was particularly ironical in that the new rulers and their Daylamite followers were Shīʿīs. They were not, however, Ismāʿīlīs, and they felt no obligations towards the Fatimids, while their attitude towards the Sunnīs remained tolerant. The nominal sovereignty of the ʿAbbasid caliph was retained.

In the middle years of the fifth/eleventh century a new power arose in north-eastern Persia, that of the Oghuz (Arabic, Ghuzz) Turcoman tribesmen under the leadership of the Seljuk family. In 447/1055 their chief, Tughrul Beg, entered Baghdad, where Buyid authority had collapsed. He received from the Caliph al-Qā'im the title of "sultan" in recognition that he was the effective "power" (Arabic, *sulṭān*) in the state. Unlike the Buyids, the Seljukids and their Turcoman followers were Sunnī Muslims, and as such intent on upholding the supremacy of the ʿAbbasid caliphate against external enemies and internal dissidents.

Under Tughrul Beg and his two successors, his nephew Alp-Arslan (455–65/1063–72) and the latter's son Malik-Shāh (465–85/1072–92), the Seljukid territories formed an extensive empire including what are now Iran and Iraq, and stretching into Syria. Meanwhile the house of Seljuk became increasingly assimilated to the Perso-Arabic Muslim society over which it ruled. The Turcoman tribesmen, the original military base of the dynasty, became an embarrassment to sultans whose economic strength depended on sedentary cultivators and urban merchants. Hence, like the caliphs before them, the Seljukids recruited standing armies of Turkish slaves, the Mamluks. The assimilation of the dynasty is epitomized in the name of the third sultan. Unlike his two predecessors, he did not bear a Turkish name but was called Malik-Shāh – a combination of the Arabic and Persian words for "king". Closely associated with Malik-Shāh throughout his reign was his wise and powerful minister, the *Wazīr* Niẓām al-Mulk – actually an honorific meaning "the Order of the Kingdom". The assassination of Niẓām al-Mulk, followed in a few weeks by the death of Malik-Shāh himself, marked the beginning of the decline of the Seljukid sultanate. A succession struggle ensued, from which in 488/1095 the eldest son of Malik-Shāh, Berkyaruk, emerged as sultan.

Even at the height of their power, the Seljukid sultans did not rule a centralized empire so much as an assemblage of provinces inhabited by diverse nationalities speaking different languages, the products of varying historical developments. The tendency towards fragmentation which showed after the death of Malik-Shāh was facilitated by the Seljukid tradition of rule by the family rather than by an individual monarch, in consequence of which members of the royal house held provinces in appanage. This was to have serious results for Syria at the time of the First Crusade.

Besides this Great Seljuk sultanate, there was in the late fifth/eleventh century another Seljukid sultanate in Anatolia (see below, Ch. 19). The westwards movement of the Oghuz Turcomans brought them up against the Armenian frontier regions of the Byzantine empire, which they penetrated and raided. Then in 463/1071 there took place a great and decisive pitched battle at Manzikert (Malāsjird) near Lake Van between the armies of Alp-Arslan and the Emperor Romanus Diogenes, in which the latter was defeated and captured. The Byzantine frontier defences were shattered, and the Turcomans broke through, no longer merely to raid but to extend permanently the range of their pastures, and ultimately to settle in Anatolia. In this they were in fact assisted by Byzantine faction-leaders during the power-struggle which followed the overthrow of Romanus Diogenes. The leadership among the Turcoman immigrants was assumed by a Seljukid prince, Süleymān, the son of a certain Kutlumush who had been killed in 456/1064 in a revolt against Alp-Arslan. It is significant of the changed situation in Anatolia that Süleymān's capital was Iznik (until recently the Byzantine city of Nicaea) in the far north-west. Like his Great Seljuk cousins, Süleymān was entitled "sultan", the territory in which he ruled being known as Rūm, i.e. the lands of the former Roman empire in the east.

Just as the ʿAbbasid caliphate in its debility had been taken over by powerful warrior-chiefs ruling in the caliph's name, the Fatimid caliphate had similarly declined and passed under military control. The original power-base of the Fatimids in North Africa had been constituted by Berber tribal warriors. After the transfer of the caliphate to Cairo, Turkish Mamluk troops were added, as well as Daylamites. Also, like previous rulers in Egypt, the Fatimids imported Blacks (Arabic, *Sūdān*) as slaves from Nubia. Risings and faction-fights among these heterogeneous forces were not uncommon. After the death of the autocratic and probably insane Caliph al-Ḥākim in 411/1021, his successors were feeble rulers, and the growing insubordination of the armed forces culminated in a long period of anarchy from 451/1060 to 465/1073. At its height the Black troops dominated Upper Egypt, into which they had been driven by their opponents, the Berbers held the Delta, and the Turks Cairo itself, where they forced the Caliph al-Mustanṣir to sell his vast treasures as they pillaged his great library. The anarchy ended only when the caliph called to his aid another war-lord, the governor of Acre (at the time a Fatimid possession), Badr al-Jamālī, a Mamluk of Armenian origin. He landed in Egypt with his own reliable Armenian troops, restored order, and ruled (formally as *wazīr*, actually as military dictator) from 466/1074 until his death twenty years later at the age of over eighty. He was succeeded in the wazirate by his son, al-Afḍal Shāhanshāh.

Al-Mustanṣir himself died a few months later. The respective powers of the caliph and the *wazīr* were demonstrated at this juncture when al-Afḍal set aside the appointed heir to the caliphate, a middle-aged man named Nizār, and installed his much younger brother, al-Mustaʿlī (487/1094). This arbitrary act of political calculation, which was followed by the revolt, defeat and death of Nizār, produced a schism in the Ismāʿīlī movement which still represented the ideological basis of the regime. Its dynamism and driving force now passed from the Fatimid caliphate in Egypt to a militant splinter group in the east. This was the organization known as the New Preaching (Arabic, *al-daʿwa al-jadīda*), founded by a Persian Ismāʿīlī named Ḥasan-i Ṣabbāḥ, who had already in 483/1090 captured the fortress of Alamūt in Daylam as a base for operations against the Great Seljuks. The New Preaching, which later developed an important branch in Syria, has passed into Western historical writing as the Order of Assassins. Lacking military power, the order had recourse to political murder to destroy its opponents and spread terror. The Assassins' first important victim was the *Wazīr* Niẓām al-Mulk.

Across the Red Sea from Egypt, western Arabia was a region of marginal historical and political importance at this time. In the Ḥijāz were the two Holy Cities of Mecca and Medina, which were of permanent significance as religious centres and places of pilgrimage, the former containing the sanctuary of the Kaʿba, to which Muslims throughout the world turn in prayer. Medina had been the first capital of the Muslim empire, but had long since lost this position. In the late fifth/eleventh century both cities, although nominally under Fatimid suzerainty, were ruled by dynasties of local origin, claiming descent from the Prophet. The Yemen in the south-west of Arabia, lying remote from the centres of Sunnī power, was a place of refuge for minority groups of the Shīʿa. At the beginning of this period the principal power in the Yemen was the Sulayhid dynasty, whose founder, ʿAlī b. Muḥammad, had captured Ṣanʿāʾ in 455/1063 and Aden in the following year. The Sulayhids were Ismāʿīlīs and nominal vassals of the Fatimid caliphs.

Thus the great powers in the Near East at the time of the First Crusade were three: the Great Seljuk sultanate, the Seljuk sultanate of Rūm and the military wazirate which ruled in the name of the Fatimid caliphate. Although Anatolia had been almost wholly lost to the Byzantine empire after Manzikert, a revival had begun with the accession of a vigorous statesman and soldier, Alexius Comnenus, in 1081. At the meeting-place of the interests and rivalries of these powers lay Syria, where the political situation had long been extremely complex. Under the Umayyad caliphs, Syria had been the seat of the caliphate, a position it lost with the ʿAbbasid revolution and never regained. When the ʿAbbasid caliphate declined, Egypt passed under the rule, first of two autonomous gubernatorial dynasties, the Tulunids (254–92/868–905) and the Ikhshidids (323–58/935–69), then of the Fatimids, and Syria became a debatable land between the power based in Iraq and the power based in Egypt. Moreover, as caliphal control weakened, there was a revival of Arab tribal rule in Syria. This did not lead to greater unity, since the tribes fell into two competing groups formed by traditional loyalties and claiming descent respectively from Qays and Yaman, the northern and southern Arabs of pre-Islamic times. The most successful and celebrated of these Arab dynasties was that of the Hamdanids, which, originating in the vicinity of Mosul, captured Aleppo from the Ikhshidids in 333/944. The Hamdanid principality, straddling northern Syria and Mesopotamia, undertook warfare against the Byzantines – a conflict which ultimately turned to its disadvantage. A prolonged Byzantine counter-offensive ensued, during which Aleppo was devastated, Antioch regained for the empire in 358/969 and a protectorate established over Hamdanid Syria. These events coincided with the

Fatimid conquest of Egypt, which was followed by expansion into Syria and the taking of Damascus. The broad result of these developments was that by the end of the fourth/tenth century the Byzantines and the Fatimids had virtually arrived at deadlock in Syria. The country was divided into two spheres of influence: that of the Byzantines in the north with their base at Antioch, and that of the Fatimids in the south with their base at Tripoli. Each power had its clients among the Arab chiefs and tribes, who remained restless and ungovernable.

A fresh turn to events in Syria was given by the westward movement of the Oghuz and the establishment of the Great Seljuk sultanate. It was not, however, a sultan who was primarily responsible for the coming of the Turcomans to Syria. War-bands had straggled into the country from 456/1064, and Atsız, the leader of one such group, was called in by Badr al-Jamālī (when still governor of Acre) to suppress an Arab tribal rising in 463/1071. Atsız captured Jerusalem, and occupied Palestine at the expense of the Fatimids. Hereupon Alp-Arslan invaded Syria to take up the Holy War against the Fatimids, and perhaps also to remove the threat posed by Atsız. He took Aleppo, and then swung back northeastwards fearing an attack by Romanus Diogenes in his rear. The outcome was the battle of Manzikert. The power of Atsız grew. He took Damascus in 468/1076, and in the next year he attempted to invade Egypt but was repulsed by Badr al-Jamālī. To secure himself, Atsız sought the protection of Malik-Shāh. The sultan's response was to send in an army under the command of his brother Tutush, who procured the killing of Atsız, and obtained his territories as an appanage in 472/1079.

In this way the centre and south of Syria were for the most part incorporated in the Great Seljuk sultanate. In the north, Antioch was taken from its last Byzantine governor by Süleymān, who was gaining recognition as sultan of Rūm. Aleppo at this time was ruled by an Arab chief, a client of Malik-Shāh, and thus formed a buffer between the two rival Seljukids. Süleymān's expansionist policy led to war. In 479/1086 he was defeated by the army of Tutush and killed. When Malik-Shāh himself arrived to make a settlement in Syria, Tutush kept his appanage with its capital at Damascus and appointed a Turcoman chief named Artuk as his vassal in Jerusalem. The three great cities of the north were placed under Mamluks of Malik-Shāh: Antioch under Yaghısıyan, Aleppo under Aksungur al-Ḥājib and Edessa under Buzan. Little was left to the Fatimids except the coastal strip from Tyre southwards, although al-Afḍal Shāhanshāh recaptured Jerusalem in 491/1098, less than a year before it fell to the Crusaders.

Two other important changes occurred a few years before the arrival of the Crusaders. On the death of Malik-Shāh in 485/1092, Kılıj-Arslan, the son of Süleymān, who had been taken hostage on his father's death, returned to Iznik and thus restored the Seljuk sultanate of Rūm. Meanwhile Tutush left Damascus in an attempt to secure the Great Seljuk sultanate for himself. He was defeated and died in battle in 488/1095, and the victor, Berkyaruk, made a new settlement in Syria. Tutush's two sons, Dukak and Riḍwān, succeeded to Damascus and Aleppo respectively. Since they were still young, the real power in their appanages was held at first by Mamluk regents known as *atabegs*. The governors whom Malik-Shāh had appointed to Aleppo and Edessa had lost their lives during the succession-struggle. Only Yaghısıyan remained at Antioch. While Aleppo had passed to Riḍwān, Edessa had been taken by an Armenian lord named Toros, who was nominally a vassal of the Great Seljuk sultan.

When the Crusaders approached Syria in the autumn of 1097, they had before them a politically fragmented land, where the rulers were for the most part men of narrow vision and little experience. Behind these petty princes and governors were the two major powers, the Great Seljuk sultanate and Fatimid Egypt, both in decline, and the former at least little interested in the fate of Syria.

CHAPTER TWO

The First Crusade 1095–1099

The initiative in launching the First Crusade came from Pope Urban II at a council of the Church held at Clermont in France in November 1095. The council was chiefly concerned with French ecclesiastical matters, and was mainly attended by French clergy – although those of the actual domain of the French king were notably absent since the excommunicated Philip I was at odds with Urban. The pope's appeal was not on the agenda of the council. It was delivered to a meeting which included many laymen, and which was held in the open air after the formal sessions. The four early reports of the pope's speech differ among themselves, and modern scholars also differ about its exact content.[1] There is agreement that Urban laid stress principally upon the oppression of the Christians under Muslim rule, and the dishonour to Christians that infidels should defile the Holy Places. Urban's appeal for succour for the oriental Christians had indeed little current justification. In the situation prevalent in the late fifth/eleventh century the Christians belonging to the Orthodox Church were viewed with some mistrust by Muslim rulers as possible agents of, or collaborators with, the Byzantines. The other oriental churches had little to complain of, and improved their position at the expense of the Orthodox. Their writers display no hostility to their Muslim masters, and prefer the Seljukids to the Byzantines.

Although the pope's summons to the Crusade came at the end of a council devoted to other business, it was not casual or unconsidered but represented an interweaving of papal policies which had been developing over some decades. These concerned the attitude of the papacy towards the Orthodox Church and the Byzantine empire; the relations between the papacy and Western rulers, especially the Holy Roman emperor; and the relations between the papacy and the Normans in southern Italy, who were to play an important part in the First Crusade.

The eleventh century was indeed the century of the Normans, when these descendants of Viking settlers in the north of France established their rule in southern Italy and Sicily, in England, and finally in Antioch. But whereas the expedition which resulted in the conquest of England was organized and commanded by the duke of Normandy, the pretender to the English throne, the Normans came to Italy in the early eleventh century as individuals or small bands, men of little or no account in their homeland, who were out to make their fortunes in a territory claimed by Byzantium, largely dominated in ecclesiastical matters by the papacy, and partly ruled by Lombard princes. Soldiers of fortune and freebooters at the outset, the Normans established themselves first in 1030 at Aversa, the nucleus from which the principality of Capua was to develop. During the same period the twelve sons of Tancred, the petty lord of Hauteville, came to Italy. The most remarkable of them, Robert Guiscard, arrived in 1047, and his son Bohemond, the future Crusader and prince of Antioch, was born a few years later. In 1053 Robert and one of his brothers in alliance with Count Richard of Aversa defeated at the battle of Civitate an attempt by Pope Leo IX to break the growing power of the Normans. Roger, Robert's younger brother, came to Italy in 1056, and went on to conquer and rule Muslim Sicily.

Recurrent clashes and episodes of tension between the popes and the Orthodox patriarchs of Constantinople culminated in open schism in 1054, when a papal legate laid a decree of excommunication on the high altar of St Sophia. Five years later three notable events took place. In April 1059 a synod of the Roman Church forbade clerics to receive investiture at the hands of laymen. In August 1059 at the synod of Melfi, Pope Nicholas II, by a change in papal tactics, received Richard of Aversa and Robert Guiscard as vassals. Finally, later in 1059 a certain Hildebrand became archdeacon of Rome – a zealous promoter of reforms to enhance papal authority. In 1073 he himself became pope as Gregory VII. His reign saw the exacerbation of relations with the Emperor Henry IV over the question of lay investiture. During his prolonged struggle with Henry, the pope needed allies, and these he found ultimately in the Normans of southern Italy, among whom Robert Guiscard was pre-eminent. Bari, the last city held by the Byzantines in Italy, had fallen to Robert in 1071. Richard of Aversa died in 1078. Two years later, Robert renewed his oath of fealty to Gregory VII, who greatly needed his support. When Henry IV captured Rome in 1084, Robert Guiscard moved against him, retook the city and devastated it. The Romans rose against this overwhelming alliance, and drove out the pope along with the Normans. Gregory died at Salerno in the following year with, it is said, the words, "I have loved justice and hated iniquity, therefore I die in exile." Robert Guiscard died later in the same year (1085).

In the meantime both men had had dealings with the Byzantines. Robert Guiscard, as mentioned above, had finally ended Byzantine rule in Italy. Gregory VII, however, in the early part of his reign sought to reach an accommodation with the Byzantine emperor which would end the schism, and establish the primacy of the Roman see throughout Christendom. This would be to his advantage in the investiture contest with Henry IV, and the pope for his part would endeavour to make a settlement between the Byzantines and the Normans. Then in 1074 Gregory announced his intention of leading an army to succour Constantinople, which was threatened by the infidels – this, of course, was three years after Manzikert. He called on the faithful to aid him but the project came to nothing, lost in the more urgent business of relations with Henry IV. Some historians have seen in this abortive scheme an anticipation of Urban II's call at Clermont twenty-one years afterwards. The Byzantine emperor with whom Gregory had friendly relations, Michael VII, was overthrown in 1078. Not only was the pope disconcerted, so also was Robert Guiscard, who had planned the marriage of his daughter to Michael's son. The result was a reversal of papal policy as shown in the alliance with the Normans in 1080, and followed by an invasion of Byzantine territory by Robert Guiscard in 1081. Like William of Normandy when invading England fifteen years before, Robert sailed with a banner blessed by the pope. He was accompanied by his eldest son, Bohemond, who continued the campaign after his father's departure, but in 1083 the Normans were defeated by the Byzantines and thrown out of the Balkans. This Byzantine victory was one of the first successes of the Emperor Alexius Comnenus. On the accession of Urban II to the papacy in 1088 better relations were established, and already before the council of Clermont Byzantine ambassadors had asked the pope for help against the infidel. Alexius was hoping for a force of mercenaries such as the Byzantines had often recruited from Englishmen, Armenians, Normans and Turks. What he got was the First Crusade.

Urban II apparently envisaged the Crusaders as forming a single army under the command of men nominated by himself. He had already been in touch with a powerful noble, Raymond of St Gilles, count of Toulouse, who four days after the end of the council announced his readiness to take part in the Crusade. Probably the pope intended that Raymond should take the military command, but the leader was to be his own legate, Adhémar, the bishop of Le Puy.

Southern France was thus the point of origin and the primary field of recruitment of the Crusade. In the following months the pope continued his appeals both in speech and writing, and the summons to the Crusade was also carried by the bishops who had attended the council.

So far the movement remained under the direction of the institutional Church, but propagandists of a very different kind were already at work. These were the *prophetae*, preachers who had a popular following among the poor, especially in north-eastern France, Flanders, Lorraine and the Rhineland. As Pope Urban II represented the role of institutional religion and political calculation in the launching of the Crusade, Peter the Hermit stood for the charismatic and irrational element. His preaching and that of the other *prophetae* tapped a flood of popular messianism which ran like an underground river through medieval Europe. The belief that mankind was living in the Last Days, and that a messianic figure, perhaps an emperor, perhaps even Charlemagne awakening from his long sleep at Aachen, would arise to overthrow the infidel and retake Jerusalem – such ideas had long been current (not only among the poor and illiterate), and now seemed about to be realized.

The emotion and excitement which impelled vast numbers of peasants, mostly unarmed and undisciplined, to leave their homes in the spring of 1096, a mass migration rather than an army, had tragic consequences. It produced in the first place a series of attacks on the Jewish communities long settled in the great towns of the Rhineland. In spite of the protection of Henry IV, of Godfrey of Bouillon (the duke of Lower Lorraine), and of the Rhineland bishops, the people of these ancient Jewries perished in their thousands at the hands of men inflamed by greed and fanaticism. But the fate of the persecutors was hardly less miserable than that of their victims. A lawless mob, they reached Hungary, where they were destroyed like vermin. Only the bands led by Peter the Hermit and his knightly companion, Walter the Penniless, reached Constantinople in July and August 1096. Encamped outside the city, they posed a problem of security to the Byzantine authorities, who transported them across the water to the camp of Civetot. From this base they raided into enemy territory as far as the Seljukid capital, Iznik. The Turkish response was not long delayed, and in October 1096 they were annihilated. The People's Crusade was at an end.

Meanwhile an expedition more in accordance with the pope's ideas was getting under way. It differed, however, in one important respect from what the pope had planned. Instead of being a single army under the command of Raymond of St Gilles, it consisted of contingents under several leaders who were unwilling to defer to one another. The pope perhaps intended the various forces to make their rendezvous at Le Puy, but in fact they first assembled at Constantinople which they reached by different routes. The first to arrive (in November 1096) was a small contingent under Hugh of Vermandois, the brother of King Philip I of France. Next, just before Christmas, came a great force from Lorraine, northern France and Germany, led by Godfrey of Bouillon, who was accompanied by his brother, Baldwin of Boulogne, and a kinsman named Baldwin of Le Bourg. Another large but homogeneous army arrived at the beginning of April 1097. It was composed of Normans from southern Italy under the command of Bohemond, so recently the defeated enemy of Alexius Comnenus. With him came his nephew, Tancred. Not until late in the same month did Raymond of St Gilles bring in the largest of the contingents, recruited from Provençals and Burgundians. The last to reach Constantinople (in May 1097; was made up of Crusaders from northern France and Flanders, and it was commanded by three of the greatest lords of the region: Count Robert of Flanders, his cousin Robert Curthose, duke of Normandy (who had pawned his duchy to his brother, William Rufus, to raise funds for his adventure), and Count Stephen of Blois, the duke's brother-in-law.

With the assembling of the Crusade of the Princes at Constantinople, two problems emerged. The first was that of the formal relations between the Crusader chiefs and the Byzantine emperor; the second, that of the relations of the chiefs among themselves. Alexius viewed the Crusaders with justifiable misgivings. In the words of his daughter, Anna Comnena:

> He heard a rumour that countless Frankish armies were approaching. He dreaded their arrival, knowing as he did their uncontrollable passion, their erratic character and their irresolution, not to mention the other peculiar traits of the Kelt [i.e. the Western European], with their inevitable consequences: their greed for money, for example, which always led them, it seems, to break their own agreements without scruple for any chance reason.[2]

As the leaders arrived, Alexius required them to swear homage to him, and to undertake to restore to him all territories formerly held by the Byzantines. With the exception of Bohemond (whose tactics were now to outbid his rivals by gaining the emperor's favour), they were reluctant to take the oath. Raymond of St Gilles, in fact, would swear only to respect the emperor's person and possessions. After this inauspicious start, however, better relations grew up between Raymond and Alexius, rooted in their common dislike and mistrust of Bohemond.

Once across the Sea of Marmara, the Crusaders started operations against Iznik. On 21 May 1097 they defeated the Sultan Kılıj-Arslan I in a pitched battle. In June Iznik surrendered to the representatives of

Alexius, and was reincorporated in the Byzantine empire. The Crusaders then started their advance across Anatolia to Syria. Two more defeats were inflicted on the Turks: at Dorylaeum (Eskishehir) at the beginning of July, and in August at Heraclea (Ereghli). Then part of the Crusader forces struck southwards through the Cilician Gates, and captured Tarsus. Baldwin of Boulogne, who had been one of the leaders of this diversion, made his way eastwards across the Euphrates to Edessa, and was formally adopted by Toros, the Armenian governor. In March 1098 Toros was killed in a rising, and Baldwin took over the government, not as a vassal of Alexius but as the independent count of Edessa. Thus was established the first of the Crusader states.

Some idea of the impression which the coming of the Crusaders made on the Muslims of the Near East, even those who were not in the front line, may be obtained from the account by the contemporary Damascene chronicler, Ibn al-Qalānisī. He opens his annal for the year AH 490 (December 1096–December 1097) with these words:

> In this year there began to arrive a succession of reports that the armies of the Franks had appeared from the direction of the sea of Constantinople with forces not to be reckoned for multitude. As these reports followed one upon the other, and spread from mouth to mouth far and wide, the people grew anxious and disturbed in mind. The king, Dā'ud b. Sulaimān b. Qutulmish [i.e. Kılıj-Arslan I], whose dominions lay nearest to them, having received confirmation of these statements, set about collecting forces, raising levies, and carrying out the obligation of Holy War. He also summoned as many of the Turkmens as he could to give him assistance and support against them, and a large number of them joined him along with the ʿaskar of his brother [i.e. the standing army of the Danishmendid ruler of northern and central Anatolia]. His confidence having been strengthened thereby, and his offensive power rendered formidable, he marched out to the fords, tracks and roads by which the Franks must pass, and showed no mercy to all of them who fell into his hands. When he had thus killed a great number, they turned their forces against him, defeated him, and scattered his army, killing many and taking many captive, and plundered and enslaved. The Turkmens, having lost most of their horses, took to flight. The King of the Greeks bought a great many of those whom they had enslaved, and had them transported to Constantinople. When the news was received of this shameful calamity to the cause of Islām, the anxiety of the people became acute and their fear and alarm increased.[3]

The main Crusader army advanced to Antioch, which guarded the approach to northern Syria. After a long and exhausting siege, which lasted from October 1097 to June 1098, Bohemond procured the betrayal of the city. The governor, Yaghısıyan, was killed but the citadel still held out, and the Crusaders found themselves besieged by a relieving force under the *atabeg* of Mosul, Kırbogha. He was, however, defeated in battle, and the citadel finally surrendered. It thereupon became clear that Bohemond intended to hold Antioch for himself and his followers, regardless alike of his oath to Alexius and of the feelings of the other leaders. The ideals of the Crusade were giving way to the personal ambitions of its chiefs. Two independent states, the county of Edessa and the principality of Antioch, had come into being. Adhémar of Le Puy, the papal legate, who might have held the Crusade together, had died in August 1098.

Finally in January 1099 a large number of the Crusaders decided to advance on Jerusalem under the command of Raymond of St Gilles. The rendezvous was at Maʿarrat al-Nuʿmān, a city between Aleppo and Ḥamāh which had been captured in the previous month. The line of march was south up the Orontes valley, then westwards by a passage between the mountains to the coast north of Tripoli. On the way the fortress of Ḥiṣn al-Akrād (Crac des Chevaliers) was taken. After an unsuccessful siege of ʿArqa, north-east of Tripoli, the Crusaders continued down the coast, meeting little opposition as they passed, and indeed receiving help from Fakhr al-Mulk, the ruler of Tripoli. Near Jaffa the Crusaders turned inland by way of al-Ramla in the plain of Palestine. Again there was no resistance until they reached the walled city of Jerusalem itself. It held out for over a month, to fall on 22 Shaʿbān 492/15 July 1099. A dreadful scene of carnage ensued as the Crusaders massacred Muslims and Jews alike. Only the defeated Fatimid governor, Iftikhār al-Dawla, and his bodyguard were granted a safe conduct. An Egyptian army under the *Wazīr* al-Afḍal Shāhanshāh entered Palestine too late to save Jerusalem, and was routed at Ascalon in the south (Ramaḍān 492/August 1099). Ascalon itself was ready to surrender to Raymond, but this aroused the resentment of Godfrey of Bouillon who had already been recognized as the ruler of Jerusalem. In consequence, Ascalon remained as an Egyptian bridgehead for over half a century.

NOTES

1. Cf. H. E. Mayer, *The Crusades*, London 1965, 9–11; J. Prawer, *Histoire du royaume latin de Jérusalem*, I, 2nd edn, Paris 1965, 168–71.
2. E. R. A. Sewter (tr), *The Alexiad of Anna Comnena*, Harmondsworth 1969, 308.
3. H. A. R. Gibb (tr), *The Damascus Chronicle of the Crusades*, London 1932, 41–2.

CHAPTER THREE

The Frankish States and the Muslim Response 1099–1128

The three small territories in the Levant which were conquered during the First Crusade (together with Tripoli, acquired later) are usually called the Frankish states, since the Muslims designated the Crusaders (and Western Europeans generally) as *al-Faranj*, "the Franks". The county of Edessa and the principality of Antioch, established by Baldwin of Boulogne and Bohemond respectively, guarded the northern and north-eastern approaches to Syria. Jerusalem with its port of Jaffa and a handful of towns along the coast and in the highlands formed a state which, since it included the Holy Places, had the hegemony among the Frankish conquests. Its first ruler, elected by the leaders of the Crusade after the capture of Jerusalem, was Godfrey of Bouillon, who assumed the title, not of king but of *advocatus Sancti Sepulchri*, "the advocate [i.e. defender] of the Holy Sepulchre". The title indicated an ambiguity in Godfrey's position, an uncertainty as to the political status of the territory which held the Holy Places. Was it to be a state of the Church, governed by the pope through his legate, or a messianic community awaiting the Second Coming of Christ, or simply a Christian kingdom in the Holy Land? Godfrey's title excluded none of these possibilities, although the death of Adhémar of Le Puy had removed from the scene the one man who at this critical period could have claimed to be the legitimate channel of papal authority, while the messianic dream appealed to the poor followers of the Crusade rather than to the politically minded clergy and nobles whose views were decisive. As it was, the title and function of an *advocatus* were well known in the lands from which the Crusaders came: he was a layman who protected and administered Church estates.

After Godfrey's accession, Robert of Normandy's chaplain, Arnulf, was uncanonically elected patriarch of Jerusalem. The best that could be said of him was that he would not compete with Godfrey to rule over the new state. Soon afterwards he was displaced by a much more powerful cleric, Archbishop Daimbert of Pisa, who arrived off the coast in command of a great war-fleet in the summer of 1099. He may have been sent as papal legate; the point is disputed. In any case Arnulf was deposed, Daimbert was elected patriarch and Godfrey did homage to him as suzerain. Thus the future of Jerusalem as a state of the Church seemed assured when the situation suddenly changed. The Pisan fleet, Daimbert's power-base, sailed for home after Easter 1100. Godfrey died in Jerusalem in July of the same year at a time when Daimbert was away from the city, whereupon Godfrey's household sent for his brother in Edessa to come and claim the inheritance. Baldwin of Boulogne duly arrived, and his assured position was made clear when on Christmas Day of 1100 he was crowned king by Daimbert in Bethlehem. So the Latin kingdom was inaugurated. It is possible that the setting of the coronation in Bethlehem (later kings before Saladin's reconquest of the city were crowned in Jerusalem) indicates a final assertion by the patriarch of his suzerainty over the Holy City. Nevertheless, from this point Daimbert's power dwindled, and in 1102 he was exiled to Antioch, where he died. On the departure of Baldwin of Boulogne to Jerusalem, the county of Edessa passed to his kinsman, Baldwin of Le Bourg. Antioch also changed rulers in 1100, when Bohemond was captured on campaign by the Danishmendid chief in Anatolia. Thereupon Bohemond's nephew, Tancred, ruled the principality on his behalf. Although Bohemond returned from captivity in 1103, he did not remain long in Antioch, of which Tancred was the effective ruler from 1108.

The formation of these three Frankish states had left unprovided one, and he the greatest, of the leaders of the First Crusade. Raymond of St Gilles had failed to establish himself in either Antioch or Jerusalem when they were conquered. The coastlands were not, however, all at once occupied by the Crusaders, and around the important port of Tripoli was a small Muslim principality ruled by a family, Banū ʿAmmār, who were by origin judges in this former Fatimid possession. It was a member of this family who had assisted the Crusaders on their southward march in 1099, and who now became the object of Raymond's hostilities. Raymond began his operations with the capture of Tortosa (Anṭarṭūs) in 485/1102, and then went on to besiege Tripoli itself. Although he was already styling himself "count of Tripoli", the city did not fall until 502/1109, four years after his death. The Muslim ruler, Fakhr al-Mulk, who had left Tripoli before its capture, made his way to Baghdad to seek help from the ʿAbbasid caliph and the Seljukid sultan.

The coming of Archbishop Daimbert with the Pisan fleet was an event of strategic as well as political significance. The Crusaders and the states they founded lacked sea-power, which was supplied (at a price) by the Italian maritime republics of Pisa, Venice and Genoa. Godfrey's need for a naval force which would enable him to secure and hold the ports and coastal plain explains his deference to Daimbert, but in June 1100, after the departure of the Pisan fleet, he began to negotiate with a Venetian squadron which had put into Jaffa, and which helped to capture Haifa. The real establishment of the Venetians in the Latin kingdom came with their participation in the blockade and capture of Tyre in 518/1124. The terms for their assistance, negotiated earlier, were confirmed by King Baldwin II, i.e. Baldwin of Le Bourg, who had succeeded the childless Baldwin I in 1118. By the agreement the Venetians received one-third of the city of Tyre, and were almost entirely exempt from the payment of customs. Twenty years earlier (497/1104) a fleet of their great rivals, the Genoese, had enabled Baldwin I to capture the important port of Acre, and had similarly received an extensive grant of privileges, as also they did from Bertram, the son of Raymond of St Gilles, on the taking of Tripoli. The consequence of these and other grants was the establishment of autonomous Italian settlements, the communes, in the trading-cities of the Frankish states. They formed enclaves withdrawn from the jurisdiction of the territorial ruler, and administered by officials appointed by the mother-cities in Italy. As time went on, the jealousies and conflicts of their parent-republics were reproduced in the Levant. Acre in particular was torn apart by communal dissension.

Military necessity led to the rise of another group of autonomous powers in the Frankish states. Although they were organized as feudal polities, they could not in this way alone obtain large fighting forces. Warriors from Europe and armed pilgrims gave their services for a season, but there was no large-scale immigration and settlement to swell the ranks of the feudal forces. In these circumstances an important, indeed, an essential, part was played by the members of the military orders. The earliest of these was the Order of St John, the Hospitallers, which developed out of a charitable foundation existing in Jerusalem before the First Crusade. The Hospitallers had originally been organized to serve the sick poor, and the order's constitution in the Latin kingdom was established by a papal bull of 1113. From 1136 at latest it was beginning to undertake military activities, and these came to overshadow, although never to exclude, its original charitable functions.

This development resulted from imitation of the Order of the Temple, the Templars, which started in 1119, when a small group of knights was organized to protect pilgrims on the roads of the Holy Land. They received the patronage of King Baldwin II, and the formal Rule of the order was promulgated in 1128. The two orders constituted a monastic knighthood, directly dependent on the papacy, and uncontrolled by the local Catholic hierarchy. They attracted recruits and gifts of property both in the Frankish states and in Europe. The orders became extremely wealthy, and the Templars in particular carried out financial and banking activities. To the defence of the Latin kingdom the two orders could contribute a force almost as numerous as the feudal levies, and they also held and garrisoned many of the castles. In the county of Tripoli and the principality of Antioch, which were even more exposed to Muslim attacks (especially after the loss of Edessa in 539/1144), their role was still more important, and they were more independent there than in the Latin kingdom. Unfortunately the mutual rivalry of Templars and Hospitallers became a constant and weakening factor in the politics of the Frankish states. A third important military order, recruited in Germany, was that of the Teutonic Knights.

In the Muslim territories lying immediately to the east of the Frankish states there were three cities of critical strategic and political importance. The first of these was Mosul, the principal city of the Jazīra, i.e. the northern region between the Euphrates and the Tigris. It was the key point for the defence of the eastern Fertile Crescent against the Crusaders, for whom Edessa formed an advanced base. Its significance in this respect was first shown when in Shaʿbān 497/May 1104 the combined forces of Mosul and Sokman, the lord of Mārdīn, defeated an attack on Ḥarrān by an alliance of Bohemond, Tancred, Baldwin of Le Bourg and his chief vassal, Joscelin of Courtenay. This defeat marked the limit of Crusader advance eastwards, and showed the Muslims that the Franks were not invincible. Sokman, who died shortly afterwards, was a son of Artuk, formerly Tutush's governor of Jerusalem.

More immediately threatened by the Frankish states were the two Syrian capitals of Aleppo and Damascus. In Aleppo, Riḍwān ruled until his death in 507/1113. His brother in Damascus, Dukak, had died in 497/1104, and was soon followed to the grave by his son. Effective power in Damascus passed to the *Atabeg* Tughtigin, a regent without a king, who founded the short-lived Burid dynasty. For several years after the First Crusade, the Muslim rulers in Syria pursued a cautious and by no means entirely hostile policy towards the Frankish states. Even when the permanence of the Frankish settlements came to be recognized, the Muslim rulers were prepared to compromise with them, and even to seek alliance. In 502/1108–9 an agreement was reached between Baldwin I and Tughtigin to partition the revenues of the grainlands lying west of Lake Tiberias and the upper Jordan. In the next year a similar agreement was made by Tughtigin and Count Bertram of Tripoli over another fertile frontier region – the vale of the Biqāʿ between Lebanon and anti-Lebanon. In 502/1109 the complexities of local politics led to a war in the north in which Riḍwān and Tancred were in alliance against the governor of Mosul and Baldwin of Le Bourg.

Not for some year after the Crusaders' conquests did the call to the *jihād* become audible, and then it was in the circles of pious Muslim teachers and writers, not in the councils of the rulers. Al-Sulamī, a teacher in the Great Mosque of Damascus, read in 498–9/1105 to groups of auditors a work which he had composed on the duty of the Holy War. In it he gave his view of the Frankish advance, not only in his own country but also in Sicily and Spain:

A number fell upon the island of Sicily at a time of difference and competition, and likewise they gained possession of town after town in Spain. When mutually confirmatory reports reached them of the state of this country – the disagreement of its lords, the dissensions of its dignitaries, together with its disorder and disturbance – they carried out their resolution of going out to it, and Jerusalem was the summit of their wishes.

Then they looked down from Syria on disunited kingdoms, hearts in disagreement and differing opinions, linked with secret resentments. Thereby their ambitions grew in strength, and extended to what they beheld. They continued assiduously in the holy war against the Muslims, while the Muslims did not trouble about them or join forces to fight them, leaving to each other the encounter until they [i.e. the Franks] made themselves rulers of lands beyond their utmost hopes. . . . Their hopes expand inasmuch as they see their enemies content to be at peace with them, so that they are convinced that all the lands will become theirs, and all the people prisoners in their hands. May God Who is near and answers in His munificence humble their thoughts by uniting the Community and setting it in order.[1]

Somewhere about the year 503/1109–10 the first signs of a change on the part of the Muslim rulers begin to appear. Tripoli had fallen to the Franks in the previous year, Fakhr al-Mulk Ibn ʿAmmār was a refugee in Baghdad, and the Sultan Muḥammad (a son of Malik-Shāh) was moved to announce his intention to wage the *jihād*. An expedition was sent against Edessa under the command of the *Atabeg* Mawdūd, governor of Mosul since 502/1108, a courageous warrior who was the nephew of Kırbogha. The city was not taken, and in 504/1111 after demonstrations in the mosques of Baghdad, another expedition against the northern Frankish territories was authorized. On this occasion Mawdūd experienced a notable lack of support from the rulers of Aleppo and Damascus, who were less disturbed by the Franks than by the prospect of a close alliance with the sultan. Riḍwān shut the gates of Aleppo against Mawdūd, while Tughtigin, hardly more cordial, sought to divert Mawdūd's army to a reconquest of Tripoli. In 507/1113 Mawdūd was murdered by an Assassin while on a third Syrian expedition. It was rumoured that Tughtigin was privy to the crime; certainly a few months later he made a new truce with Baldwin I.

The death of Riḍwān marked for all practical purposes the end of Seljukid rule in Syria. Of the two sons who succeeded him, one was assassinated, the other a minor. Real power lay in the hands of the *Atabeg* Lu'lu', one of Riḍwān's freedmen, until he too was assassinated in 510/1117. For several years Aleppo was the object of a confused and complicated power-struggle. Within the city itself there were two important groups. One was headed by the Shīʿī *qāḍī* Ibn al-Khashshāb, who played a large part in the politics of Aleppo until his death in 519/1125. He was one of the earliest spokesmen of the religious opposition to the Frankish conquests and settlement, and during Riḍwān's reign had pressed him to resist the Crusaders. Riḍwān for his part had sought the support of the Assassins, who at this time were securing a foothold in Syria. After Riḍwān's death, a popular rising against the Assassins led to their expulsion from Aleppo, although traces of their influence there remained for another decade.

The political future of Aleppo was thus an open question. The Sultan Muḥammad sponsored another expedition into Syria in 509/1115. This provoked an immediate reaction from the Syrian rulers, Franks and Muslims alike. The *Atabeg* Lu'lu' in Aleppo was aided by Tughtigin and Roger of Salerno, the regent of Antioch, as well as by Ilghāzī, who had succeeded his brother Sokman as lord of Mārdīn. The sultan's army withdrew but in Rabīʿ II 509/September 1115 it was routed with great slaughter by Roger at the battle of Dānīth. So ended the counter-crusade which Mawdūd had begun, and so too ended the direct involvement of the Great Seljuk sultanate in Syrian affairs. As the events of this year showed, the rulers of Damascus and Antioch could not be indifferent to the fate of Aleppo, but while Tughtigin was on the whole anxious to maintain the status quo in the north (since his more direct concern was his relations with the Latin kingdom), Roger of Salerno would have been very ready to bring Aleppo under his own control. Early in 512/1118 he seemed about to do this, and the citizens, advised by Ibn al-Khashshāb, appealed for help to Ilghāzī. His response inaugurated six years of Artukid domination over Aleppo.

The Artukids were the ruling clan of the most important group of

Turcomans in the region at the time. The original centre of their power had been in Palestine, where Artuk and his sons, Ilghāzī and Sokman, had, as already mentioned, been vassals of Tutush. They lost Palestine when al-Afḍal Shāhanshāh took Jerusalem in 491/1098. They then established themselves in Diyār Bakr, the northern part of the Jazīra, where they acquired the great strongholds of Mārdīn and Ḥiṣn Kayfā. Artukid relations with the Great Seljuk sultan were unstable and opportunist, and Ilghāzī was now to all intents and purposes the independent ruler of Diyār Bakr. His territories marched with the principality of Antioch, and in Rabīʿ I 513/June 1119 he met Roger of Salerno in battle. The Crusaders were taken by surprise, and completely defeated at the pass of Sarmadā between Antioch and Aleppo. Roger himself was killed in the fighting, and with him perished the flower of the chivalry of Antioch. The battle was remembered by the Franks as *Ager Sanguinis*, the Field of Blood. It was significant as a victory won by a local Muslim ruler without the support of the Great Seljuk sultan.

But the Artukid domination of Aleppo, which seemed to presage a new counter-crusade in northern Syria since Ilghāzī made full use of propaganda for the *jihād*, rested on the sole personality of Ilghāzī himself. He died in 516/1122, and the Artukid hold over the city soon crumbled. In Shaʿbān 518/September 1124 Aleppo was once again besieged by a coalition of Frankish and Muslim forces led by King Baldwin II and Joscelin of Courtenay, who had succeeded the king as count of Edessa. The resistance was headed by the *qāḍī* Ibn al-Khashshāb, who denounced the Muslim ally of the Franks, Dubays b. Ṣadaqa, an Arab tribal ruler, who was lord of al-Ḥilla on the Euphrates. Ibn al-Khashshāb sent an appeal for aid, first and ineffectively to his nominal ruler, the son of Ilghāzī at Mārdīn, then to the governor of Mosul, Aksungur al-Bursuqī, who arrived in Dhu'l-Ḥijja 518/January 1125, and raised the siege. It was not, however, Aksungur who was to resume the *jihād* against the Franks. He was murdered in Mosul, another victim of the Assassins, in 519/1126. Another but briefer period of uncertainty followed in Aleppo, where Ibn al-Khashshāb also had been assassinated in the previous year. Then in Muḥarram 522/January 1128 Aleppo was occupied by the troops of the new ruler of Mosul, the *Atabeg* ʿImād al-Dīn Zangī, son of Malik-Shāh's former governor, Aksungur al-Ḥājib. Once more the two great northern cities at the head of the Fertile Crescent were united to form a base for military action in Syria.

NOTE

1. E. Sivan, "La genèse de la contre-croisade: un traité damasquin du début du XIIe siècle", *Journal Asiatique*, 1966, 207 (Arabic text), 215–16 (French trans.). English version P. M. Holt.

CHAPTER FOUR

Outremer and its People

Outremer, "the land beyond the sea", consisted of the four Frankish states set up as a result of the First Crusade: the county of Edessa, the principality of Antioch and the Latin kingdom of Jerusalem, to which was added a few years later the county of Tripoli, The first of these, Edessa, which straddled the upper Euphrates and was most vulnerable, was to have the shortest life. Its first two counts, Baldwin of Boulogne (1098–1100) and Baldwin of Le Bourg (1100–18) went on to become successively kings of Jerusalem. Baldwin of Le Bourg was succeeded in the county by his cousin Joscelin of Courtenay (1118–31), and he by his son Joscelin II, whose loss of the city of Edessa to Zangī in 539/1144 marked for all practical purposes the end of the county. Antioch under the princes of the house of Hauteville survived, albeit with a diminishing territory, until the city itself was captured in 666/1268 by al-Ẓāhir Baybars from Bohemond VI, a descendant in the sixth generation of Bohemond I, the founder of the principality. Tripoli, the only Frankish state centred on a maritime city, was ruled by the descendants of Raymond of St Gilles until 1187, when the direct line came to an end, and the county passed to the house of Hauteville. After the loss of Antioch Bohemond VI and his son Bohemond VII (1275–87) continued to rule in Tripoli. Bohemond VII died childless, and the political troubles which ensued formed a prelude to the conquest of Tripoli by Kalavun in 688/1289.

The history of the Latin kingdom falls into two parts divided by Saladin's victory at Ḥaṭṭīn, his capture of Jerusalem and his almost complete reconquest of the kingdom in 583/1187. Thereafter the capital of the restored kingdom was at Acre. In the first phase of its history, after the death of King Baldwin II in 1131, the crown passed to his daughter Melisend and her husband, Count Fulk of Anjou, the grandfather of King Henry II of England. The failure of the male line had not on this occasion any serious political or military consequences. Half a century later, when the succession again passed to a woman, the outcome was to be very much different. King Fulk had been succeeded by his sons, Baldwin III (1143–63) and Amalric I (1163–74). Amalric left a son, Baldwin IV (1174–85), who was a leper and died young and childless, and a daughter, Sibyl, whose child, Baldwin V (1185–86) had a brief and nominal reign. Already in 1180 Sibyl had taken as her second husband a young nobleman from Poitou, Guy of Lusignan, who in 1186 obtained the crown in right of his wife. The conflict with Saladin and the disaster of Ḥaṭṭīn took place in the following year. In 1190 Queen Sibyl died, and Guy had little personal following in the kingdom. During the Third Crusade he was set aside, and received the kingdom of Cyprus in compensation.

Queen Sibyl's next heir was her half-sister Isabel – the second of four successive descents of the crown in the female line. The restored kingdom was ruled by two of her four husbands, Count Henry of Champagne (1192–97) and Aimery, alias Amalric II (1197–1205), the brother of Guy of Lusignan. Isabel's daughter, Mary called "La Marquise", had as husband John of Brienne. John ruled first as king (1210–12), then after his wife's death as regent for their daughter, another Isabel (alias Yolanda), until her marriage in 1225 to the Emperor Frederick II of Hohenstaufen. At this point the crown passed to absentee rulers (if we except the few months of Frederick's "crusade" in the Holy Land) until the execution of the emperor's grandson Conradin by Charles of Anjou in 1268 ended the Hohenstaufen line.

Thereupon the kingdom was claimed by King Hugh III of Cyprus, a descendant of the house of Lusignan and (on his mother's side) of the much-married Isabel. Cyprus and the Latin kingdom were thus linked in a personal union like that between Antioch and Tripoli. The king was still usually an absentee, represented by a *bailli* or regent at Acre. Finally in 690/1291, Kalavun's son, al-Ashraf Khalīl, conquered Acre and what remained of Outremer.

As we have seen, the First Crusade did not consist of a unified military force operating under a single command but of distinct contingents drawn from different regions and headed by noblemen jealous of their independent authority. The piecemeal conquests reflected this structure of the invading forces, to which also the four resulting Frankish states bore witness. Thus Antioch was settled mainly by Normans, while the Franks of the Latin kingdom came originally (like its ruling house) from Lorraine and northern France, and those of Tripoli had followed Raymond of St Gilles from Provence. Edessa had been an Armenian lordship, and was usurped rather than conquered by Baldwin of Boulogne, so that Armenians continued to form an important part of the population in the Frankish county. Among the four states, the Latin kingdom had a certain primacy of status, and we are best informed about its history and institutions.

Coming from the feudal society of Western Europe, the Crusaders brought with themselves its ideas and institutions, and implanted them in their Syrian territories. Yet apart from variations between one Frankish state and another, the feudalism of Outremer was distinguished from the feudalism of Europe by characteristics resulting from the circumstances in which it developed. In the first place, the Frankish settlers were always a minority, and the feudal military resources of the rulers were correspondingly limited. Few reliable statistics exist or can be deduced. It has, however, been surmised that the Frankish population consisted at most of about 250,000, about half of whom were in the kingdom of Jerusalem. The three great cities of the kingdom were Acre, which probably had over 60,000 inhabitants in the twelfth century, Tyre and Jerusalem itself with 20,000 to 30,000. Contemporary evidence shows that around 1170 there were about 675 knights in the feudal forces of the kingdom, augmented by rather over 5,000 sergeants (who were probably foot-soldiers) provided by the ecclesiastical communities and the towns.

The social structure of Outremer was also unusual by comparison with feudal Western Europe. Among the Frankish settlers there were only two classes, the nobles (from simple knights upwards) and the burgesses. Apart from the four ruling families of the Frankish states, the nobles were almost entirely parvenus – men of modest origin who had bettered themselves by settlement in the conquered territories. Even the Ibelin family, who rose to outstanding importance in the later Latin kingdom, had an obscure ancestry, being descended perhaps (although this was not what they themselves claimed) from Pisan merchants or Norman knights of Sicily. While most of the founders of the Frankish aristocracy had come out in the First Crusade, its ranks were recruited by energetic newcomers, who sought a career open to talent in Outremer. Their relations with the older nobility were not always cordial, as the latter had learnt to accept and value some measure of coexistence with their Muslim neighbours, which the bellicose and inexperienced new arrivals found hard to stomach. In addition there was sometimes rivalry for profitable marriage alliances. Guy of Lusignan was one such interloper, and won a crown by a fortunate marriage. Another, who like Guy was partly responsible for the catastrophe of the first Latin kingdom, was Reynald of Châtillon. In 1153, soon after his arrival in Syria, he married Constance, the widowed princess of Antioch, which he ruled as regent until he was captured by the Muslims in 1160. Released (and long a widower) in 1176, he married another heiress, Stephanie, the lady of Oultrejourdain (Transjordan), by whom he obtained the great castle of al-Karak, the indirect cause of his destruction.

The burgesses, in spite of the name, were not merely the town-dwellers but included all the Franks outside the aristocracy. Their numbers were constantly being increased by fresh immigrants. In the Latin kingdom they formed the bulk of the city population, but in Tripoli, Antioch and Edessa they were outnumbered by the local Christians. They handled chiefly the small-scale domestic trade of the towns, while the larger international commerce was managed by the communities of Italian (and later other Western) merchants, who had established themselves in a privileged position soon after the conquest.

A third factor which differentiated the feudal society of Outremer from that of Western Europe was its situation in an environment that was ethnically and linguistically wholly alien, and hardly less so in religion, since even the native Christians did not belong to the familiar Roman Church of the Crusaders' homelands. This situation had two consequences. The Frankish rulers and nobles could not intermarry with the great Muslim families of the hinterland, nor could they easily obtain brides from the West. There were some marriages with Armenian and Byzantine ladies; for example, the wife of Amalric I and mother of Isabel was Maria Comnena of the imperial house, while in the following century Sibyl, an Armenian princess, married Bohemond VI and was regent of Tripoli after his death. For the most part, however, the Frankish aristocracy wedded within its own restricted circle. Consanguinity, strictly defined by canon law, became increasingly difficult to avoid, and annulment of marriage correspondingly easy. The role of royal and noble ladies in Frankish politics was all the greater in that they were often left as sole heirs in a society where male children tended to die young and grown men were exposed to the constant hazards of warfare. The history of the royal house of Jerusalem is a case in point. Hence in Outremer not only could property, fiefs and even the crown descend in the female line but also (unlike the West) the right of primogeniture, as opposed to the equal sharing of the inheritance, obtained as between sisters.

In quite another way the alien environment of the settlers in Outremer affected their feudal practice. Almost the whole of the rural population and part of the townspeople were not Franks but natives of the conquered territories. The taking of a town during the First Crusade was usually followed by the slaughter of its inhabitants, and the progress of the invasion produced a flight of refugees to lands still under

Muslim rule. Nevertheless, many of the indigenous people stayed or returned. Muslims, native Christians and Jews formed a subject population on whom the agriculture in particular of the Frankish states depended. There was some attempt at Frankish rural settlement in fortified villages, but only 50 or 60 of these out of a total of about 1,200 villages were established in the Latin kingdom. The Syrian Christians gained little by exchanging a Muslim for a Christian master, while the Muslims ironically found themselves paying the poll-tax which in Islamic states was levied from the Christians as *dhimmīs*.

Although villages were granted as fiefs to the Frankish aristocracy, there were two important differences from Western usage. The lords lived in the towns, not in manor-houses on their estates. Hence no part of the land of the village formed the lord's demesne to be cultivated by his peasantry, nor in consequence were there the personal ties which, for better or worse, existed in Europe between a lord and his people. The village existed to produce revenue (usually one-third of the crops) for its absentee lord. In practice if not in origin, the Frankish fief had much in common with the *iqṭāʿ* in contemporary Muslim Syria (see below, pp. 68–69). A large number of fiefs, however, were not in any case grants of landed estates as was usual in the West. Outremer was carved out of a region which, unlike Western Europe in the Dark Ages, had never ceased to have a money economy. Cultivable land was scarce but the towns and their trade offered abundant sources of revenue. Hence money-fiefs, i.e. assignments of such financial sources, were a frequent form of remuneration so that in effect the king could call on the services of a body of salaried knights who had done homage to him.

The feudalism of Outremer was thus constrained by the circumstances in which it developed to become something rather different from the feudalism of Western Europe, while an almost unbridgeable gap separated the Frankish superstructure from indigenous society. There was indeed a certain ironical resemblance between these Frankish rulers and warriors sustained by a native Arabic-speaking peasantry, and their opponents across the border – Turkish rulers and warriors also sustained by a native Arabic-speaking peasantry. Between Muslims and Franks there was little cultural contact such as occurred in Sicily and Spain. The extent and the limits of mutual understanding at the aristocratic level are well illustrated in an anecdote recounted by Usāma b. Munqidh, a warrior from a noble Arab family of twelfth-century Syria:

> In the army of King Fulk . . . was a Frankish reverend knight who had just arrived from their land in order to make the holy pilgrimage and then return home. He was of my intimate fellowship and kept such constant company with me that he began to call me "my brother". Between us were mutual bonds of

amity and friendship. When he resolved to return by sea to his homeland, he said to me:

"My brother, I am leaving for my country and I want thee to send with me thy son (my son, who was then fourteen years old, was at that time in my company) to our country, where he can see the knights and learn wisdom and chivalry. When he returns, he will be like a wise man."

Thus there fell upon my ears words which would never come out of the head of a sensible man; for even if my son were to be taken captive, his captivity could not bring him a worse misfortune than carrying him into the lands of the Franks. However, I said to the man:

"By thy life, this has exactly been my idea. But the only thing that prevented me from carrying it out was the fact that his grandmother, my mother, is so fond of him and did not this time let him come out with me until she exacted an oath from me to the effect that I would return him to her."

Thereupon he asked, "Is thy mother still alive?" "Yes," I replied. "Well," said he, "disobey her not."[1]

Immediately after the taking of Jerusalem by the Crusaders, there seemed a possibility that it would become the capital of an ecclesiastical state headed by the Latin patriarch and immediately dependent on the pope. The coronation of Baldwin I as king of Jerusalem removed this from the realm of practical politics, and thereafter although lawyers might assert that the kingdom had two chief lords, the patriarch and the king, this was no more than a legal fiction. The patriarch's lordship was in fact limited to the quarter of Jerusalem around the Church of the Holy Sepulchre. Still more illustrative of the political weakness of the Latin Church in the kingdom was the fact that during this period when the papacy was struggling with European rulers to secure the freedom of episcopal elections, it was the king of Jerusalem who in the last resort chose the candidate he wished for consecration as patriarch.

The Latin Church nevertheless occupied a privileged and wealthy position in the Frankish states, mainly at the expense of the hierarchy and religious foundations of the Orthodox Church. Latin patriarchs took the place of Greeks at Jerusalem and Antioch, and Latin bishops were appointed to the sees, while the pious endowments of the formerly predominant Church were granted by the new rulers to its rival. At the lower levels, however, especially in rural areas, the Orthodox clergy and churches were little disturbed, and a number of Greek monasteries continued to exist. As well as the Orthodox Christians, there were other churches which were regarded as heretical by both Rome and Constantinople, particularly the Jacobites and Armenians, the latter being especially numerous in Edessa and Antioch. On the whole and in spite of their heresy, these oriental churches were more favourably regarded than the Orthodox by the Frankish rulers – following Islamic precedents, for instance, the kings of Jerusalem confirmed the Jacobite patriarchs in office. Yet it can hardly be said that the situation of the oriental Christians was better under the Franks than it had normally been under the Muslims. Mostly Arabic-speaking, and to Frankish eyes indistinguishable from their Muslim fellow-countrymen, the native Christians of Outremer were second-class citizens in religious as in political status. It was a curious outcome of a movement which had been evoked, at least in part, to help the Christians of the East.

NOTE

1. Philip K. Hitti, *An Arab–Syrian gentleman and warrior in the period of the Crusades*, New York 1929; repr. as *Memoirs of an Arab–Syrian gentleman*, Beirut 1964, 161.

CHAPTER FIVE

Zangī and Nūr al-Dīn 1128–1154

During most of the sixth/twelfth century the history of Syria is dominated by a succession of three names: those of the *Atabeg* Zangī, ruler of Mosul and Aleppo, of his son Nūr al-Dīn and of the latter's vassal and successor, Ṣalāḥ al-Dīn b. Ayyūb – the Saladin of European writers. There has been a tendency to see these men as primarily champions of Islam, leaders in the *jihād* against the infidel intruders into Syria–Palestine, men whose aim was above all the eviction of the Franks, and whose task was largely achieved, if not finally completed, by the victories of Saladin. Although there is truth in this view (particularly with the advantage of hindsight), it is an over-simplification of complex events and shifting relationships. These men were concerned to maintain and extend their dominions by manipulating the tangled politics of the region. The Frankish states were only one category of their opponents, and in their time as previously the relations of Franks and Muslims were by no means always hostile.

The conventional presentation of these three men as forming a kind of apostolic succession as liberators of Syria–Palestine from the Franks is not specifically the work of modern writers. Its origins go back to the century after Saladin's death, and it arose from the conflation of rival historiographies. Already in the months immediately following the death of Saladin, his secretary, ʿImād al-Dīn al-Iṣfahānī, completed a eulogistic account (begun during his master's lifetime) of the final years of Saladin's career from 583/1187 to 589/1193. He also wrote a seven-volume chronicle of Saladin's life and times. Another courtier, the army judge Bahā' al-Dīn Ibn Shaddād, also wrote a biography within a few years of Saladin's death. These works, produced in the afterglow of victories over the Latin kingdom and of warfare against the Third Crusade, created the picture of Saladin as the redeemer of Jerusalem and the captain in the Holy War. At this same time one of the great Arabic historians was setting forth another view. Ibn al-Athīr (555–630/1160–1233) lived in Mosul, where Zangī's descendants still ruled after the Syrian possessions of Nūr al-Dīn's branch of the family had been usurped by Saladin. Subtly in his universal chronicle, openly in his dynastic history of the *atabegs*, Ibn al-Athīr wrote as a partisan of the Zangids, and in particular described at length the exemplary career of Nūr al-Dīn. In this he may have been deliberately responding to statements made about Saladin by Ibn Shaddād.

The reconciliation of these two rival presentations was achieved sixty years after Saladin's death by Abū Shāma, a religious scholar of Damascus. The purpose of his work was essentially didactic – a warning and a summons to the Muslim rulers of his time, who were placing in jeopardy the gains of their heroic predecessors. When Abū Shāma finished his book in 651/1253, Egypt had been taken from the Ayyubids by the Mamluks. St Louis, after the defeat of his crusade in Egypt, was restoring the defences of the Latin kingdom, and was being sought as an ally by both the Mamluks and the Ayyubids, who alike offered to retrocede Saladin's conquests to him. In the east the Mongols, infidels far more dangerous than the Franks, were beginning their inexorable advance, which was to culminate in the capture of Baghdad and the overthrow of the ʿAbbasid caliphate in 656/1258. At that time of present danger and impending catastrophe, Abū Shāma combined the two partisan historiographies to form an interpretation of the roles of Zangī, Nūr al-Dīn and Saladin which has dominated much subsequent writing to our own day.

Besides the Muslim and Frankish rulers, there was in Syria in this period another force which played an important, if ambiguous, part. This was the Order of the Assassins. The chaotic situation in Syria on the eve of the First Crusade, and the instability which continued after the establishment of the Frankish states, provided an opportunity for the Ismāʿīlī propagandists. With the tolerance and indeed the patronage of Riḍwān, as we have seen, they made Aleppo the base of their operations. Soon after his death in 507/1113 the Assassins were proscribed, although they were not at once completely purged from the city. Their next base was Damascus, where they received the protection of Tughtigin. Here also the death of their patron in 522/1128 was followed by a proscription. Tughtigin was succeeded as ruler by his son Böri (arabicized as Būrī, whence the name of the Burid dynasty), and in the next year thousands of Assassins were killed. Thereafter the Assassins of Syria, like their brethren in Persia, made their bases in remote and impregnable mountain fortresses. Their strongholds were mostly in

Jabal Bahrā' (now Jabal Anṣāriyya), the coastal range of northern Syria. The chief of them was Maṣyāf, which they captured from the family of Usāma b. Munqidh in 535/1140. Their relations were especially critical with the rulers of Mosul, who as Sunnī Muslims detested Shī'ī extremists, and who threatened communications between the Syrian Assassins and the parent organization in Persia. The Assassins were almost certainly responsible for the murder of Aksungur al-Bursuqī, and their hostility continued towards his successors, Zangī and his sons.

'Imād al-Dīn Zangī, who became master of Aleppo in 522/1128, was the son of Aksungur al-Ḥājib, whom Malik-Shāh had appointed as governor of that city in 480/1087. When the struggle for the succession to the sultanate broke out after Malik-Shāh's death in 485/1092, Aksungur was captured in battle, and put to death by Tutush (487/1094). Zangī, a boy of seven at the time, was brought up under the guardianship of the *atabeg* of Mosul, Kırbogha. After serving in forces of later governors of Mosul including Mawdūd, Zangī was himself appointed governor and *atabeg* at the request of a delegation from the city to the sultan's court. This was in 521/1127. In Aleppo meanwhile, anarchy reigned. A governor appointed by the sultan was besieged in the city by the townspeople. By Dhu'l-Ḥijja 521/December 1127 Zangī's representatives were at Aleppo, and in Jumādā II 522/June 1128 he made his state entry into the city. It is not clear whether he had been formally appointed as governor by the sultan. In any case he asserted the legitimacy of his rule by bringing back to Aleppo the remains of his father, the memory of whom was cherished there, and by marrying the daughter of Riḍwān, thus linking himself with his Seljukid predecessors. The link between the Jazīra and northern Syria which had briefly existed under Ilghāzī and Aksungur al-Bursuqī was restored.

Zangī's establishment of a personal union of Mosul and Aleppo had two consequences. First, Aleppo after many years of instability ceased to be the object of competition among the neighbouring Christian and Muslim rulers. That unhappy condition had now passed to Damascus, and to bring Damascus under his control was the principal aim of Zangī's Syrian policy. But secondly, Zangī's possession of Mosul involved him in the affairs of the eastern Fertile Crescent and the Great Seljuk sultanate, and these occupied him for more of his seventeen years' reign than did developments in Syria. His contribution to the counter-crusade was thus incidental to his other interests as a ruler.

It is, however, his part in the history of Syria that must here be dealt with. He made his first attempt to dominate Damascus in 524/1130, when he invited Böri to co-operate with him in the *jihād*. Zangī then seized Ḥamāh, having treacherously captured its ruler, who was one of

Böri's sons. This was all that Zangī was able to achieve on that occasion, and for the next four years he was occupied in the east. In the meantime Böri died from wounds received in an attack by Assassins (526/1132). His son and successor, Shams al-Mulūk Ismāʿīl, facing growing unpopularity, invited Zangī's intervention. But when Zangī arrived with his army early in 529/1135, Ismāʿīl had been murdered at his mother's instigation, and his brother Shihāb al-Dīn Maḥmūd, had been installed in his place. Resistance to Zangī was organized by the Amir Muʿīn al-Dīn Önör. A message from the caliph bidding Zangī return to Mosul provided him with a face-saving pretext for withdrawal from a fruitless campaign.

The front-line city between the territories of Zangī and the Burids was Ḥimṣ, which he attacked, devastating the neighbourhood, in Shawwāl 529/August 1135. Shortly afterwards the city passed under the control of Önör, who succeeded in holding it against another attack and siege by Zangī in 531/1137. In Dhu'l-Qaʿda 531/August 1137, however, Zangī captured the strategically important Crusader castle of Baʿrīn, known to the Franks as Montferrand, on the route from Tripoli to Ḥamāh. Just at this time the situation in northern Syria was complicated by the arrival of a Byzantine army under the Emperor John Comnenus (1118–43), the son and successor of Alexius. Resuming his father's policy towards the Crusaders, he compelled Raymond of Poitiers, the consort of the heiress of Antioch, to become his vassal. John and Raymond agreed that if the emperor succeeded in conquering Aleppo, Ḥimṣ and Ḥamāh, he would grant them to Raymond in fief, in lieu of Antioch itself. The agreement was followed by a short and unrewarding campaign in northern Syria, and so came to nothing.

Zangī at last obtained possession of Ḥimṣ by diplomacy when in 532/1138 he negotiated a marriage alliance with Böri's widow, who brought him the city as her dowry. This was a strategic and political gain, but Zangī soon found that the marriage in no way strengthened his hold over Damascus. There another turn was given to the development of the situation when Shihāb al-Dīn Maḥmūd was murdered in a palace conspiracy in Shawwāl 533/June 1139. Urged by his wife, Zangī brought up his forces to besiege Damascus, and Önör again led the resistance. The siege lasted from Rabīʿ II 534/December 1139 to Shawwāl 534/June 1140. In this extremity Önör purchased Frankish aid by a formal alliance with Fulk of Anjou, king of Jerusalem. In the face of this new danger Zangī raised the siege, and finally withdrew to Mosul. From this campaign he had gained two things: the empty mention of his name in the *khuṭba* as the overlord of Damascus, and the garrison town of Baʿlabakk which dominated the fertile Biqāʿ. Zangī appointed as its governor one of his Kurdish followers, Najm al-Dīn Ayyūb b. Shādhī, the eponym of a family, the Ayyubids, who were to play a leading part in Near Eastern history in the ensuing decades.

So the possession of Damascus continued to elude Zangī, and his later exploits were in the north. Here a coincidence of events brought him his greatest prize. The Artukid lord of Ḥiṣn Kayfā, Dāwūd b. Sokman, with whom Zangī had recently been in conflict, died in Muḥarram 539/August 1144, and his son, Kara-Arslan, negotiated with Count Joscelin II of Edessa to secure his position. Joscelin moved with a strong force to the west of his county. Seizing the opportunity of Joscelin's absence from his capital, Zangī descended on the city of Edessa and captured it in Jumādā II 539/December 1144. This was the first Frankish capital to be retaken by the Muslims, and Zangī at once assumed the character of a champion of Islam. Formal recognition of his services appeared in the titles conferred upon him by the caliph: Zayn al-Islām, Nāṣir Amīr al-Mu'minīn, al-Malik al-Manṣūr – "the Ornament of Islam, the Auxiliary of the Commander of the Faithful, the Divinely Aided King". Less than two years later Zangī was dead, murdered by a Frankish slave while he lay drunk on the night of 6 Rabīʿ II 541/14 September 1146.

The death of Zangī was followed by the partition of his dominions between his eldest son, Sayf al-Dīn Ghāzī, who took Mosul and the territories in the Jazīra, and his second son, Nūr al-Dīn Maḥmūd, who succeeded to the government of Aleppo. This settlement, which was followed by generally amicable relations between the Zangid princes, had two consequences. Nūr al-Dīn was able to concentrate on the affairs of Syria and the prosecution of the *jihād* against the Frankish states in a way that had been impossible to his father, distracted as he was by developments in the eastern Fertile Crescent. On the other hand, the narrower base of Nūr al-Dīn's economic and military power limited his capacity to undertake an aggressive and expansionist policy in Syria–Palestine. Unlike Zangī, he could not draw on the resources of the eastern Fertile Crescent.

The military forces which Nūr al-Dīn had at his disposal were similar in structure and composition to those of his father Zangī, and of his successor, Saladin. The army which he put into the field resembled in some respects the feudal forces of medieval Europe, since it was not a standing army, recruited and paid directly by the ruler, but an assemblage of contingents brought together annually for a summer campaign, and dispersing when the winter rains brought mud and cold. The principal contingent, the nearest equivalent to a standing force, was the ruler's *ʿaskar*, a body of cavalrymen who formed his personal and permanent guard, composed of both free-born warriors and Mamluks. The Turkish Mamluk element was counterbalanced by the recruitment of free Kurdish warriors such as the Ayyubids. There were also Arab and Turcoman tribesmen, chiefly serving as auxiliaries. The Yürük (Arabic, Yarūq) Turcomans played a particularly important part as irregular cavalry. At the end of his reign Nūr al-Dīn had 3,000 men in his *ʿaskar*. On campaign this force was augmented by the *ʿaskars* of his amirs and provincial governors; Asad al-Dīn Shīrkūh, the Kurdish lord of Ḥimṣ and uncle of Saladin, for example, had an *ʿaskar* of 500 men. An amir maintained his *ʿaskar* from a grant of the revenues of an estate, known as an *iqṭāʿ*, on which see further (pp. 68–69). The field army might also be supplemented by *ajnād*, second-class cavalrymen, who were apparently a locally recruited militia armed with spears and swords, unlike the *ʿaskarīs* who were mounted archers. The pitched battles of the period were cavalry encounters, in which the heavily armed Frankish knights charged with their couched lances the lighter and more mobile Muslim bowmen. Infantry were of significance only during sieges, when men with technical skill were required to work the siege-engines, to sap and mine the enemy's fortifications, and to handle the devices for throwing Greek fire, a combustible naphtha compound.

At the outset Nūr al-Dīn's hold over the Zangid possessions in Syria was threatened. Urged on by the Armenians in Edessa, Joscelin attempted to retake the city, but Nūr al-Dīn, acting resolutely and promptly, brought up his army, and dealt a crushing blow, not only to the Frankish forces but also to the native Christians, thousands of whom were massacred. Önör of Damascus also saw an opportunity to regain territory and influence in central Syria, and forced Najm al-Dīn Ayyūb out of Baʿlabakk. In the following year (541/1147), however, a reconciliation was effected, and sealed by a dynastic marriage.

A few months later the Second Crusade made its impact on Syria. The chief figure in its promotion, which was the reaction to the loss of Edessa, was the Cistercian abbot, St Bernard of Clairvaux. Unlike the First Crusade, its main contingents were led by two of the greatest rulers in Europe, Louis VII of France and Conrad III of Germany. In June 1148 an assembly in Jerusalem of the leading Crusaders and the dignitaries of the Latin kingdom unwisely decided to attack Damascus. The decision was suicidal for the Second Crusade, and perhaps fatal in the long term to the Latin kingdom itself. On the whole Jerusalem and Damascus had hitherto managed to live together, and since Zangī had threatened Önör in 534/1139 there had been an alliance between the two neighbouring states. Now Önör appealed to Nūr al-Dīn for help. The

Crusaders abandoned the siege of Damascus while Nūr al-Dīn was advancing southwards.

Ibn al-Qalānisī, a contemporary and a native of Damascus, describes in these words the turn of the tide for his city:

Meanwhile reports had reached the Franks from several quarters of the rapid advance of the Islamic armies to engage in the Holy War against them and of their eagerness to exterminate them, and they became convinced of their own destruction and of the imminence of disaster. Having taken counsel of one another, they found no way of escape from the net into which they had fallen and the abyss into which they had cast themselves save to retreat in disorder at dawn on the Wednesday, the following day, and to flee, broken and forsaken. When the Muslims learned this, and the signs of the retreat of the Franks became clear to them, they moved out to attack them on the morning of the same day and hastened towards them, pursuing them with arrows, so that they slew a large number of men, horses, and other animals in their rear files. In the remains of their camps, moreover, and along their highroads there were found such uncountable quantities of burial pits of their slain and of their magnificent horses, that there were stenches from their corpses that almost overcame the birds in the air. They had also burned down al-Rabwa and al-Qubba al-Mamdūdīya [suburbs of Damascus] during the night. The people rejoiced at this mercy which God had bountifully bestowed upon them, and multiplied their thanks to Him for having vouchsafed to them an answer to the prayers which they had offered up without ceasing during the days of this distress, and to God be praise and thanks therefor.[1]

In a military sense the Second Crusade was indecisive but it demonstrated that Damascus was now the key to Syria. Three events changed the situation. In Ṣafar 544/June 1149 the army of Nūr al-Dīn, reinforced by contingents from Damascus, won an important victory at Inab, a fortress in the principality of Antioch. Raymond of Poitiers, the prince of Antioch, was killed in the battle. Passing through the ravaged principality, Nūr al-Dīn bathed symbolically in the Mediterranean. The Frankish coastal states were now threatened by the new champion of Islam. Then in Rabīʿ II 544/August 1149 Önör died, and in Jumādā II/November Sayf al-Dīn Ghāzī. A clash between Nūr al-Dīn and his younger brother, Quṭb al-Dīn Mawdūd, who succeeded as ruler of Mosul, was narrowly averted, and the previous coexistence between the two Zangid states was restored.

Four more years elapsed before Nūr al-Dīn obtained possession of Damascus, and in the meantime the remains of the county of Edessa were brought under his rule. Then in 548/1143 the Frankish rulers of the coast won a last belated victory when King Baldwin III captured Ascalon, the Fatimid bridgehead in Palestine which had so nearly fallen in 492/1099. Damascus now found itself caught between two aggressive military powers. Among the people of the city there was a growing desire for the rule of Nūr al-Dīn. The last Burid, Mujīr al-Dīn Uvak, endeavoured to maintain his position in spite of the opposition of his subjects, the blandishments of Nūr al-Dīn and the danger from the Franks. The end of the dynasty came in Ṣafar 549/ April 1154, when Nūr al-Dīn's army, besieging Damascus, was admitted into the city by collaborators from among the townspeople (see below, p. 71).

Nūr al-Dīn had at last united Muslim Syria under his personal rule and his prestige was at its height. As well as being the champion in the *jihād*, he impressed himself upon his subjects as the paragon of a Muslim ruler. In Damascus as in Aleppo he sponsored a revival of Sunnī Islam, and endowed schools, mosques and Ṣūfī convents, as well as a palace of justice (*dār al-ʿadl*), where the grievances of the people might be heard and redressed (see further, p. 73). It is this aspect of his rule which is denoted by the title bestowed on him by the caliph – al-Malik al-ʿĀdil, "the Just King". But the fall of Ascalon had indicated a new shift in the power-struggle between the Franks and their neighbours. From Aleppo the centre of conflict had moved to Damascus; from Damascus it now moved to Egypt.

NOTE

1. H. A. R. Gibb (tr), *The Damascus Chronicle of the Crusades*, London 1932, 286–7.

CHAPTER SIX

Nūr al-Dīn and the Rise of Saladin 1154–1174

The fall of Ascalon to Baldwin III and the acquisition of Damascus by Nūr al-Dīn indicated that in the coming period Egypt would play an important part in the policy of its northern neighbours as the pivot of relations between the Frankish and the Muslim rulers in Syria. The crisis was, however, delayed for nearly ten years, during which time Nūr al-Dīn maintained the truce with Baldwin III which had existed under the Burids, and he even continued to pay tribute as his predecessors in Damascus had done.

The initiative as regards Egypt was, in fact, taken by the Latin kingdom under Baldwin III and, after his death in 1163, by his brother and successor Amalric, who had been count of Jaffa and Ascalon, and as such was experienced in the affairs of the south of the kingdom and the Egyptian frontier. Politically, the Fatimid caliphate was at this time in a sorry condition. The caliph was no longer an autocratic ruler or even the real holder of power. Al-Ḥāfiẓ, the last adult caliph, died in 544/1149. Of his three successors, al-Ẓāfir was sixteen on his accession, al-Fā'iz four (549/1154), and al-ʿĀḍid nine (555/1160). From the time of Badr al-Jamālī in the late fifth/eleventh century, the military *wazīr* had been the effective ruler, but the wazirate itself had become the object of contention among the great amirs, so that periods of strong government and political stability were rare. Shortly before al-Ẓāfir's accession the governor of Alexandria, a Kurd named Ibn al-Salār, usurped the wazirate, and held it for four years until he was murdered in a conspiracy between his stepson, ʿAbbās b. Abi'l-Futūḥ, and the latter's son. ʿAbbās then became *wazīr*. In a murky episode that ensued ʿAbbās's son murdered the caliph, while ʿAbbās carried out a massacre of the Fatimid princes, reserving as nominal caliph the baby al-Fā'iz. The event provoked a revolt, and the Armenian governor of Middle Egypt, Ṭalā'iʿ b.

Ruzzīk, moved on Cairo. ʿAbbās fled and was subsequently killed, and Ṭalāʾiʿ became *wazīr*. He was in his turn murdered in 556/1161, and was succeeded as *wazīr* by his son Ruzzīk. Then in 558/1163 the governor of Upper Egypt, an Arab named Shāwar, marched on Cairo. He overthrew Ruzzīk and made himself *wazīr*, but not for long as, a few months later, he was ousted by a powerful courtier of Arab descent, the chamberlain Ḍirghām. Shāwar fled to seek help from Nūr al-Dīn, while Ḍirghām succeeded to the wazirate.

It was at this point that the Zangid ruler of Syria became involved in the affairs of Egypt, although Ibn al-Salār during his brief wazirate had opened abortive negotiations with Nūr al-Dīn. By contrast the Latin kingdom was already an important factor in Egyptian politics. In 1155 Ṭalāʾiʿ b. Ruzzīk had undertaken to pay tribute to the Latin kingdom, and this was reimposed after his murder. The year of crisis came in 558/1163. The split between Shāwar and Ḍirghām, the flight of the former to Nūr al-Dīn and the refusal of Ḍirghām to pay tribute to the Latin kingdom encouraged Amalric, the vigorous new king, to undertake an invasion of Egypt. The Frankish army reached Bilbays, which guarded the approaches to Cairo, but the defenders cut the dikes to release the Nile flood (Shawwāl 558/September 1163), so that the invaders were compelled to retreat.

Nūr al-Dīn had been reluctant to interfere, and to burden his compact Syrian kingdom with the military and strategic problems of intervention in Egypt. Early approaches to him from Ibn al-Salār and Ṭalāʾiʿ b. Ruzzīk had come to nothing. But on this occasion he was won over by his great Kurdish vassal Shīrkūh, who may have hoped to make himself independent in Egypt. So, accompanied by his nephew Saladin (then in his mid-twenties), Shīrkūh set out with Shāwar in Jumādā I 559/April 1164 to invade Egypt. Cairo was captured, Ḍirghām killed and Shāwar restored to the wazirate. But to evade the payment of an indemnity which he had promised to Nūr al-Dīn, Shāwar now sought the help of the Franks against Shīrkūh. Amalric again invaded Egypt, and besieged Bilbays, but the military operations of Nūr al-Dīn in Palestine prevented him from pressing his advantage. An armistice was arranged in Dhuʾl-Ḥijja 559/October 1164, and both the Frankish and the Muslim army evacuated Egypt. Shīrkūh's ambition had now been whetted, and in 562/1167, with the backing of the ʿAbbasid caliph, he won Nūr al-Dīn's approval for another expedition into Egypt. Faced by this threat, Shāwar again sought the help of Amalric. This time both armies penetrated more deeply into Egypt: there were operations around Cairo, a major battle (in which the Franks were defeated) at al-Bābayn in Middle Egypt (Jumādā I 562/March 1167), and a siege of

Alexandria, where Saladin was governor. Once again, however, no decisive result was obtained, and the two armies evacuated Egypt in Shawwāl 562/August 1167. The Franks had nevertheless a tangible sign of their domination: the tribute to the Latin kingdom was increased, a Frankish resident was installed in Cairo and Frankish troops garrisoned the gates of the city.

In the following year Amalric, under pressure from the grand master of the Hospitallers, led his forces into Egypt for the fourth time, intending on this occasion to make a complete conquest and to annex the country. Bilbays fell on 1 Ṣafar 564/4 November 1168 after a three days' siege, and a massacre followed. The Franks advanced on Cairo, where Shāwar played for time with negotiations, while the Caliph al-ʿĀḍid sent a personal appeal to Nūr al-Dīn and Shīrkūh for help. This time there was no delay in the response. Shīrkūh and his army started from Syria (Ṣafar 564/December 1168), and in the next month Amalric began to withdraw his depleted forces. The Franks' great gamble had failed, and the Latin kingdom had in the end gained nothing from an enormous expenditure of blood and treasure. Shāwar was also a loser. He was arrested by Saladin, and put to death at al-ʿĀḍid's command by Shīrkūh, who was thereupon appointed *wazīr* (Rabīʿ II 564/January 1169). A few weeks later the obese and gluttonous old warrior was dead. The wazirate with the honorific of al-Malik al-Nāṣir and the title of "sultan" (usually conferred on Fatimid *wazīrs*) devolved on his nephew Saladin.

With Shīrkūh and Saladin the Ayyubid family moved to the centre of the Near Eastern stage. Their origins were obscure, and began with Saladin's grandfather, Shādhī, who was a Kurd living near the town of Dvin, north of the River Araxes and Mount Ararat, near the meeting-point of the modern frontiers of Turkey, Iran and Russia. The rulers of the region were at that time a Kurdish dynasty, the Shaddadids, whose power was on the decline. Shādhī and his two sons, Najm al-Dīn Ayyūb and Asad al-Dīn Shīrkūh, migrated to the eastern Fertile Crescent, where Shādhī was appointed castellan of Tikrīt on the Tigris. On his death, the office passed to Ayyūb, who in early 526/1132 facilitated the crossing of the river by Zangī after an unsuccessful campaign. This was a fateful action, for when six years later Ayyūb lost Tikrīt, he and his brother made their way to Zangī, taking with them Saladin, who according to tradition was born on the night of their departure. Something has already been said of their fortune under Zangī and Nūr al-Dīn. Ayyūb was given Baʿlabakk when Zangī took it, and subsequently entered the service of the Burids. Shīrkūh remained with Nūr al-Dīn but negotiated with his brother over the capitulation of Damascus in

549/1154. Ayyūb became governor of Damascus, while Shīrkūh received Ḥimṣ in *iqṭā'*. Although Nūr al-Dīn granted the town to another of his followers after Shīrkūh's death, Saladin later gave it to the son of Shīrkūh, whose descendants ruled there until the early Mamluk sultanate. The Ayyubid family thus had a background of military and political experience under the Shaddadids and the Zangids which prepared Saladin for the part he was to play.

Saladin's succession to the wazirate had not been an entirely straightforward matter. On Shīrkūh's death, several of the senior officers of the Syrian expeditionary force coveted the chief command. Saladin's claims were advanced by an influential Kurdish jurist, 'Īsā al-Hakkārī, and his appointment indicated the ascendancy of the Kurds and the *'askar* of Shīrkūh, the Asadiyya, over the Turks and Turcomans who were the Mamluks or clients of Nūr al-Dīn. Some of these remained irreconcilable, the commander of the Turcoman cavalry, 'Ayn al-Dawla al-Yarūqī, being the most important of the amirs who returned to Syria rather than serve under Saladin. The investiture of the new *wazīr* took place three days after Shīrkū's death. Saladin was neither young nor inexperienced. At over thirty years old he was a middle-aged man by medieval standards, and he had served in Shīrkūh's three expeditions, playing an important part in the fighting at al-Babayn and in the defence of Alexandria. We hear of his hesitation to participate in the hurly-burly of warfare and politics, but his reluctance was never insuperable. Once installed in office, he set about securing his position with equal resolution and ruthlessness.

At the start there seemed no reason why his wazirate should long endure. Politically there was a profound ambiguity in his position. He was the commander of an alien expeditionary force, the agent of the Syrian Nūr al-Dīn. Like his master he was a Sunnī Muslim, deriving legitimate authority ultimately from the 'Abbasid caliph. At the same time, as *wazīr* he was the delegate of the Ismā'īlī Fatimid Caliph al-'Āḍid, from whom he held in theory plenary civil and military authority in Egypt. More immediately important was the uncertain base of his actual power. He had no effective control over the Fatimid armed forces, which comprised 40,000 cavalrymen (including probably several thousand Arab auxiliaries) and 30,000 infantrymen, who formed the garrison of Cairo. These latter were the Black troops, the *Sūdān*, sometimes anachronistically designated "Sudanese".

Against these potentially overwhelming forces, Saladin could rely only on his much smaller Syrian contingent. This had originally consisted of 2,000 troopers from the Nūriyya (i.e. the *'askar* of Nūr al-Dīn), al-Yarūqī's 6,000 Turcomans and Shīrkūh's own Asadiyya. The expeditionary force was depleted, however, not only by casualties but also by the withdrawal to Syria of the Turcomans and dissident amirs. To compensate for these losses and defections, Saladin built up his own *ʿaskar*, the Ṣalāḥiyya. To maintain his troops, and at the same time to weaken the Fatimid military establishment, Saladin began to seize the revenues of the Egyptian amirs, and to grant them in *iqṭāʿ* to his own followers. The resentment this caused resulted in a conspiracy fomented by a member of al-ʿĀḍid's household, a Black eunuch, Mu'tamin al-Khilāfa, who tried to establish an agreement with the Latin kingdom. The plot was discovered, Mu'tamin al-Khilāfa hunted down and killed and an ensuing revolt of the Black troops bloodily suppressed (564/1169). A remnant of the Blacks escaped to Upper Egypt, which was the scene of revolts for some years to come.

The leading part in this action in Cairo was taken by Shams al-Dīn Tūrān-Shāh, Saladin's younger brother, who with the other sons of Najm al-Dīn Ayyūb had been allowed by Nūr al-Dīn to go to Egypt a short time previously. It had not been an easy decision for the *atabeg*; he seems very early to have recognized and mistrusted Saladin's ambition. He recalled the Nūriyya amirs from Egypt, and confiscated the Syrian *iqṭāʿs* of Shīrkūh and Saladin, thus depriving the Asadiyya of their financial resources, and necessitating Saladin's seizure of the Egyptian revenues. He was at first reluctant to let Saladin's brothers join him, rightly foreseeing that they might transform Egypt into an immense family holding. Several months later the patriarchal Najm al-Dīn Ayyūb himself arrived in Egypt. Representing the older generation, which had found security and prosperity in the service of Nūr al-Dīn, he acted as a brake on his son's ambitions, and prevented a breach between the *atabeg* and his viceroy in Egypt. The conversion of the country into a family domain, however, proceeded apace. Najm al-Dīn Ayyūb received in *iqṭāʿ* the revenues of the great ports of Alexandria and Damietta and the province of the Buḥayra lying west of the Delta. The *iqṭāʿ* of Tūrān-Shāh was, significantly, the troublesome region of Upper Egypt.

With the elimination of the Black troops, the Fatimid caliphate had lost its basis of military support, and its formal extinction could not long be delayed. Nūr al-Dīn had had this in mind even in the time of Shīrkūh: he was now pressing Saladin to take the decisive step of substituting the name of the ʿAbbasid caliph for that of the Fatimid in the *khuṭba*. Saladin had for some time been making preparations for the return of Egypt to the fold of Sunnī Islam. In Jumādā II 566/March 1171 two key offices were given to members of his entourage: that of chief judge (hitherto held by a Shīʿī) to a Kurdish jurist, Ṣadr al-Dīn al-Hadhabānī, and that of head of the caliph's chancery to a man who had already served Shāwar and Shīrkūh. His name was Abū ʿAlī ʿAbd al-Raḥīm but he is always known by his official style of al-Qāḍī al-Fāḍil, "the Excellent Judge". By the autumn the Caliph al-ʿĀḍid was mortally ill, and Saladin was ready to make the change. The exact chronology and course of events are by no means clear, but on 10 Muḥarram 567/12–13 September 1171 al-ʿĀḍid died, and certainly on the following Friday (but perhaps on the previous Friday) the name of the Caliph al-Mustaḍīʾ was pronounced in the *khuṭba*. He was the first ʿAbbasid caliph to be publicly recognized in Egypt since 358/969.

The suppression of the Fatimid caliphate ended the ambiguity in Saladin's position: he now governed Egypt as the deputy of his Sunnī overlord under the nominal sovereignty of the ʿAbbasid caliph, who formally invested Nūr al-Dīn with the rule over Syria and Egypt, and sent a robe of honour to Saladin. The death of his brother Quṭb al-Dīn Mawdūd (565/1170) enabled Nūr al-Dīn to intervene in Mosul, and to install his nephew, a second Sayf al-Dīn Ghāzī, as his vassal. The dominions of Nūr al-Dīn were now at their widest extent. But it was becoming clear that mistrust between Nūr al-Dīn and Saladin was growing. Several developments in these years suggest that Saladin was playing for his own hand. Immediately after the overthrow of the Fatimid caliphate, Saladin led his forces into Transjordan in a combined operation with Nūr al-Dīn against the great castles of al-Karak (known to the Franks as Crac des Moabites) and al-Shawbak (Crac de Montréal). Then suddenly, alleging the danger of a rising in Cairo, he withdrew, to the anger of Nūr al-Dīn. It seems that Saladin realized that the taking of these castles would remove a useful buffer territory from between the domains of his overlord and his own, while close co-operation between Nūr al-Dīn and himself would limit his military and political initiative. A second invasion of Transjordan in 568/1173 was similarly broken off. It is also perhaps significant that at this period Saladin and his family were endeavouring to gain possession of territories outside the Zangid sphere of influence – possibly to serve as a refuge if events went against them. A revolt of the remnants of the Blacks in Upper Egypt followed by a Nubian invasion led to the despatch of an army under Tūrān-Shāh in 568/1173, which penetrated Nubia, and installed a Kurdish garrison in the fortress of Ibrīm between the First and Second Cataracts (see below, p. 132). In the same year another army invaded the territories lying to the west of Egypt. The most successful and most lasting in its results of these expeditions was one sent out in 569/1174, again under Tūrān-Shāh, into the Yemen. The country was conquered, and Ayyubid princes ruled there for over half a century.

Meanwhile Nūr al-Dīn continued to feel resentment at what seemed to him an inadequate contribution from the Fatimid treasures and the Egyptian revenues. Matters came to a head when he sent one of his chief treasury officials to carry out an audit and fix the annual tribute due from Saladin. In the meantime he was mustering his troops. Nūr al-Dīn and Saladin were spared the imminent clash when the *atabeg* died in Damascus on 11 Shawwāl 569/15 May 1174.

CHAPTER SEVEN

The Ascendancy of Saladin 1174–1193

Less than two months after Nūr al-Dīn's death in Damascus, King Amalric died in Jerusalem on 11 July 1174. The passing of the leaders of Muslim and Christian Syria created a new political situation. The heirs of both were minors: al-Ṣāliḥ Ismāʿīl was eleven years old, Baldwin IV was thirteen and a leper. The accession of a child was ominous of a period of instability for a medieval state, but at this juncture the advantage lay with the Latin kingdom, where there were established constitutional forms and usages. There was no such security for the dominions of the *atabeg*. In Jerusalem the regency until Baldwin IV came of age in 1176 was held by Count Raymond of Tripoli, who was also lord of Tiberias in right of his wife Eschiva. He was supported by the native barons, the higher clergy and the Hospitallers – a faction with a good understanding of the Frankish states and their position as an enclave in the Muslim Near East. They were inclined to a policy of coexistence rather than military adventure. There was, however, an opposing faction, more aggressive in its attitude, and composed chiefly of the recent arrivals in Outremer and the Templars. Its first leaders were Joscelin of Courtenay (son of Count Joscelin II of Edessa) and the rash and irresponsible Reynald of Châtillon. They had been Nūr al-Dīn's captives in Aleppo from 1160 until their release in 1176, when, as mentioned earlier (p. 34), Reynald by a prompt marriage acquired the lordship of Oultrejourdain and its key castles of al-Karak and al-Shawbak.

On the Muslim side there was also division. Possession of the person of al-Ṣāliḥ Ismāʿīl was a matter of competition among Nūr al-Dīn's officers, and in Dhu'l-Ḥijja 569/July 1174 the prize was secured by the eunuch Gümüshtigin, who forthwith took the young *atabeg* off to Aleppo. Meanwhile Sayf al-Dīn Ghāzī of Mosul seized the opportunity to annex Nūr al-Dīn's former territories beyond the Euphrates. But of the contenders for power, the most formidable was Saladin. Biding his time, he formally acknowledged al-Ṣāliḥ Ismāʿīl as his overlord.

Saladin's behaviour in the dozen years following the death of Nūr al-Dīn rendered him a controversial figure in his own day, and differences of opinion about his motives and character appear in the writings of modern historians. From 569/1174 to 581/1186 events seem to show that Saladin's preoccupation was not the *jihād* but the reunification of the Zangid domains under his own overlordship. He may have intended this to be what in fact it was, the prelude to a great campaign against the Latin kingdom, but it is gratuitous to assume that this was his sole, or perhaps even his primary, intention. From a purely political point of view, the Frankish states were not essentially different from the other obstacles to his creation of an empire in Egypt and the Fertile Crescent. There were some hostilities against the Franks during these years. In 573/1177 Saladin took the initiative with a raid up the Palestine coast. Leaving Gaza and Ascalon untaken in his rear, he was surprised and routed, narrowly escaping with his life, at Mont Gisard near al-Ramla (2 Jumādā II 573/25 November 1177). But Baldwin IV, who had fought in the battle, lacked the resources to follow up the victory. Two years later there was another encounter. The Franks constructed a stronghold (called in the Arabic sources Bayt al-Aḥzān) at Jisr Banāt Yaʿqūb, the crossing of the Jordan on the way from Damascus to the Palestinian coast. A clash between Saladin's troops and Baldwin IV in the Jawlān (Golan) region resulted in a Muslim victory (Shawwāl 574/April 1179). The Franks were again defeated at Marj ʿUyūn in the upper Jordan valley on 3 Muḥarram 575/10 June 1179, and two months later Bayt al-Aḥzān was captured and destroyed. In general, however, an armistice prevailed, and as late as 1185 a four-year truce was made between Saladin and the Latin kingdom.

The real interest and significance of these years lie in Saladin's pertinacious extension of his ascendancy over the Zangid realms. The first step came in Rabīʿ I 570/October 1174 after Gümüshtigin had taken al-Ṣāliḥ Ismāʿīl to Aleppo. The amirs in Damascus, who had already unsuccessfully sought the protection of Sayf al-Dīn Ghāzī, invited the help of Saladin. He entered the city almost without opposition, asserting that he was the rightful guardian of the young *atabeg*, and thereafter he intervened continually in the affairs of Syria and the eastern Fertile Crescent. His first attempt to gain control of Aleppo was foiled by an alliance between Gümüshtigin and Sayf al-Dīn Ghāzī, but the allies were defeated at the Horns of Ḥamāh (19 Ramaḍān 570/13 April 1175), after which Saladin again besieged Aleppo. This time he was able to impose his terms: al-Ṣāliḥ was to remain lord of Aleppo but his forces were to join Saladin against the Franks. This may have been a veritable plan for an alliance in the *jihād* or no more than a face-saving formula to cover the dependence of the *atabeg* on his former vassal. The Zangid suzerainty was officially abrogated a few days later, when Saladin received a diploma from the Caliph al-Mustaḍī' investing him with his holdings in Egypt and the Yemen, the territories which he would liberate in the future, and the Syrian lands except for al-Ṣāliḥ Ismā'īl's actual possessions in and around Aleppo. The matter was, however, not yet at an end. The Zangid alliance was re-established, and was again defeated by Saladin at the battle of Tall al-Sulṭān, south of Aleppo (10 Shawwāl 571/22 April 1176). Another siege of Aleppo was ended by a renewal of the former agreement. On his return to Damascus, Saladin married the widow of Nūr al-Dīn (who was also Önör's daughter), thereby symbolically affirming his position as the legitimate successor of both the Zangids and the Burids.

Some years passed before Saladin improved his position in the north. Then a number of significant events occurred. In 575/1180 the Caliph al-Mustaḍī' died, and was succeeded by his son, al-Nāṣir, during whose long reign (until 622/1225) the 'Abbasid caliphate had an Indian summer of power and authority. In Ṣafar 576/June 1180 Sayf al-Dīn Ghāzī died, and was succeeded at Mosul by his brother 'Izz al-Dīn Mas'ūd, who tried in vain to obtain Saladin's recognition of his rule over the lands annexed on the death of Nūr al-Dīn. Saladin had in fact already gained a foothold to the north of Mosul. During that summer, after making a truce with the Latin kingdom, he intervened to protect Nūr al-Dīn Muḥammad b. Kara-Arslan, the Artukid lord of Ḥiṣn Kayfā (who was actually a vassal of the Zangids of Mosul) from the sultan of Rūm, Kılıj-Arslan II. The two sultans met on the Gök Su (a tributary of the Euphrates), and settled their differences. Thus the Artukid territory passed from the Zangid sphere of influence into that of Saladin. Then in Rajab 577/December 1181 al-Ṣāliḥ Ismā'īl died in Aleppo. Within a month 'Izz al-Dīn Mas'ūd had annexed the city, married the mother of al-Ṣāliḥ Ismā'īl (thereby countering Saladin's pretensions to the succession) and carried off the treasure to Mosul.

A clash between the two rulers was now inevitable. Saladin took the offensive, and in 578/1182 he laid siege to Mosul. On the intervention of the caliph he withdrew, but he went on to campaign in the Jazīra, where he was assisted by the Artukids. He captured the great fortress of Āmid, which he promptly delivered to Nūr al-Dīn Muḥammad, but Mosul still eluded him. The caliph would not grant him a diploma of investiture to legitimate his claims, so Saladin turned back to Syria to settle accounts with Aleppo. Although the Nūriyya veterans there were prepared to fight, the governor, a brother of ʿIzz al-Dīn Masʿūd, surrendered on terms, and at last in Ṣafar 579/June 1183 the capital of northern Syria passed into Saladin's hands. Mosul remained, and it was not until 581/1185 that Saladin launched another attack against it. Although yet again he failed to force Mosul to surrender (and indeed he fell desperately ill during the winter), he obtained by negotiation at least the formal recognition of his claims. Agreement was reached in Dhu'l-Ḥijja 581/March 1186 that Saladin's name should be recited in the *khuṭba* as overlord of Mosul.

The position of the Latin kingdom had deteriorated since the death of Amalric. Like the other Frankish states, it had found no solution to the perpetual problem of the lack of manpower. For some years the absence of adequate help from the West had been compensated by the assistance of the Byzantine Emperor Manuel Comnenus. But in 1176 Manuel was heavily defeated in battle by Kılıj-Arslan II at Myriokephalon – a second Manzikert (see below, p. 171). He was a broken man, and his death four years later meant that the Frankish states had lost their last effective ally. In the Latin kingdom Baldwin IV asserted his authority over his factious nobles with remarkable resolution, but he was leprous and childless and his days were clearly numbered. In 1180 his sister, Sibyl, married a newcomer to the country, Guy of Lusignan, who adhered to the adventurous faction of Joscelin of Courtenay and Reynald of Châtillon. In March 1185 the king died, and once again a minor succeeded – Baldwin V, Sibyl's child by her previous marriage. He was only eight years old, and Count Raymond of Tripoli again assumed the regency. So Reynald and his bellicose associates were held in check, but not for long. Baldwin V died in the summer of 1186. Sibyl became queen, and crowned Guy of Lusignan king.

In the events leading to the imminent clash between the Latin kingdom and Saladin, Reynald of Châtillon played a fateful part. His castle of al-Karak was a thorn in the side of the Muslims, being a base from which the routes linking Damascus with Egypt and the Ḥijāz were threatened. In 578/1183, moreover, Reynald had launched a naval squadron on the Red Sea, sacked the port of ʿAydhāb on its African coast (by which pilgrims passed to Jedda), sunk a pilgrim-vessel, and threatened the immunity of Mecca and Medina. Exceptionally odious in Muslim eyes, he is significantly one of the very few Franks to receive a notice in al-Ṣafadī's voluminous biographical dictionary, *al-Wāfī bi'l-wafayāt*, compiled in the eighth/fourteenth century. The account there given of "the prince of al-Karak" goes on to describe the decisive campaign of Ḥaṭṭīn, which laid the Latin kingdom open to Saladin:

The prince of al-Karak . . . was the most malicious, evil and treacherous of the Franks. He intercepted a caravan coming from Egypt to Syria, in which were many people and much wealth, and seized the lot by killing, capturing and robbing. The Sultan Saladin sent to rebuke him for what he had done, saying, "Where are the covenants? Return what you have taken." He paid no heed, raiding the Muslims and slaughtering them, so the sultan swore to have his blood. This deed of his was in the year 582 [1186–7].

Then the battle of Ḥaṭṭīn took place in the year 583. The Franks came out of Acre leaving no adult male behind: it is said that there were 80,200 of them, knights and footsoldiers. They encamped at Ṣaffūriyya. The sultan advanced to Tiberias with 12,000 horsemen and many footsoldiers. He mounted mangonels against Tiberias, ruined its walls, and took it on Thursday [2 July 1187]. The citadel in which were the wife of the count and the commander of the Franks held out against him. He took up his position at Lūbiya at sunrise. The Muslims cut them [i.e. the Franks] off from water; it was a hot day and fires were started against them. Muẓaffar al-Dīn [Gökböri] set fire to the cultivation. They passed the night surrounded by the Muslims, and when the dawn came on Saturday, they fought until noon. They went up the hill of Ḥaṭṭīn with the fire blazing around them, and perished, falling one after another from the hill. The Count [Raymond of Tripoli] was with them. He was carried along, and Saladin opened a way for him, so he went up to Ṣafad. The swords of the Muslims were at work dealing death to the Franks. There were captured of their rulers Guy and his brother Geoffrey,[1] the prince of al-Karak, Humphrey [of Toron] and the lord of Jubayl, Beirut and Sidon, the grand masters of the Templars and the Hospitallers, and others. The cross of the Crucifixion was brought to the sultan; it was adorned with jewels and rubies in a golden case.

When the rulers were driven as prisoners before the sultan, he dismounted, knelt and kissed the ground in thanks. He came to a tent, and summoned them. He seated the rulers at his right hand, and the prince of al-Karak at his side. The sultan noticed that the king, who was glancing around, was consumed with thirst. He ordered him to be brought a goblet of iced water. He drank of it, and gave to the prince to drink. The sultan said to him, "I did not grant you permission to give him to drink." He had sworn to slay him with his own hand, so he said to him, "Accursed and treacherous one. You have sworn and betrayed and broken your oath." He went on to enumerate his treacheries to him. Then he arose, and struck him with his sword, cleaving his shoulder, and the Mamluks made an end of him. They cut off his head, and fed his carcase to the dogs. When the king saw him slain, he was filled with fear and confusion. The sultan promised him safety, saying, "This was a treacherous liar, who betrayed on more than one occasion." Then the sultan offered Islam to the Templars and Hospitallers. Those who accepted conversion were spared, and those who did not were slain. He slew a great number, and sent the rest of the rulers and prisoners to Damascus.[2]

After this overwhelming victory, it seemed that all the Latin kingdom would fall to Saladin. Acre was surrendered by Joscelin of Courtenay. Jerusalem withstood siege for a time but yielded on terms on 27 Rajab 583/2 October 1187. In contrast to the Crusaders, eighty-eight years before, the troops of Saladin did not signalize their victory by massacre and rapine. Even the Church of the Holy Sepulchre remained intact, and the tombs of the Frankish rulers from Godfrey of Bouillon to Baldwin V were as yet inviolate. By the end of 1187, of the cities of the Latin kingdom only Tyre remained in Frankish hands. It had been saved by the defence put up by Conrad of Montferrat, the uncle of Baldwin V, newly arrived by sea. Saladin's siege of Tyre ended when his eastern allies withdrew their contingents. The problem of keeping his army in the field was constantly to beset him in the next five years.

The defeat at Ḥaṭṭīn and the fall of Jerusalem produced a new upsurge of crusading enthusiasm, and on this occasion the cross was taken by the three most powerful monarchs of Western Europe: the Emperor Frederick Barbarossa, Philip Augustus of France and Richard Lion-heart of England. The great German army, led across Europe and Anatolia by Frederick, broke up when he drowned in June 1190 before reaching Syria. Philip and Richard, quarrelsome and mutually resentful allies, reached Palestine by sea in April and June 1191 respectively, Richard on the way conquering Cyprus from Isaac Comnenus, the self-styled Byzantine "emperor" of the island. The immediate goal of the Third Crusade was Acre, where the Muslim garrison had been besieged by King Guy, who had been released by Saladin after swearing that he would not again take up arms against him – a pledge which he did not keep. Guy in his turn had been beset by Saladin since the late summer of 1189. The Crusader reinforcements, culminating in the arrival of the kings, finally brought victory to the Franks at Acre. In Jumādā II 587/July 1191 the city capitulated. It was to enter upon a new phase of its history as the capital for the next century of the restored Latin kingdom.

Very shortly after the recapture of Acre, King Philip returned home. The Crusade, now under Richard's leadership, moved into its second stage. Richard's primary aim was to clear the Muslim forces from the coastlands – a necessary preliminary to an attempt to retake Jerusalem. As the Crusaders advanced southwards from Acre there were engagements with Saladin's troops, who were defeated at the battle of Arsūf, after which Richard took Jaffa (17 Shaʿbān 587/10 September 1191). From this base he twice struck up into the hills towards Jerusalem, and twice halted at Bayt Nūba, a few miles from the city, and withdrew. The native barons and the knights of the military orders advised the king soundly and sadly that Jerusalem could become a trap. A place of far greater strategic importance to both sides was Ascalon, lying as it did on Saladin's lines of communications with Egypt. As the Crusaders advanced, he demolished it; Richard soon afterwards fortified it again. Both the leaders tacitly recognized that the position was one of stale-

mate. Already after the taking of Jaffa negotiations had been begun, Saladin being represented by his brother, al-ʿĀdil Sayf al-Dīn, known to the Franks as Saphadin. After much bargaining a three years' truce was concluded in Shaʿbān 588/September 1192. The Latin kingdom retained the coast as far as Jaffa, but Ascalon and Gaza, their fortifications razed, passed to Saladin. The Crusade was over, and the leading actors departed. Richard left (for captivity in Austria) a week after swearing to the truce, Saladin died in Damascus on 27 Ṣafar 589/4 March 1193.

The restored and diminished Latin kingdom was not under the rule of Guy of Lusignan, whose right had lapsed with the death of Queen Sibyl in 1190. Richard compensated him with the crown of Cyprus. Sibyl's sister, Isabel, the heiress to the Latin kingdom, had been compelled to marry Conrad of Montferrat. He thereby acquired a claim to the throne but was murdered by Assassins in Tyre in April 1192. A few days later his widow married Count Henry of Champagne, a leading French Crusader. Although he never assumed the title of king, he was the ruler when Richard departed.

NOTES

1. Not Geoffrey, who did not reach the Holy Land until the summer of 1188, but his brother Aimery (Amalric), later Latin king.
2. Al-Ṣafadī, *al-Wāfī bi'l-wafayāt*, VI, ed. S. Dedering, Wiesbaden 1972, 182–4. English version P. M. Holt.

CHAPTER EIGHT

The Later Ayyubids 1193–1249

After Saladin's death in 589/1193 his family, the Ayyubids, continued to rule in Egypt until 648/1250, and in Muslim Syria for a further decade. The various territories which he had gradually and laboriously brought under his control did not form part of a closely united monarchy but were partitioned under the rule of different members of the Ayyubid clan. The government of the Ayyubids was therefore similar to that of the Buyids and Seljukids before them, and like these earlier ruling clans, the Ayyubids were frequently at odds among themselves. During the greater part of the period of their ascendancy, three Ayyubids maintained (often with difficulty) their supremacy over their kinsmen and fellow-rulers. These were: first, Saladin's brother, al-ʿĀdil Sayf al-Dīn from 596/1200 to 615/1218; secondly, al-ʿĀdil's son, al-Kāmil Muḥammad from 615/1218 to 635/1238; and thirdly, al-Kāmil's son, al-Ṣāliḥ Ayyūb from 637/1240 to 647/1249.

Saladin himself had relied mainly on his close kinsmen for the government of his growing empire, and at the time of his death the territories were distributed among them as appanages. Saladin's own sons had the three chief provinces: al-Afḍal ʿAlī ruled in Damascus, al-Ẓāhir Ghāzī in Aleppo and al-ʿAzīz ʿUthmān in Cairo. The northern territories at the head of the Fertile Crescent forming the link between Syria and the Kurdish homeland of the Ayyubids, were in the hands of al-ʿĀdil Sayf al-Dīn, whose son (Saladin's nephew), al-Muʿaẓẓam Īsā, held Transjordan – another region of strategic importance. The collateral branch, the Asadī dynasty, i.e. the descendants of Saladin's uncle Asad al-Dīn Shīrkūh, ruled the central Syrian province of Ḥimṣ. The remote and detached Yemen, which had been conquered by Saladin's brother Shams al-Dīn Tūrān-Shāh, had subsequently passed to another brother, and plays no part in the history of the Ayyubids in Egypt and Syria.

The dispositions made by Saladin during his lifetime thus seemed to assure supremacy within the clan to his own sons, and among them to the eldest, al-Afḍal ʿAlī of Damascus. But this was not to be. Saladin's sons had their failings as rulers, of which we are informed by contemporary and later historians, deferential as ever to events. They had also a subtle, powerful and experienced kinsman in al-ʿĀdil, who drew his strength from their weaknesses. In the clan-struggles which ensued during the ten years following Saladin's death, an important part was played by the shifting loyalties of the *ʿaskars*. Chief among these were the Asadiyya and the Ṣalāḥiyya, which had been constituted in the heroic days of the dynasty by Shīrkūh and Saladin respectively. There is no need to detail the intrigues and alliances of these unstable years, but the broad outlines may be indicated. In 592/1196 al-Afḍal ʿAlī was driven out of Damascus, which was then held by al-ʿĀdil in the name of his nephew, al-ʿAzīz ʿUthmān of Egypt. But al-ʿAzīz died in 595/1198, and in 596/1200 al-ʿĀdil usurped the throne of Egypt from his son al-Manṣūr Muḥammad, a minor, and assumed the title of sultan. Finally in 598/1202 al-Ẓāhir Ghāzī of Aleppo was forced to accept al-ʿĀdil's supremacy, and in return was permitted to retain his principality, which indeed continued to be held by his son and grandson until the cataclysm of the Mongol invasion in 658/1260.

Al-ʿĀdil in this way overthrew Saladin's settlement in Egypt and southern Syria, and he made new territorial dispositions in favour of his own sons. Of these, al-Kāmil Muḥammad was his father's deputy in Egypt, al-Muʿaẓẓam ʿĪsā received Damascus and al-Ashraf Mūsā the Jazīra. A fourth son, al-Ṣāliḥ Ismāʿīl, held at this time only the minor lordship of Buṣrā in Ḥawrān. The Asadīs continued to rule in Ḥimṣ, and a junior branch of the Ayyubids, descendants of Saladin's nephew, Taqī al-Dīn ʿUmar, had the other central Syrian province of Ḥamāh.

The great renown achieved by Saladin in his last years, and the unquestioned supremacy which he then enjoyed, have perhaps falsified the historical perspective so that the clan-struggles of 1193–1202 appear as aberrations from the true pattern of Ayyubid monarchy, whereas a good case might be made for the view that the partition of rule was (at least in the eyes of the Ayyubids themselves) the norm, and the domination of one member of the clan an anomaly. A similar case might be stated in regard to external policy. Traditional Muslim historiography, followed by modern writers, has tended to emphasize Saladin's victory in the *jihād*, and so by implication to suggest that the usual relationship between the Muslim and Frankish rulers was one of unremitting warfare. This presentation of Saladin is, as indicated earlier (see p. 54), an over-simplification. Until the eve of Ḥaṭṭīn the relations of Saladin and the Franks were the ordinary earthy relations of competitive neighbours, not cordial but marked with the usual incidents of medieval diplomacy and warfare. This was the situation that was restored after (or even before) Saladin's death, and it continued on the whole until the middle of the seventh/thirteenth century, when the two factors of the establishment of the Mamluk sultanate and the Mongol invasion of Syria gave a new turn to events. As a corollary, it is perhaps wrong to regard the Frankish states in the later Ayyubid period as progressively enfeebled enclaves. The contraction of the Latin kingdom's frontiers after Ḥaṭṭīn was not necessarily a military or strategic disadvantage to the Franks, whose continuing tenure of the ports gave them a significant economic relationship to the Muslim hinterland.

It is also misleading to concentrate on the dealings of the Ayyubids with the Frankish states as if these constituted the sum of their external relations. They themselves certainly made no such mistake. They had a sensitive frontier region in the north, where Ayyubid territory marched with the diminished realms of earlier dynasties, the Artukids and the Zangids, with the Christian states of Lesser Armenia and Georgia, and with the powerful Seljuk sultanate of Rūm. The north-east was the direction from which two movements of steppe-peoples were to enter the Ayyubid dominions: first the Khwarazmians, then the invaders who had set them in motion, the Mongols themselves.

Once al-ʿĀdil had attained supremacy among the Ayyubids, and his sons had been installed in the chief provinces, progress was made both on the northern march and in dealings with the Franks. A repulse of the Georgians in 606/1209–10, followed by a thirty-year truce, secured Ayyubid control of the north-eastern sector. Meanwhile the end of the Third Crusade had been followed by a decline in Western support for the Latin kingdom. A crusade launched (but not led) by the Emperor Henry VI succeeded in retaking Sidon and Beirut in 593/1197, thereby strengthening the Frankish hold of the coastlands. In the following year Innocent III commenced his pontificate with a call to a new crusade. One was indeed organized, but what ensued was something very different from what he had envisaged. The Fourth Crusade was diverted by its Venetian paymasters to Constantinople, the Byzantine empire was overthrown, and Baldwin of Flanders was installed as the first Latin emperor (1204). By a significant contrast, in the same year al-ʿĀdil concluded a formal truce with King Aimery by which Lydda and al-Ramla as well as Nazareth were retroceded to the Latin kingdom. This was the second of three truces, which in all lasted for almost the whole of al-ʿĀdil's reign. At the same time the sultan maintained commercial relations with Venice and Pisa.

The death of al-ʿĀdil in Jumādā II 615/August 1218 occurred at a critical time. Innocent III, disappointed at the outcome of the Fourth Crusade, had sought since 1213 to promote another. He died in 1216 but his successor, Honorius III, maintained papal interest in the Crusade, and in 1218 it was decided to strike at the centre of Ayyubid power in Egypt by an attack on Damietta. While operations were proceeding in the Delta against the forces under al-Kāmil's command, the Seljuk sultan of Rūm, Kay-Kāvūs I, in collusion with the exiled Ayyubid, al-Afḍal ʿAlī, marched on Aleppo. At this juncture al-ʿĀdil died. The imminent danger in Syria passed; Aleppo was relieved and Kay-Kāvūs withdrew. But in Egypt pressure on Damietta increased as more Crusaders arrived from Europe, among them the papal legate, Pelagius of Albano, who assumed a dominating position among the Christian leaders. He was largely responsible for the rejection of very advantageous terms offered by al-Kāmil: the restoration of all the former territories of the Latin kingdom west of the Jordan in return for the evacuation of Egypt and a thirty-year truce. Pelagius's obduracy seemed at first to be justified by success. Damietta fell in Shaʿbān 616/November 1219. Then (as before when al-Kāmil's offer had been under consideration) quarrels broke out between Pelagius and John of Brienne, the regent of the Latin kingdom. The Crusade had lost its momentum, and in the summer of 618/1221 the Crusaders found themselves cut off by the Nile flood outside al-Kamil's camp at al-Manṣūra, between Damietta and Cairo. Only the exhaustion of their opponents saved them. An eight-year truce was negotiated with Pelagius, who was allowed to evacuate Egypt with the Crusaders.

The threat from the Crusaders had deferred but not removed the outbreak of a new Ayyubid clan-struggle, this time among the sons of al-ʿĀdil. In this phase the chief competitors for power were al-Kāmil and al-Muʿaẓẓam of Damascus, with al-Ashraf Mūsā in the Jazīra generally allied to al-Kāmil. But al-Muʿaẓẓam died in Dhu'l-Qaʿda 624/November 1227, and in the following year al-Kāmil and al-Ashraf, conferring at Tall al-ʿAjūl near Gaza, decided to oust his son, al-Nāṣir Dāwūd, from Damascus, which was to go to al-Ashraf, while al-Kāmil was to annex Palestine and Transjordan. The plan was executed in 626/1229. This joint supremacy of al-Kāmil and al-Ashraf over the Ayyubids lasted, not without strain, until the death of al-Ashraf in Muḥarram 635/August 1237. He was succeeded by his brother, al-Ṣāliḥ Ismāʿīl, who was ousted by al-Kāmil in Jumādā I 635/December 1238, but retook the city in 637/1239.

The execution of the agreement of Tall al-ʿAjūl was delayed by an episode which has seemed extraordinary to both contemporary and modern writers, Christian and Muslim alike, but which represents later Ayyubid policy as operated by its most skilful practitioner. Since 1215 the Emperor Frederick II of Hohenstaufen had been under a vow to go on crusade. In 1225 by his marriage to Isabel (Yolanda), the heiress of the Latin kingdom, he became king of Jerusalem in right of his wife. After the failure of the Damietta Crusade, he was under papal pressure to fulfil his vow. In addition to these reasons for going on crusade, Frederick received a call from an unusual source – none other than al-Kāmil himself, who in 623/1226 sent an embassy under one of his chief officers, the Amir Fakhr al-Dīn Yūsuf b. Shaykh al-Shuyūkh, with the offer made vainly to Pelagius of a restoration of the territories taken by Saladin. This startling gesture was a calculated act of policy. At that time al-Kāmil wanted Frederick's support against al-Muʿaẓẓam, while by a pre-emptive diplomatic strike he hoped to avert the armed Crusade which he knew to be in preparation. Frederick in return sent his own envoys to Cairo, and in Shawwāl 625/September 1228 he landed at Acre.

By that time the situation had changed in two important respects. The death of al-Muʿaẓẓam had removed al-Kāmil's most dangerous opponent, and Frederick had been excommunicated by Pope Gregory IX, Honorius III's successor. The formal reason for the excommunication was Frederick's return in 1227 as a sick man from a previous attempt to leave for the Holy Land. Frederick's final departure did nothing to mollify the pope, since on this occasion the emperor was acting independently, whereas it had been papal policy from the start of the Crusades to maintain their direction. So on his arrival at Acre, Frederick had to undertake long and humiliating negotiations before al-Kāmil consented to the treaty of Jaffa (Rabīʿ I 626/February 1229), which retroceded Jerusalem to the Latin kingdom but retained a Muslim enclave including the Dome of the Rock and al-Aqṣā Mosque. Bethlehem and a corridor linking Jerusalem with the coast were also restored. It was a triumph of diplomacy, and it aroused resentment and disgust on both sides – by pious Muslims because it ceded Jerusalem, and by pious Christians because it did not cede the religious heart of the city. The Latin patriarch laid an interdict on his own metropolis, which Frederick entered on 17 March 1229. On the following day, although denied the consolations of religion, he wore his crown in the Church of the Holy Sepulchre. In strict constitutional law he was no longer king of Jerusalem, since Queen Isabel had died in childbirth the previous year, and he was now regent for his infant son, Conrad of Hohenstaufen. On May Day, among hostile demonstrations, he set sail from Acre. Even in his own lifetime his supporters saw him as the Emperor of the Last

Days, whose liberation of the Holy Sepulchre would inaugurate the Millennium, and when he died in 1250 the popular belief of both friends and enemies was that he was sleeping in Etna or Kyffhäuser, and would return at the end of time. So Frederick joined the undying heroes.

Some idea of the impression that Frederick made on the Muslims may be obtained from the contemporary chronicler, Ibn Wāṣil. In his account of the negotiations between al-Kāmil and Frederick, he says:

> He who went to and fro on embassies between him [al-Kāmil] and the king-emperor was the Amir Fakhr al-Dīn b. al-Shaykh, and discussions on various matters went on between the two of them. In the meantime the emperor sent al-Malik al-Kāmil questions of philosophy and difficult questions of geometry in order to test his men of learning thereby. So al-Malik al-Kāmil passed the arithmetical questions he had sent him to Shaykh ʿAlam al-Dīn Qayṣar b. Abi'l-Qāsim, who was foremost in this discipline. He passed the rest to a company of eminent scholars, and they answered the lot. . . .
>
> When the matter of the truce was concluded, the emperor sought leave of the sultan to visit Jerusalem. Leave was granted him, and the sultan commissioned the judge Shams al-Dīn, the judge of Nablus (God's mercy be on him), a man of eminence in the state and in high honour with the Ayyubid kings, to attend on the emperor until he had visited Jerusalem and returned to Acre. Shams al-Dīn (God's mercy be on him) told me, saying, "When the emperor came to Jerusalem, I attended on him as the Sultan al-Malik al-Kāmil had commanded me, and I entered the Holy Sanctuary [i.e. the Dome of the Rock] with him, and he saw the places of pilgrimage in it. Then I entered the Aqṣā Mosque with him, and its construction and the construction of the Dome of the Sacred Rock delighted him. When he reached the *miḥrāb* of the Aqṣā, its beauty and the beauty of the pulpit delighted him. He went up the stairs to the top. Then he came down, and took my hand, and we came out of the Aqṣā. He saw a priest with the gospels in his hand, who wanted to enter the Aqṣā, so he shouted disagreeably to him, 'What's that you've brought here? By God, if one of you tries to get in here without my leave, I'll have his eyes out. We're the vassals and slaves of this Sultan al-Malik al-Kāmil. He has granted these churches to me and to you as an act of grace. Don't any of you step out of line.' The priest made off shaking with fear."[1]

The death of al-Kāmil in 635/1238 was followed by another period of struggle among the Ayyubids, in which the principal contender was his eldest son al-Ṣāliḥ Ayyūb, whom he had removed from the succession and sent to govern the territories in the Jazīra. Al-Ṣāliḥ Ayyūb, however, succeeded (although not without difficulty) in ousting his brother, al-ʿĀdil Abū Bakr, and establishing himself as sultan in Egypt in 637/1240. While still in the Jazīra, he had established an alliance with a host of freebooting warriors known as the Khwarazmians. Originally recruited from the Kıpchak Turks in Central Asia by the Khwārazm-Shāhs, who ruled the lower Oxus region, they had accompanied the last of the dynasty, Jalāl al-Dīn, when the kingdom was overrun by the

Mongols in 617/1220. After his death in 628/1231 in Diyār Bakr, they remained there as a band of mercenaries. In the service of al-Ṣāliḥ Ayyūb they came on to the Syrian stage. In 642/1244 under their chief, Berke Khan, they invaded Syria, captured Jerusalem (where they desecrated the Christian Holy Places and the tombs of the Latin kings), joined al-Ṣāliḥ's forces at Gaza, and then defeated an allied army of the Syrian Ayyubids and Franks at Ḥarbiyya, known to the Latins as La Forbie. The ferocity and turbulence of the rootless Khwarazmians were in the end too much even for their allies and paymasters, and in 644/1246 they were annihilated by the Ayyubid troops of Ḥimṣ and Aleppo. By that time al-Ṣāliḥ Ayyūb was paramount in Syria, having taken Damascus from al-Ṣāliḥ Ism'ā'īl in 643/1245, and only the young ruler of Aleppo, al-Nāṣir Yūsuf, gave some indications of ambition and independence. Damascus had fallen to al-Ṣāliḥ Ayyūb in Jumādā I 643/October 1245.

The sultan's troubled career was, however, soon to close, as he was stricken by a fatal disease. At his juncture he was threatened by an invasion from Europe. French Crusaders under King Louis IX (St Louis) wintered in Cyprus in 646/1248–9. In the spring they launched their attack, which like the Crusade of 1218 was directed against Egypt. Fakhr al-Dīn b. Shaykh al-Shuyūkh, now commander of the sultan's forces, did not attempt to hold Damietta, which the Crusaders occupied in Ṣafar 647/June 1249. As before, al-Manṣūra was the base for the Egyptian resistance, and there al-Ṣāliḥ Ayyūb died in his camp in Sha'bān 647/November 1249. At this critical time the Ayyubid cause in Egypt was saved by a military group whose day was about to dawn. Even during his father's lifetime, al-Ṣāliḥ had recruited numerous Mamluks (mostly from Kıpchak Turks) for his *'askar*. He had continued their recruitment subsequently, and the Baḥriyya, as they were called, became his most efficient and reliable troops. They had already played an important part in the Syrian campaign of 642/1244, and now they saved Egypt from the Crusaders.

NOTE

1. Ibn Wāṣil, *Mufarrij al-kurūb fī akhbār Banī Ayyūb*, IV, ed. Hassanein Rabie [Cairo] 1972, 242, 244–5. English version P. M. Holt.

CHAPTER NINE

Institutions from the Seljukids to the Ayyubids

POLITICAL AND MILITARY INSTITUTIONS

The two decades before the First Crusade marked both the establishment and the turning-point of Seljukid rule in Syria. Originally the house of Seljuk had regarded their empire as pertaining to the family as a whole rather than to a single individual. In practice as time went on, the regime became increasingly monarchical in character as the Turkish clan-chief was transmuted into the Islamic sultan, and appropriated the despotic ideas and arbitrary methods of government which had developed under the ʿAbbasid caliphs. One surviving application of the concept of familial sovereignty is to be seen in the grant of frontier provinces as appanages to Seljukid princes, who bore the title of *malik*, that of sultan being held by the paramount ruler alone. Central and southern Syria with Damascus as the capital, conquered by Tutush, the brother of Malik-Shāh, were formally granted to him as an appanage. After Tutush's death in 488/1095, when his appanage was split between his two sons, Riḍwān at Aleppo and Dukak at Damascus, they continued to hold the status of *maliks*, nominally vassal rulers under the Great Seljuk sultans, who were Malik-Shāh's increasingly ineffective successors.

With the Seljukid *maliks*, two characteristic institutions were introduced into Syria: the office of *atabeg*, and the assignment of revenue known as *iqṭāʿ*. Both of these were connected in different ways with an institution which the Seljukids had copied from earlier Islamic regimes, the recruitment of military slaves or Mamluks. The original Seljuk conquests had been the consequence of a great westward migration of the Turcoman Ghuzz (Turkish, Oghuz) tribesmen, but when the conquests had been achieved, the sultan as ruler of an extensive territorial empire felt the need of a disciplined standing force (*ʿaskar*), loyal to his person, to form the nucleus of his army and to keep the Ghuzz themselves in check. The great majority of these Mamluks were at this time recruited from the Turkish tribes of Central Asia. As they were heathens, their enslavement was permissible under Islamic law. Their conversion to Islam was, however, accomplished along with their military training. Once this was completed, they were probably emancipated; certainly there was no obstacle to their rising to high military commands as amirs in the ruler's *ʿaskar*, to governorships of provinces and the great offices of the royal household and the state, and to positions of confidence in the court.

The most powerful office which came to be held by Mamluks was that of *atabeg*. Its origins are obscure but it first comes clearly into view with the Seljukids, and the title itself is purely Turkish, being composed of two elements meaning respectively "father" (*ata*) and "commander" or "lord" (*beg*). The function of the *atabeg* was to act as tutor and guardian of a young Seljukid prince, and where his ward was the holder of an appanage, the *atabeg* was in effect a regent with plenary powers. The *atabeg* was usually a military chief; hence as the Mamluk institution was implanted in the Seljukid military establishment, the office became a perquisite of the great Mamluk amirs. In Seljukid Syria both Riḍwān and Dukak had *atabegs*, although neither prince was an infant when Tutush died. The position of an *atabeg* in regard to an adult *malik* was anomalous, as is shown by the respective fates of Janāḥ al-Dawla, *atabeg* of Riḍwān, and Tughtigin, *atabeg* of Dukak. Riḍwān and Janāḥ al-Dawla quarrelled. The *atabeg* established himself as the independent lord of Ḥimṣ (490/1097), where he was slain in 496/1103 by three Assassins, probably at Riḍwān's instigation. Tughtigin, by contrast, remained influential with Dukak, whose mother he married (a procedure not uncommon among *atabegs*), and whom he survived. After Dukak's death in 497/1104, Tughtigin continued to rule in Damascus as *atabeg* to his infant son, who, however, died shortly afterwards. Henceforward although there was no Seljukid *malik* in Damascus, Tughtigin remained in power until he himself died in 522/1128. He was succeeded as ruler by his son Böri (Būrī) and later descendants until Damascus fell to Nūr al-Dīn b. Zangī in 549/1154. The title of *atabeg*, which would in any case have been inappropriate, was not used by his successors, the Burids.

The term *iqṭāʿ* has a number of different but related significances in the history of the Islamic Near East. It is sometimes rendered "fief" by Western historians, but this is misleading since it suggests analogies with European feudalism which are superficial. It may be better translated "assignment", and in the period under consideration it means primarily an assignment of revenue levied on *kharāj* lands, i.e. estates which at the time of the Arab conquest had been left in the hands of their non-Muslim owners, and which were taxed at a higher rate than lands which had passed into Muslim proprietorship. Although most of the owners of *kharāj* land sooner or later became Muslims, the fiscal liability of the land as such did not change. The grant of an *iqṭāʿ* upon such land did not (legally at least) alter its status, i.e. it remained the property of its owners who, however, henceforward paid what tax was due not to the agents of the government but to the assignee (*muqṭaʿ*). This assignment of revenue (*iqṭāʿ al-istighlāl*) was not an innovation of the Seljukid rulers. It had been practised by the preceding regime in the central region of the ʿAbbasid caliphate, that of the Buyids, who had granted assignments of this type to ensure the payment of their soldiery.

The Seljukids extended the practice throughout their wider empire, and also showed themselves more ready than the Buyids to confer whole provinces in *iqṭāʿ*, so that both administrative and fiscal functions were exercised by the governor. The great appanages of the Seljukid *maliks* were the final term of this development. There thus grew up the autonomous provincial holdings which, as we have seen in Syria, became hereditary principalities ruled by atabeylical dynasties. In the meantime the method by which the value of the assignment was calculated had changed. Instead of a fixed sum being granted to the *muqṭaʿ* out of the taxes levied, the assignment was now deemed to be sufficient to enable him to provide certain services or to maintain a military household of so many persons. Thus each *iqṭāʿ* had an estimated assessment of revenue called the *ʿibra*. The spread of the *iqṭāʿ* system was harmful to the peasantry, since it eroded their status as free cultivators. As the *muqṭaʿ* was not strictly speaking the possessor of an estate but merely the recipient of its revenue, as moreover he was almost always resident in a distant town, he lacked the contact with the peasantry felt by a feudal lord of a manor. His dealings with the cultivators would be through his household staff, who would go down to the estate, and levy the taxes due with more or less honesty and equity.

There is no contemporary description of the governmental institutions in Syria under the Seljukids and their immediate successors, but passing remarks by the Damascene chronicler of the period, Ibn al-Qalānisī (d. 555/1160) and others indicate that the provincial institutions were modelled upon those of the Great Seljuk sultanate, which were themselves largely derived from those of the Ghaznavids in the east and the Buyids. As in other regimes established by warriors in Islamic territory, there were two distinct classes of institutions: on the one hand, the ruling and military establishment, staffed mainly by Turks (either freemen or more usually Mamluks); on the other, the civilian establishment, staffed in Syria by native speakers of Arabic.

The mainspring of the military establishment was the ruler's court, which probably reproduced in miniature the *dargāh* of the Great Seljuk sultans. The *ʿaskar* of the ruler, his military household, was both his guard and his standing army. It was recruited mainly from Mamluks, and officered by the amirs. The chief officer was the *ḥājib* (a term which signified "chamberlain"), also known in Damascus as the *sālār* (Persian, "chief"), and in Aleppo as the *isfahsalār* (Persian, *sipahsālār*, "army-chief"). The *ḥājib* in Damascus was also the military governor (*shaḥna*). *Ḥājib* (in this sense), *sipahsālār* and *shaḥna* were all Seljuk terms. The maintenance of the amirs and troopers came from their *iqṭāʿs* as described earlier, and also from their *jāmakiyyāt*, a term derived from the Persian *jāma*, "garment", which at this time probably meant an allowance of clothing or cloth, although later under the Mamluk sultanate it signified simply a salary.

The head of the civilian establishment was the *wazīr*, whose title went back to the early ʿAbbasid caliphate. Under a military regime such as that of the Syrian Seljukids his functions were much diminished. He was no longer an omnicompetent minister but merely the head of a bureaucracy dominated by the arbitrary will of the ruler. If, as is probable, the provincial administrative system in Syria resembled that of the Great Seljuk sultanate, he presided over four departments (sing., *dīwān*): the chancery (*dīwān al-rasāʾil*), of which incidentally Ibn al-Qalānisī was at one time the head (*ʿamīd*) in Damascus; the revenue department (*dīwān al-istifāʾ*), headed by the *mustawfī*; a supervisory (or possibly security) department (*dīwān al-ishrāf*), headed by the *mushrif*; and the army department (*dīwān al-ʿarḍ*), headed by the muster-master (*ʿāriḍ*). The officials and clerks in these departments were for the most part Muslims, who had received their education in a religious school (*madrasa*) (see p. 78). They thus formed part of the same social class as the jurists (sing., *faqīh*; pl., *fuqahāʾ*), the Islamic judges (sing., *qāḍī*), the mosque officials such as the prayer-leaders (sing., *imām*) and the preachers (sing., *khaṭīb*).

The military and civilian establishments were the two arms of government, but in the late fifth/eleventh century the powers which had formerly dominated Syria, the Seljukids and the Fatimids, were both in decline. In this situation there appeared a movement towards urban independence and the acquisition of control by the upper bourgeoisie. In the coastal towns, still nominally under Fatimid sovereignty, successful revolts in Tyre and Tripoli in 462/1070 were headed by the local Shīʿī *qāḍīs*, who thereupon became the rulers of what effectively were city-states, Tyre was regained with some other coastal towns by the Fatimids in 482/1089. Tripoli had a longer period of independence under the ruling family, Banū ʿAmmār. The *qāḍī* al-Ḥasan b. ʿAmmār (462–4/1070–2) was succeeded by his nephew Jalāl al-Mulk ʿAlī (464–92/1072–99), and he by his brother Fakhr al-Mulk, who left Tripoli in 501/1108, when the city was shortly to fall to the Crusaders.

The bourgeois leaders in the great towns of the interior, Damascus and Aleppo, did not claim formal independence of the Seljukids and Burids, but confronted them or collaborated with them by means of two indigenous urban institutions, the *ri'āsa* (or office of *ra'īs*) and the *aḥdāth*. The *ra'īs* (pl., *ru'asā'*), a term sometimes inappropriately translated "mayor", was as the term indicates, a "chief" of the townspeople. His influence derived not only from his personal standing but also from his control of a local urban militia, the *aḥdāth*. *Ru'asā'* and *aḥdāth* developed out of movements of local resistance to external authority in the troubled times of the fourth/tenth and fifth/eleventh centuries, and became quasi-autonomous institutions. Five members of one family, Banu'l-Ṣūfī, held the *ri'āsa* in Damascus between 488/1095 and 548/1154, and Ibn al-Qalānisī himself twice held the post. The *ra'īs* in this period received formal recognition from the ruler. In 548/1154 a newly appointed *ra'īs* (Ibn al-Qalānisī's brother) was summoned to the citadel of Damascus, where he was invested with the insignia of office. He rode thence in a state procession to his home, while an *iqṭāʿ* and honorifics were bestowed on him by a patent of appointment. The capture of Damascus a few weeks later by Nūr al-Dīn had been preceded by secret negotiations with the *ra'īs* and the *aḥdāth*, so that only a token resistance was offered when he assaulted the city (see above, p. 45). In Aleppo no family of *ru'asā'* comparable to Banu'l-Ṣūfī emerged, as the Sunnīs and the Shīʿa had their respective leaders in the families of Banū Badīʿ and Banu'l-Khashshāb.

Ibn al-Qalānisī gives some indications that the distinctions between the military and civilian institutions became relaxed (if indeed they had been strictly maintained) during the sixth/twelfth century. In 511/1117–18 the muster-master of Damascus, who bore an Arabic name, and whom one would expect to be a civilian, is entitled *al-amīr* and takes over the military appointment of *iṣfahsalār* of Aleppo. He combined this with a financial post, that of *nāẓir al-amwāl*, perhaps a synonym for *mustawfī*. A still more striking combination of offices demonstrated the ascendancy of Banu'l-Ṣūfī. In 531/1136–7 a member of this family was restored to the *ri'āsa* and given the title of amir. In

524/1129–30 another member of the family had combined the posts of *ra'īs* and *wazīr*, although his incompetence in the latter function soon led to his dismissal. The combination of offices reappeared, however, twenty years later.

Muslim Syria was consolidated under the rule of Nūr al-Dīn. Aleppo and the north fell to him in 541/1146, when Zangī's territories were partitioned between his sons. He obtained Ḥimṣ by exchange with his nephew, the Zangid ruler of Mosul, in 544/1149. His taking of Damascus in 549/1154 gave him the centre and south of Syria. Two later and minor acquisitions were of the fortress of Shayzar on the Orontes in 432/1157, after its Arab ruling family, Banū Munqidh, had been wiped out in an earthquake, and Qalʿat Jaʿbar on the middle Euphrates, obtained in 564/1148 by barter from another Arab clan, Banū ʿUqayl. This kingdom-building was a process of personal union rather than of political centralization and institutional fusion.

Like the Burids, Nūr al-Dīn came of an atabeylical family (see above, p. 40). An indication of the decline of the Seljuk sultanate and the rise of the *atabegs* to independent sovereignty is given by the Caliph al-Muqtafī's conferment on Zangī of the title of al-Malik al-Manṣūr, "the Divinely-Aided King", after the taking of Edessa. Nūr al-Dīn himself, originally styled "amir", received the title of al-Malik al-ʿAdil, "the Just King". The use of the title of *malik*, originally a prerogative of the Seljukid princes, was to spread even more widely among the Ayyubids, and then later to be restricted very narrowly by the Mamluk sultans.

Under the rule of Nūr al-Dīn, a successful war-lord, the urban institutions which had developed under the preceding regimes began to decline. The *ra'īs* and the *aḥdāth*, indigenous holders of civil authority and military power, gave place to the *shaḥna*, the military governor, and his deputy, the chief of police (*ṣāḥib al-shurṭa*). Two innovations which are particularly associated with Nūr al-Dīn are essentially older institutions which he developed and reorganized. The first of these was the pigeon-post. The need for the rapid communication of intelligence to autocratic rulers threatened by external enemies and internal dissidents had been felt by the Umayyad and ʿAbbasid caliphs in their heyday, and had resulted in the establishment of a great department of state, the *barīd*, the head of which (*ṣāḥib al-barīd*) controlled an elaborately organized system of post-horses, which brought reports from all parts of the empire. With the decline of the caliphate, the *barīd* fell into desuetude. The Syrian Seljukids and also Zangī made occasional use of carrier-pigeons as a means of official communication. In 567/1171–2 Nūr al-Dīn organized the service on a regular basis, linking together the whole of his dominions, and providing him with early warning of Frankish incursions.

Nūr al-Dīn's other innovation was in a very different field. The tradition that aggrieved subjects should have direct access to their ruler is both ancient and widespread. In Islamic lands the recognition of this right was embodied in a system of jurisdiction supplementing the administration of the *Sharī'a* by the *qāḍīs'* courts. This *maẓālim* jurisdiction, sanctioned by the authority and power of the ruler, never produced a body of precedents recognized as binding, like equity in the development of English law; it remained throughout a personal function of the ruler in response to petitions of grievances by individuals. It was not, however, wholly arbitrary in its exercise; Nūr al-Dīn, for example, sat with the judges and jurists of the *Sharī'a* to hear petitions. His innovation was to establish a fixed locality, *dār al-'adl* (the Palace of Justice), in which he sat twice weekly to redress wrongs. The Palace of Justice in Aleppo was constructed early in his reign, that in Damascus soon after his conquest of the city.

Nūr al-Dīn's effective successor, Saladin, as the ruler of both Muslim Syria and Egypt, was the heir to two different groups of political institutions: those derived immediately from the Zangids, and ultimately from the Great Seljuk sultanate; and those of the Fatimid caliphate. The Fatimid court and the caliphal household were staffed by a hierarchy of office-holders, and an elaborate departmental system provided for the secretarial and fiscal functions of the administration. The office-holders fell into two great categories, the Men of the Swords (*arbāb al-suyūf*) and the Men of the Pens (*arbāb al-aqlām*). The Men of the Swords included not only the amirs, the military officers properly speaking, but also the caliphal retinue, who formed the military household and were part of the court establishment. They comprised over 1,000 eunuchs, 500 pages and about 5,000 troopers in barracks. The great officers of the household and the Fatimid state were drawn from the Men of the Swords. The chief of them was the *wazīr*. Although in the earlier Fatimid caliphate the wazirate had usually been held by a civilian, from the time of Badr al-Jamālī (see above, p. 12), who assumed office in 567/1074, a succession of military *wazīrs* with plenary powers effectively ruled Egypt. The last of these was Saladin, whose title of sultan and honorific of al-Malik al-Nāṣir were conferred on him as the *wazīr* of the Fatimid caliph. Another of the great officers was the commander-in-chief (*isfahsalār*). Several of the great court and public offices were held by eunuchs.

The Men of the Pens staffed the religious establishment, which was headed by the chief judge (*qāḍī al-quḍāt*). A religious office which had its origin in the early propagandist days of the Fatimid movement was that of the chief missionary (*dāʿī al-duʿāt*). With the movement's transformation into a settled territorial monarchy, the chief missionary, resident in Cairo, was responsible for the official transmission of Ismāʿīlī doctrine and for the reception of converts. By combining this office with the wazirate and the chief military command, Badr al-Jamālī (himself, of course, a Man of the Swords) emphasized his control of both the ruling and the religious establishments. Besides the religious offices, the departmental offices were also held by Men of the Pens, some of whom, particularly in the financial departments, were Copts. The chancery (*dīwān al-inshā'*) was headed by its chief clerk, a confidential official who had the right of direct access to the caliph. The army department (*dīwān al-jaysh*) had mainly financial duties, and provided for the maintenance of the officers and soldiery. Its head was required to be a Muslim. The finances of the Fatimid caliphate appear to have been originally administered by a court department (*dīwān al-majlis*), from which other financial departments developed. A general control over them was exercised by an official known as the supervisor of the departments (*nāẓir al-dawāwīn*).

How much of the elaborate structure of Fatimid institutions survived the ascendancy of Saladin and the extinction of the caliphate? The court with its hierarchy of officials (the eunuchs among them) probably largely disappeared. The palace officials, notably the eunuch Mu'tamin al-Khilāfa, had been the centre of opposition to Saladin at the start of his wazirate. In any case, as a Kurdish warrior-chief, almost continually on campaign, Saladin could have had little time or use for the protocol and staff of a palace in Cairo. The Ismāʿīlī religious establishment was swept away as Sunnī Islam was restored in Egypt. In Jumādā II 566/February–March 1171 a Sunnī jurist was installed as chief judge, and others were appointed as his subordinates. These belonged to the Shāfiʿī legal system (*madhhab*), which predominated in Egypt. Like other religious colleges, the great mosque of al-Azhar, built immediately after the Fatimid conquest of Egypt, became henceforth a centre of Sunnī religious teaching. The Fatimid military forces ceased to exist. Saladin's Syrian army of occupation took the place of the Fatimid cavalry, while the Black infantry regiments were destroyed when the rising of 564/1169 was suppressed.

The element of continuity between the institutions of the Fatimid and Ayyubid regimes lies rather in the secretarial and fiscal organization. It was personified in al-Qāḍī al-Fāḍil, "the Excellent Judge". A Sunnī Muslim of Palestinian origin, he was born in 529/1135, and he began his career in the Fatimid chancery in Cairo. He served both

Shīrkūh and Saladin during their wazirates, and was appointed head of chancery in 566/1171. Throughout Saladin's reign, al-Qāḍī al-Fāḍil worked closely with him as his chief minister, his *wazīr* in all but title. The revenues of Egypt continued to be exploited for the benefit of the new ruler and his army. Saladin had, of course, grown up acquainted with the system of military and administrative *iqṭā*'s, which had developed in Syria for a century or more. As master of Egypt, he proceeded to assign its landed revenue in *iqṭā*'. Apart from exceptionally large assignments to his kinsmen, *iqṭā*'s of varying values were assigned to his officers for the maintenance of their military households. The introduction into Egypt of the Seljukid type of *iqṭā*' has traditionally been seen as an innovation by Saladin. Although the term was already current in Egypt, it denoted strictly a different kind of fiscal arrangement, the *qabāla*, by which an individual advanced the tax due from a locality, and subsequently reimbursed himself from the revenue as it came in. It is, however, possible that the first introduction of the Seljukid type of *iqṭā*' goes back to a fiscal reform carried out by the *wazīr* al-Afḍal Shāhanshāh (d. 515/1121), and that Saladin did no more than complete and render universal a process that had already begun.[1] In effect, a system ensuring the payment of revenue due to the state developed into a system ensuring the payment of salary due to a military officer.

With the revenues of Egypt at his disposal, Saladin was able to build up and maintain the military forces which enabled him to establish his rule over Muslim Syria also, and in the end to reconquer much of the Latin kingdom. The core of his forces was formed by his own *'askar*, of which the original constituents were drawn from the troops which Nūr al-Dīn had sent to Egypt, from Shīrkūh's own *'askar*, the Asadiyya, and from the Ṣalāḥiyya which Saladin himself formed after achieving power in Egypt. During campaigns, contingents were provided by the *muqṭa*'s in Syria and Egypt, and also after 581/1186 by the Zangid ruler of Mosul, who had perforce recognized Saladin as his overlord. The *'askars* of this period were recruited from both Mamluk (in effect Turkish) and free-born Kurdish horsemen. There were also auxiliary troops of various kinds: Turcoman and Arab cavalry, Kurdish soldiers of fortune and volunteer fighters in the Holy War. Foot-soldiers as such played little part in the war of movement which characterized the period; their chief importance was in siege-warfare.

A field army constituted from these elements had obvious organizational weaknesses. There was no true chain of command; the discipline of the force depended largely on the personality of the ruler and the circumstances in which the army found itself. Saladin, while engaged during the Ḥaṭṭīn campaign in a victorious Holy War, effectively held together his assemblage of diverse contingents, but the subsequent operations around Tyre clearly demonstrated their lack of staying power (see above, p. 59). Another problem which arose from time to time was hostility between Kurds and Turks or Turcomans. There were in this period no significant developments in military technology or tactics. Essentially, the Muslim horseman, armed with a light lance and bow, was pitted against the Frankish knight carrying a heavy lance and mounted on a great horse. The concerted charge of a company of knights could sweep their opponents from the field, but they were vulnerable to the Muslim tactic known as *al-karr wa'l-farr*, i.e. feigned retreat before the enemy, followed by his encirclement.

Already during Saladin's lifetime there was foreshadowed the political structure of the Ayyubid realm under his successors. The system of familial rule, characteristic, as we have seen, of the Great Seljuk sultanate, reappeared on a smaller scale, and with it the political fragmentation of Muslim Syria as in the days before Nūr al-Dīn. Egypt, Damascus, Aleppo, Ḥimṣ, Ḥamāh and the Jazīra were so many autonomous principalities, each under its own Ayyubid ruler (Ḥimṣ, strictly speaking, under the collateral line of Shīrkūh), and with its own administrative system, chancery and treasury. For three long periods there was a paramount Ayyubid ruler: al-ʿĀdil Sayf al-Dīn (596–615/1200–18), al-Kāmil Muḥammad (615–35/1218–38) and al-Ṣāliḥ Ayyūb (637–47/1240–9). Theirs, however, was a personal ascendancy, won by political skill and opportunism; it did not indicate any institutional centralization. The title of sultan, acquired by Saladin by virtue of his appointment as the last Fatimid *wazīr*, was subsequently held by several Ayyubid princes, in effect as a self-bestowed courtesy title. Only in 643/1245 as the dynasty approached its end, was the title bestowed on al-Ṣāliḥ Ayyūb by the Caliph al-Mustaʿṣim, and not until four years later did it appear on his coinage. The vulgarization of the title of *malik* was even more widespread, as every male member of the Ayyubid clan bore an honorific of this kind.

The Ayyubid dominions were thus fragmented into a confederation of principalities, each local ruler commanding the military forces of his territory. The recruitment of Kurds and Turks (both Turcoman tribesmen and Mamluks) continued throughout the period, but as time went on the Mamluk element began to preponderate. This development is particularly associated with the third and last of the Ayyubid overlords, al-Ṣāliḥ Ayyūb, who recruited unusually large numbers of Mamluks, and placed marked reliance on them to the disadvantage of the Kurds. This Mamluk *corps d'élite*, perhaps 1,000 strong, was quartered in the island-fortress of the Nile by Cairo, and it may have obtained its name of the Baḥriyya from the Arabic name for the river, Bahr al-Nīl. Having been recruited by al-Ṣāliḥ Ayyūb, it was also styled the Ṣāliḥiyya. The French Crusader, Joinville, in his account of the Baḥriyya equates this corps with the *Ḥalqa*, which in Saladin's time apparently meant the troops under his personal command. By this shift to Mamluks as the military basis of his rule, al-Ṣāliḥ Ayyūb foreshadowed the future. This was true also of the political changes in his time. When he conquered Damascus in 643/1245, it ceased to be the seat of an autonomous Ayyubid prince, and became a provincial capital under a governor whom he appointed. Other autonomies in southern Syria were ended in the following years, and the region received a centralized administrative structure depending on the ruler of Egypt. Although al-Ṣāliḥ Ayyūb never succeeded in extending his domination over northern Syria, and although his system collapsed after his death, his administrative changes anticipated the more extensive and durable centralization developed by the Mamluk sultanate after 658/1260.

RELIGIOUS INSTITUTIONS

In the second half of the fifth/eleventh century, Shiʿism seemed to be strongly entrenched in the Muslim lands of the eastern Mediterranean. The Fatimid caliphs reigned in Egypt, where Ismāʿīlī Shiʿism was the religion of the court, if not of the mass of the people. A militant splinter-group, organized by the Persian Ḥasan-i Ṣabbāḥ, captured the fortress of Alamūt in 483/1090, and made it the centre of their movement, the New Preaching (*al-daʿwa al-jadīda*) (see p. 12). Members of the group, better known as the Assassins, moved into schism from the parent-body in 487/1094, when on the death of the Caliph al-Mustanṣir the all-powerful *wazīr*, al-Afḍal Shāhanshāh, brought al-Mustaʿlī to the throne in place of the designated heir, Nizār. Within a few years the Assassins were a power in Syria also. They were influential in Aleppo under Riḍwān b. Tutush (d. 507/1113), established a base in Damascus rather later, and went on to acquire more secure centres of power in the Syrian mountain strongholds. The political murders committed by the Assassins made them a terror to Sunnī rulers and notables. Another offshoot of Fatimid Ismaʿilism was the Druze community, which had originated as the cult of the Caliph al-Ḥākim (d. 411/1020), and found a refuge in the mountains of Lebanon. Further north, the range now known as Jabal Anṣāriyya sheltered another dissident group, the

Nuṣayrīs, a schism of Twelver Shiʿism. Among the Arab tribesmen, Shiʿism was also widespread.

The turn of the tide had already come with the westward advance of the Seljuk Turks, whose leaders were staunch Sunnīs. Their overthrow of the Buyid domination of the ʿAbbasid caliphate ended the control of the Islamic heartlands by a Shīʿī power. The extension of Seljukid rule to the greater part of Syria marked the first step in the weakening of Shīʿī influence in that region, although the relations between Riḍwān and the Assassins of Aleppo show that the victory of Sunnism was in some places and for some time an open question. The withdrawal of the Assassins to their mountain fortresses, however, meant that they like the Druze and Nuṣayrīs were henceforth a marginal group, sometimes troublesome but no longer a constant danger to the authorities in the Syrian cities. The reign of Nūr al-Dīn, the model of a just and pious ruler, marked the victory of Sunnism in Muslim Syria. The suppression of the Fatimid caliphate by his lieutenant, Saladin, ended a period of a little over two centuries during which Egypt had been the seat of a major Shīʿī power. Thereafter it was the external enemies of Islam, the Christian Franks and the heathen Mongols, who caused difficulties to the Sunnī rulers of Egypt and Syria.

The victory of Sunnism was not obtained by political and military means alone but also by institutions by which its doctrines could be propagated. To some extent the development of these institutions must have been a response to methods employed, at first with such success, by the Ismāʿīlīs, who had relied largely on extensive propaganda directed by the chief missionary. It is significant that within a year of his conquest of Egypt, Jawhar, the victorious Fatimid general, laid the foundations of the great mosque of al-Azhar to be a seminary for Ismāʿīlī teaching (359/970). Other seminaries (sing., *dār al-ʿilm*) existed in Syria; one was founded in Tripoli by al-Ḥasan b. ʿAmmār as Fatimid domination there came to an end. The principal institution of the Sunnī revival was the *madrasa*, i.e. the school of religious learning, founded and maintained by Muslim rulers and notables – hence with the staff under the patronage and control of the authorities. The first Syrian *madrasas* were set up under the Seljukids at the end of the fifth/eleventh century, and their number was greatly augmented by Nūr al-Dīn. At the beginning of his reign, Aleppo had one *madrasa* and Damascus eleven – an indication of the relative strength of Sunnism in the two cities. When he died, seven new *madrasas* had been founded in Aleppo and eleven in Damascus. Of these, Nūr al-Dīn himself founded four and six in Aleppo and Damascus respectively. He was also the originator of a new Sunnī institution known as *dār al-ḥadīth* for the teaching of the

Traditions of the Prophet. He founded the first of these in Damascus in 566/1170–1, and attended the lectures in person accompanied by his amirs. Another example of the close association of the dominant military group with the Sunnī revival is provided by the *madrasas* which incorporate the tombs of rulers or notables. Zangī had in 522/1128 transferred the remains of his father, Aksungur al-Ḥājib, to an already existing *madrasa* in Aleppo. Nūr al-Dīn was buried in Damascus in the Nūriyya *madrasa*, which takes its name from him. Later examples are the ʿĀdiliyya containing the tomb of Saladin's brother, al-ʿĀdil Sayf al-Dīn, and (from the Mamluk period) the Ẓāhiriyya, where al-Ẓāhir Baybars was buried. Both of these are in Damascus.

The patronage which the military rulers extended to Sunnī institutions appears in their relations with the judges who administered the Holy Law of Islam. The title of chief judge (*qāḍī al-quḍāt*), originally restricted to one judge in the ʿAbbasid capital of Baghdad, had during the sixth/twelfth century been assumed by the heads of the judiciary in the various polities which emerged from the break-up of the ʿAbbasid and Fatimid caliphates. As law based upon divine revelation, the *Sharīʿa* was theoretically absolute in the Muslim states of this period, and it conferred upon its practitioners, the judges and jurists, precedence in the official hierarchy. In practice the Holy Law was supplemented by customary usages and the decrees of the ruler, who also appointed and dismissed the judges at his arbitrary discretion. The deficiencies of the *Sharīʿa* courts had long been supplied by the *maẓālim* jurisdiction exercised by the ruler or his personal representative. The formal deference paid to the Holy Law and its officers was thus subject in practice to significant limitations, the *maẓālim* courts having the advantages of more flexible procedure, greater speed in decision and the executive power to ensure the carrying out of their judgments.

Beside the *qāḍī* there was in the towns another functionary whose office was regarded as a religious institution. This was the *muḥtasib*, whose duties lay in the application of the Qur'anic precept enjoined upon all Muslims to "promote good and forbid evil". Thus he was responsible for ensuring the observance of religious obligations, such as the performance of prayer and the keeping of the Ramaḍān fast, and for the maintenance of public decency and order. In addition the *muḥtasib* had assumed the responsibility for a rather different range of duties which made him in effect a market inspector, supervising trades and tradesmen and checking commercial fraud. These latter functions were the *muḥtasib*'s most prominent, and in practice most important, activities. They linked his office closely to that of the *qāḍī* on the one hand and the chief of police on the other. The office of *muḥtasib* was in fact sometimes combined with that of judge or chief of police, the holder usually being a jurist. It is noteworthy that in the Frankish states, the title of *muḥtasib* (usually written *mathesep*) was held by a Frankish official, who like his Muslim counterpart was mainly responsible for the supervision of the market.

The institutions so far described embodied the formal and legalistic aspects of Sunnī Islam, but beside them there was a later development representing individual devotion and emotional mysticism, which was also evolving institutions of its own. This was Sufism. At the outset it was viewed with suspicion by theologians and jurists, and it was to be found on both sides of the schism between the Sunnīs and the Shīʿīs. Here also the Seljukid period marked a turning-point. A reconciliation was effected between the Ṣūfis on the one hand, and the theologians and jurists on the other, a reconciliation symbolized by the career of the outstanding scholar and theologian, Abū Ḥāmid al-Ghazālī, who spent part of his life as a professor in the Niẓāmiyya *madrasa* in Baghdad, one of the greatest Muslim religious schools, and part in retirement as a poor Ṣūfī.

The institutionalization of Sufism proceeded under the Seljukids and their successors. Convents (sing., *khānaqāh* or *ribāṭ*) were founded for the benefit, and indirectly for the control, of Ṣūfī devotees, where they were lodged and fed, and where they performed their rituals. The reign of Nūr al-Dīn, which witnessed the proliferation of *madrasas* in Muslim Syria, as we have seen, was also notable for the foundation of Ṣūfī convents, some of them for women. The original loose associations of Ṣūfis inspired by individual teachers of mysticism gave place in this period to organized systems (sing., *ṭarīqa*, literally "a way") of initiation, instruction and ritual, which took their names from their real or supposed founders. Each *ṭarīqa* developed a hierarchy of teachers, who derived their spiritual authority by a kind of apostolic succession from the founder. An early *ṭarīqa* was the Suhrawardiyya, founded by Shihāb al-Dīn ʿUmar al-Suhrawardī (539–632/1145–1234). He was favoured by the Caliph al-Nāṣir, who sent him as ambassador to Sultan Kay-Qubād I of Rūm and to al-ʿĀdil Sayf al-Dīn the Ayyubid. The Rifāʿiyya, founded in southern Iraq by Aḥmad al-Rifāʿī in the sixth/twelfth century, soon spread into Syria and Egypt. Also popular in Syria was the Qādiriyya, which took its name from ʿAbd al-Qādir al-Jīlānī (d. 561/1166), a Persian teacher who came to be widely regarded as a saint and miracle-worker.

A religious institution of universal importance with particular significance for Egypt and Syria was the annual Pilgrimage (*Ḥajj*) to Mecca. The performance of the Pilgrimage at least once was then as now an obligation upon every Muslim, and every year thousands of men and women made their way from all parts of the Islamic world to the remote city in the barren Ḥijāz. Many of them also visited the tomb and mosque of the Prophet in Medina. For their greater safety, the pilgrims travelled in organized caravans, each directed by a commander of the pilgrims (*amīr al-ḥājj*), whose duty it was by a combination of military and diplomatic means (not least by payments to the Arab tribes for safe conduct) to convoy his caravan to the Holy Cities, and bring it safely back. Cairo and Damascus were the rallying-points of two such caravans, which between them comprised pilgrims from all the Muslim lands around the Mediterranean as well as from trans-Saharan Africa. From Cairo the traditional route ran eastwards through the Sinai Desert to al-ʿAqaba at the head of the north-eastern gulf of the Red Sea. Thence it continued south-eastwards along the sea-coast, finally turning inland to Mecca, a distance of nearly 1,000 miles in all. The still longer Pilgrimage route from Damascus ran southwards through Transjordan, Maʿān, Tabūk, Madāʾin Ṣāliḥ and Medina, following very much the line that was to be taken by the Ḥijāz railway at the beginning of the twentieth century.

The conquests made by the First Crusade severely dislocated both these routes. The Syrian caravan had to pass along the fringe of Frankish territory dominated by the Crusader castles of al-Karak and al-Shawbak. The Egyptian caravan could no longer take the accustomed land-route. Instead the pilgrims made their way up the Nile to Qūṣ, at this time the principal town of Upper Egypt, then by a difficult journey across the eastern desert to the Red Sea port of ʿAydhāb, whence they crossed to Jedda, the port of Mecca. Not until the reconquest of territory by Saladin were the old land-routes again fully secured.

Before the ʿAbbasid decline, the protection of the pilgrims and the guardianship of the Holy Cities were functions of the caliphs, but they subsequently passed to local rulers, who appointed the commanders of the pilgrims, and displayed their banners at Mecca. The city was, however, for all practical purposes independent under a succession of local dynasts. Ironically, few Near Eastern Muslim rulers ever found the opportunity to make the Pilgrimage in person. Nūr al-Dīn did so in 556/1161 during a peaceful interval in his reign, but Saladin never realized his hope of entering the Holy Cities.

NOTE

1. Claude Cahen, *Makhzūmiyyāt*, Leiden 1977 [168]–[169].

CHAPTER TEN

The Inauguration of the Mamluk Sultanate 1249–1260

The death of al-Ṣāliḥ Ayyūb opened a period of political change during which, in little over a decade, the Ayyubids lost power first in Egypt, then in Syria, and the territories which had been dispersed among various members of the clan were united under a single ruler, the Mamluk sultan. This undivided empire was to subsist until its conquest by the Ottoman sultan, Selīm the Grim, in 922/1516–17.

The immediate consequence of al-Ṣāliḥ Ayyūb's death was a military and political crisis. Louis IX and his Crusaders were advancing on Cairo from their base at Damietta. The heir to the throne, al-Muʿaẓẓam Tūrān-Shāh, was in his remote lordship of Ḥiṣn Kayfā in the Jazīra. At this point the situation was saved by the resolute action of the sultan's widow, a Turkish woman named Shajar al-Durr. In agreement with the Amir Fakhr al-Dīn b. Shaykh al-Shuyūkh and a confidant of al-Ṣāliḥ Ayyūb's, she concealed the death of the sultan, forged his signature to decrees, imposed an oath of loyalty to him and to al-Muʿaẓẓam Tūrān-Shāh as his heir, and obtained the recognition of Fakhr al-Dīn as commander-in-chief (*atābak al-ʿasākir*) and administrator of the kingdom. The military resistance to the Crusaders continued, and a decisive engagement took place on 5 Dhu'l-Qaʿda 647/9 February 1250. Fakhr al-Dīn was killed in the fighting but the Crusaders' attack on al-Manṣūra failed. A deadlock ensued, during which on 20 Dhu'l-Qaʿda/24 February the new sultan arrived at al-Manṣūra. Unable either to advance or to hold their position, the Crusaders began a disastrous retreat to Damietta, in the course of which Louis himself was captured. His queen in Damietta negotiated for the surrender of the town and the release of her husband, and in Ṣafar 648/May 1250 the Crusaders evacuated Egypt. Before returning to France, Louis with a few hundred men went to Acre, where he spent nearly four years strengthening the defences of the Latin kingdom.

Some of the repercussions of the defeat of St Louis and his Crusaders were described by an eyewitness, the historian Abū Shāma:

On 16 Muḥarram [648/20 April 1250] the cloak of the captured king of the French arrived at Damascus, sent by the Sultan al-Muʿaẓẓam to his governor in Damascus, the Amir Jamāl al-Dīn Mūsā b. Yaghmūr. He put it on, and I saw it on him. It was of red woollen material lined with ermine, and it had a gold buckle. . . .

On 20 Muḥarram [24 April] the people went into the church of Mary with joy and pleasure, accompanied by singers and musicians, rejoicing at what had happened. They intended to demolish the church. I heard that the Christians in Baʿlabakk blackened and daubed with soot the faces of the icons in their church out of grief at what had happened to the Franks. The chief of police heard of that. He laid a heavy fine [?] on them, and ordered the Jews to strike and beat and humiliate them.[1]

Before St Louis left Egypt, a dramatic political change had occurred. On 28 Muḥarram 648/2 May 1250, al-Muʿaẓẓam Tūrān-Shāh had been murdered in a conspiracy by the Mamluks of the Baḥriyya, and the Ayyubid sultanate in Egypt had come to an end. The reasons for the coup are not hard to find: at bottom it was a power-struggle between the Baḥriyya (or Ṣāliḥiyya), the Mamluk military household of the dead sultan, and that of his successor. It marked the emergence of the Baḥriyya as the dominating group in the political as well as the military affairs of Egypt. In retrospect, the death of Fakhr al-Dīn may have contributed to this development, as he was the last of the great amirs who was not a Mamluk. The Baḥriyya had played a decisive part in the resistance to the Crusaders, and they were linked by ties of ethnic loyalty to their countrywoman, Shajar al-Durr. The arrival of Tūrān-Shāh with his own household, the promotion of his Mamluks to high office at the expense of the Baḥriyya, his harassment of Shajar al-Durr herself – all these things provoked the resentment and hostility of the Baḥriyya. His murder ensued, one of the conspirators being a young Mamluk named Baybars al-Bunduqdārī, of whom more was to be heard.

The killing of al-Muʿaẓẓam Tūrān-Shāh was followed by an event which is almost unique in Islamic history – the election of a woman as ruler. For almost three months Shajar al-Durr reigned in her own name as "queen of the Muslims" (*malikat al-Muslimīn*), signing decrees as Umm Khalīl, "the Mother of Khalīl". Khalīl was the son, now dead, whom she had borne to al-Ṣāliḥ Ayyūb. This formula and the fact that she was mentioned in the *khuṭba* as "the spouse of the Sultan al-Malik al-Ṣāliḥ" indicate that she regarded herself (or her supporters sought to present her) as the legitimate heiress to the Ayyubid sultanate. Her situation as the openly acknowledged ruler was unprecedented, although an Ayyubid princess, Ḍayfa Khātūn, had recently exercised power as the regent of Aleppo for her grandson al-Nāṣir Yūsuf.

Shajar al-Durr came to the throne at an unpropitious moment. The fighting with the Crusaders had not yet ended, and as she could not lead the army in person, there was need of another commander-in-chief. The choice fell on one of the Baḥriyya, the Amir Aybeg al-Turkumānī. The evacuation of the Crusaders, which soon followed, did not, however, secure Shajar al-Durr's position. When her accession was notified to Damascus, the Qaymariyya, a powerful Kurdish tribal contingent, invited al-Nāṣir Yūsuf of Aleppo to take possession of the city. The local Baḥriyya were ejected from power. Confronted with this threat, the Baḥriyya in Cairo decided that they must have a man as sultan. Shajar al-Durr thereupon abdicated, and Aybeg was enthroned with the title of al-Malik al-Muʿizz at the end of Rabīʿ II 648/July 1250. Only five days later, he too abdicated, since an important faction of the Baḥriyya headed by their commanding officer, the Amir Fāris al-Dīn Aktay al-Jamadār, and Baybars al-Bunduqdārī insisted on a nominal restoration of the Ayyubids in the person of al-Ashraf Mūsā, a ten-year-old great-grandson of al-Kāmil. Aybeg formally resumed his post of *atābak* but in fact he ruled Egypt, while Shajar al-Durr ruled him. At an uncertain date the two married.

If the installation of al-Ashraf Mūsā as sultan had been intended to conciliate the Syrian Ayyubids, it failed, but it marks a stage in internal political developments – the appointment of a shadow-sultan, while the real issue was fought out between the holders of power, the rival factions of Aktay and Aybeg. This political device was frequently to be utilized throughout the Mamluk sultanate. For the time being, however, the factions united in face of the threat from Syria, since al-Nāṣir Yūsuf was marching on Cairo. In a battle at al-ʿAbbāsa in the approaches to the Delta (10 Dhu'l-Qaʿda 648/3 February 1251), Aybeg inflicted a defeat on the invaders, who withdrew. Peace was not concluded until 651/1253, when the Caliph al-Mustaʿṣim in Baghdad, seeing the approach of the Mongols, acted as a mediator between the Mamluks and the Ayyubids. This was not to be the end of hostilities.

Meanwhile Aybeg was carefully strengthening his position by the accumulation of treasure and the promotion of his own Mamluks, the Muʿizziyya. One of them, Kutuz, was installed in the key position of viceregent in Egypt (*nāʾib al-salṭana bi-Miṣr*). These developments inevitably threatened the Baḥriyya and their leader Aktay, who for his part achieved a dramatic political success in obtaining as a bride an

Ayyubid princess from Ḥamāh. Aktay seemed to be moving to claim the sultanate in right of his Ayyubid wife. He began to adopt a regal title, and to display the royal insignia. Finally he demanded that his wife as the daughter of kings should have her residence in the Citadel of Cairo, which Saladin had built, and which had ever since been the dwelling-place of the rulers of Egypt. Aybeg hastily contrived his murder, which was accomplished by Kutuz with two confederates on 3 Shaʿbān 652/18 September 1254. Taken by surprise and at a disadvantage, many of the chief Baḥriyya fled from Cairo, some to the Seljuk sultan of Rūm, others to al-Nāṣir Yūsuf in Syria. Among the latter was Baybars al-Bunduqdārī, who now began to assume the leadership of the dispersed Baḥriyya. In Syria they incited al-Nāṣir Yūsuf to undertake another campaign against Aybeg. The crisis was again resolved by the caliph, whose envoy negotiated another peace treaty between Aybeg and al-Nāṣir Yūsuf in 654/1256. As a consequence of this settlement, al-Nāṣir Yūsuf withdrew his support from the refugee Baḥriyya, who thereupon transferred their services to another Ayyubid, al-Mughīth ʿUmar, the lord of al-Karak, a grandson of al-Kāmil Muḥammad.

Already before this, probably after the murder of Aktay but perhaps even earlier, Aybeg had resumed the sultanate by deposing al-Ashraf Mūsā, who was sent into exile in the Byzantine empire of Nicaea. Aybeg was now at the height of his power, which he sought to confirm by a marriage alliance with a daughter of Badr al-Dīn Lu'lu', a Mamluk who had succeeded to the Zangids as *atabeg* of Mosul. This was Aktay's policy all over again, and it led to the same fatal conclusion. Shajar al-Durr saw in this marriage a threat to her own position, and had recourse to the usual expedient of murder. Aybeg was killed in the bath of his palace on 23 Rabīʿ I 655/10 April 1257, but Shajar al-Durr's triumph was short-lived. Aybeg left a son, ʿAlī, by another wife, and around him a faction opposed to Shajar al-Durr immediately began to form. The Muʿizziyya raised ʿAlī to the sultanate with the title of al-Malik al-Manṣūr, and although Shajar al-Durr was at first protected by the remnant of al-Ṣāliḥ Ayyūb's Mamluks in Cairo, her corpse was found lying outside the Citadel on 11 Rabīʿ II 655/28 April 1257. Later chroniclers embellished the story of her end with picturesque details which are not found in the contemporary source.

Al-Manṣūr ʿAlī, aged fifteen years, played the same role that al-Ashraf Mūsā had played earlier – that of a shadow-sultan around whom the Mamluk magnates fought for power. The chief of them was Kutuz, who retained the office of vicegerent and administered the state. The accession of a minor necessitated the appointment of a commander-in-chief. The first holder of this post, Sanjar al-Ḥalabī, was ousted after a few days, since his colleagues suspected him of aiming at the sultanate. His place as *atābak al-ʿasākir* was taken by another Fāris al-Dīn Aktay, distinguished from the former commander of the Baḥriyya by the *nisba* of al-Mustaʿrib. Like Sanjar al-Ḥalabī, he originated from the household of al-Ṣāliḥ Ayyūb – an indication that the ascendancy of the Muʿizziyya was not complete, and that tension between the two factions would continue.

The main body of the Baḥriyya, however, were at this time in Syria, where like the Khwarazmians earlier they formed an unruly and bellicose company without a lord of their own. They were a danger to the rulers in Cairo, Damascus and al-Karak alike. In the service of al-Mughīth ʿUmar, they found al-Karak a useful base for operations against Egypt. In Dhu'l-Qaʿda 655/November 1257, a raid in which Baybars took part was defeated at al-Ṣāliḥiyya (strategically situated like Bilbays and al-ʿAbbasā in the approaches to the Delta from the east) by Kutuz and Aktay al-Mustaʿrib. Baybars returned to al-Karak, and built up his force of refugees until he felt strong enough to urge al-Mughīth to take the offensive again. In Rabīʿ II 656/April 1258 a second battle took place at al-Ṣāliḥiyya with a similar result, and this time Kutuz opened a fatal rift among the Mamluks by putting to death the leading members of the Baḥriyya who fell into his hands. Meanwhile al-Nāṣir Yūsuf witnessed with lively apprehension the growing military strength of al-Mughīth, whose forces included not only the Baḥriyya but also a body of Kurdish tribesmen, the Shahrazūriyya. These had fled from their homeland when it was overrun by the Mongols, and had found refuge at Damascus. Al-Nāṣir found them insubordinate, and they soon abandoned his service for that of al-Mughīth, who saw in them the means of conquering Damascus. Early in 657/1259 the armies of the rival Ayyubids met near Jericho. Al-Mughīth was defeated, and fled to al-Karak. Negotiations took place, the upshot of which was that al-Mughīth agreed to surrender the Baḥriyya to al-Nāṣir and to dismiss the Shahrazūriyya, who left for Palestine. Baybars adroitly made terms for himself and a few companions, and re-entered the service of al-Nāṣir Yūsuf. About this time his relations with the Shahrazūriyya were sufficiently close for him to take a wife from their tribe.

The hostilities between al-Nāṣir and al-Mughīth were insignificant in comparison with the great events that were taking place in the east and north, for it was at this time that the Mongol tempest raged in the heartlands of Islam, blowing away its established dynasties and even the venerable ʿAbbasid caliphate itself. Nomadic tribesmen of central Asia like their Turkish neighbours, the Mongols were united into a formidable military and political force by a warrior-chief named Temujin, better known by his title of Chingiz Khan, under whose direction petty raids gave place to ambitious schemes of world conquest. Between 1206, when Chingiz Khan's supremacy was recognized in a Mongol tribal assembly (*quriltai*), and 1227, when he died, he conquered northern China and overthrew the kingdom of the Khwārazm-Shāhs in the west. This opened the way to further advances in western Asia, which did not, however, immediately occur. A *quriltai* in 1229 elected one of his sons, Ögedei, to succeed him as Great Khan. The conquests were partitioned among Ögedei's brothers and nephews, and one nephew, Batu, carried out a great invasion of Russia and eastern Europe between 1236 and 1241. Ögedei died at the end of 1241, and after the five years' regency of his widow, he was succeeded as Great Khan by his son, Güyük. In the meantime one of Batu's generals, Bayju Noyan, had defeated the Seljuk sultan of Rūm, Kay-Khusraw II, at the battle of Köse Dagh in 641/1243, and turned his realm into a Mongol protectorate (see below, p. 173). Güyük died in 1248, and his widow in her turn became regent until in 1251 their son, Möngke, was elected Great Khan.

It was during Möngke's reign that the last great thrust of the Mongols into western Asia took place. The Mongol forces commanded by Hülegü, Möngke's brother, set out on their career of conquest in 1255. Alamūt, the headquarters of the Assassins, was captured, and its chief put to death. Baghdad fell on 6 Ṣafar 656/12 February 1258. Soon afterwards al-Mustaʿṣim was executed, and the caliphate came to an end. The Mongol advance continued northwards and westwards around the Fertile Crescent. Already in 656/1258 al-Nāṣir Yūsuf had sent his son with gifts to Hülegü. He came back in the following year with a menacing and humiliating letter from the Mongol conqueror. At first al-Nāṣir determined to resist, and sought help from Egypt. In Cairo, Kutuz responded to the Mongol threat and furthered his own ambitions by deposing al-Manṣūr ʿAlī and usurping the sultanate with the title of al-Malik al-Muẓaffar (Dhu'l-Qaʿda 657/November 1259). Al-Nāṣir led his army out of Damascus but he had no stomach for a fight. As the Mongols advanced, Syrian refugees began to stream southwards before them.

By this time Hülegü had taken al-Bīra (the modern Birejik), which gave him the crossing of the Euphrates. He marched on Aleppo. Its old governor, a son of Saladin, attempted resistance but the city was taken by storm on 9 Ṣafar 658/25 January 1260. At the news, al-Nāṣir's army melted away. He himself fled to Gaza and then to Transjordan, whence he was sent as a prisoner to Hülegü. Baybars meanwhile had entered into communication with Kutuz, and on 22 Rabīʿ I 658/17 March 1260 he returned to Egypt under an oath of safety sworn by the sultan. A few days earlier Damascus had surrendered to the Mongols, who were raiding as far south as Hebron and Gaza. About this time Hülegü heard of the death of his brother Möngke, and left his army in order to participate in the settlement of the succession.

The Mongol conquest of Syria was a disaster for the Muslims: it was less obnoxious to the oriental Christians and the Franks. During the siege of Aleppo, the Mongols had been reinforced by Christian allies, King Hethoum I of Lesser Armenia and his son-in-law, Bohemond VI of Antioch–Tripoli. By contrast, the Latin kingdom showed no inclination to welcome or assist the Mongols. After the taking of Damascus, the native Christians rejoiced in the special protection of Hülegü, and displayed an imprudent arrogance, drinking wine openly in Ramaḍān and compelling Muslims to stand as the cross passed in procession through the streets.

The Ayyubid prince of Ḥimṣ was formally appointed governor of Syria by the Mongols, but after Hülegü's departure the substance of power remained in the hands of his commander, Ket-Buqa Noyan. Hülegü had sent an embassy to Cairo, summoning Kutuz to surrender, but the sultan, strongly backed by Baybars, resolved on resistance. The Mongol ambassadors were put to death – an act of glaring defiance – and on 15 Shaʿbān 658/26 July 1260 Kutuz left the Citadel at the head of his army. As they advanced along the coast of Palestine, the Frankish authorities in Acre hastened to offer their support, which was not accepted. Baybars pressed ahead with an advance party, and carried out a reconnaissance of the Mongol army, which was encamped at ʿAyn Jālūt in the valley of Jezreel, north of Mount Gilboa. On 25 Ramaḍān 658/3 September 1260 the two armies confronted one another in battle. The meeting has been described as a conflict of two steppe-peoples, one invading and the other defending the lands of Islam.[2] By nightfall Ket-Buqa Noyan was dead and his army in flight. The Mongol hold over Syria was broken, and Egypt was freed from the threat of invasion.

There was one important, if unintentional, result of Hülegü's invasion. Ayyubid rule over the two principal Syrian cities of Aleppo and Damascus had been brought to an end, and Muslim Syria as a whole fell into the hands of the Mamluk sultan without a conquest. Kutuz proceeded to make a settlement of his new dominion. Sanjar al-Ḥalabī went as governor to Damascus. Aleppo had been promised to Baybars but in fact was allotted to ʿAlāʾ al-Dīn ʿAlī, a son of Badr al-Dīn Luʾluʾ. Ayyubid princes were allowed to retain the three smaller lordships of Ḥimṣ, Ḥamāh and al-Karak. Then Kutuz set out for Cairo. But the precarious unity of the Mamluks before the Mongol threat was already crumbling. The old factional hostility of Baḥriyya and Muʿizziyya revived, and Baybars, resenting his treatment by Kutuz, fomented a conspiracy. A hunting-party on the way back to Egypt gave him his opportunity. On 15 Dhu'l-Qaʿda/24 October Baybars and his confederates slew Kutuz in the desert, and he returned to the royal tent to claim the sultanate.

NOTES

1. Abū Shāma, *Tarājim rijāl al-qarnayn al-sādis wa'l-sābiʿ*, ed. Muḥammad Zāhid al-Kawtharī, Cairo 1366/1947; repr. Beirut [1974], 184. English version P. M. Holt.
2. Bernard Lewis (citing Abū Shāma and Ibn Khaldūn) in P. M. Holt, Ann K. S. Lambton and Bernard Lewis (eds), *The Cambridge history of Islam*, I, Cambridge 1970, 214.

CHAPTER ELEVEN

The Reign of al-Ẓāhir Baybars 1260–1277

When Baybars killed Kutuz and took the throne, he was about thirty-two years old. By origin he was a Kıpchak Turk from the territory lying to the north of the Black Sea. When the Mongols conquered this region about 1241, Baybars's people fled across the Black Sea and sought refuge with a Turcoman chieftain in Anatolia, who proved treacherous, and turned on the fugitives with fire and sword. Baybars was among the captives. He was then about fourteen years of age, and his journey southwards can be traced through the slave-markets of Sivas, Aleppo, Damascus and Ḥamāh. Here the young Ayyubid prince, al-Manṣūr Muḥammad (who was later to be Baybars's vassal) was about to buy him, when he was dissuaded by his mother. "Have nothing to do with that swarthy fellow," she said, "he has an evil eye." In fact Baybars was bought by one of the Sultan al-Ṣāliḥ Ayyūb's Mamluks named Aydigin al-Bunduqdār. Soon afterwards his master fell into disgrace, and in 644/1247 Baybars entered the sultan's own household, where he attained rapid promotion and was made head of the Jamadāriyya, i.e. the pages of the Wardrobe. Something has already been said of his subsequent career in the stormy decade which opened with the murder of al-Muʿaẓẓam Tūrān-Shāh and ended with that of Kutuz.

The success of the conspiracy against Kutuz did not of itself secure the sultanate for Baybars. It marked the re-establishment of al-Ṣāliḥ Ayyūb's military household, the Baḥriyya or Ṣāliḥiyya, in place of the rival Muʿizziyya, headed by Kutuz himself. The election of Baybars as sultan was principally due to the Mamluk elder statesman, the *Atābak* Aktay al-Mustaʿrib. He broke into the royal tent, where the Mamluk magnates were about to elect a sultan, and urged the claim of Baybars as the slayer of Kutuz. On his advice, mutual oaths were exchanged by which Baybars undertook to assist his supporters, and the magnates in turn entered into a covenant of loyalty to him. Again on Aktay's advice, Baybars pushed on ahead of the army to secure the Citadel of Cairo and its treasury. He met with no resistance, and was formally enthroned the next morning (19 Dhu'l-Ḥijja 658/25 November 1260). Several weeks later he made a state procession through the city with the royal insignia.

Baybars's comrades (*khushdāshiyya*) from the Mamluk household of al-Ṣāliḥ Ayyūb remained an important political factor throughout his reign, and it was his policy to maintain good relations with them. In the words of his court biographer, Ibn ʿAbd al-Ẓāhir:

> When it pleased God to grant the advent of the sultan's reign, he gathered the fugitives, and brought in those who were afar; he promoted those who lacked advancement, and gave office to those who had been set aside. He returned to them the possessions, wealth and favours of which they had been deprived. He appointed the deserving to amirates, and promoted the competent. He set up a special department of state for them. They formed his immediate entourage, who guarded his Citadel, whether he was absent or present.[1]

Among the Ṣāliḥiyya, Aktay al-Mustaʿrib remained the sultan's chief minister for many years. He retained the title of *atābak*, although there was no need of anyone to carry out the traditional functions of this office, since Baybars was in vigorous command of his own army. When Baybars's four-year-old son, Baraka Khān, was appointed titular joint sultan in Shawwāl 662/August 1264, an *atābak*, i.e. an *atabeg* in the old Seljukid sense, was duly appointed. This was not Aktay but another leading member of the Ṣāliḥiyya, Aydemir al-Ḥillī. Meanwhile Baybars was placing increasing reliance on one of his own military household, the Ẓāhiriyya, Bilik al-Khāzindār, who understudied Aktay, shared his emoluments and succeeded him as the chief minister on his death (672/1273–4).

Throughout Baybars's reign, Syria remained his principal preoccupation. The annexation of Muslim Syria to the Mamluk sultanate was, as has been seen, a consequence of the Mongol invasion and the Mamluk victory at ʿAyn Jālūt. Although the remaining Ayyubids were quiescent, Baybars was immediately challenged by separatist movements. His own *khushdāsh*, Sanjar al-Ḥalabī, whom Kutuz had appointed governor of Damascus, proclaimed himself sultan there, and assumed the royal title of al-Malik al-Mujāhid (Dhu'l-Ḥijja 658/November 1260). He may have seen himself as no more than a vassal-ruler under the paramountcy of the sultan in Cairo, after the Ayyubid pattern. In any case, he did not reign for long. Al-Manṣūr Muḥammad of Ḥamāh refused to support him, saying, "I am with the ruler of Egypt, whoever he may be." Within Damascus a faction which included the

Qaymariyya (now reaching the term of their political importance) and Baybars's former master, Aydigin al-Bunduqdār, and which was furnished with Egyptian gold, ousted Sanjar and established the rule of Baybars. In Aleppo, the course of events was more complicated and prolonged. The Mamluk households of the last two Ayyubids, the ʿAzīziyya and the Nāṣiriyya, retained considerable power. They overthrew the governor appointed by Kutuz, ʿAlāʾ al-Dīn ʿAlī, and put one of themselves in his place. Their project of establishing an independent regime in northern Syria was cut short by a second Mongol invasion, which scattered the conspirators. Aleppo and Ḥamāh fell, but the Mongols were held and defeated at the first battle of Ḥimṣ by an army composed of the forces of the Ayyubids of Ḥimṣ and Ḥamāh with troops from Aleppo (5 Muḥarram 659/10 December 1260).

After the withdrawal of the Mongols from Aleppo a few weeks later, the city fell into the hands of a Mamluk adventurer, Akkush al-Barlī, who had already tried and failed to gain the support of the Ayyubids of Ḥimṣ and Ḥamāh. It was retaken on 3 Shaʿbān 659/17 July 1261 by none other than Sanjar al-Ḥalabī – pardoned, restored to favour and appointed governor by the sultan. Shortly afterwards he withdrew from Aleppo, which was again occupied by al-Barlī. It was finally retaken by Aydigin al-Bunduqdār in Dhu'l-Qaʿda 659/October 1261, and he then became its governor. Al-Barlī and his supporters moved to the frontier-town of al-Bīra on the Euphrates, where they held out for over a year. In the end, however, al-Barlī submitted to Baybars, who received him honourably in Cairo (2 Dhu'l-Ḥijja 660/18 October 1262), and treated him at first with great favour. He ceded to the sultan his rights to al-Bīra. When no further danger was to be feared from him, the sultan's attitude changed, and in Rajab 661/May–June 1263 al-Barlī was arrested.

In the meantime a development had occurred which was to be of much service to Baybars in both his external and his internal policy – the restoration of the ʿAbbasid caliphate under his patronage. Although after the death of the Caliph al-Nāṣir in 622/1225, the caliphate had sunk back into its previous condition of political impotence, it remained an institution of considerable juridical significance. The caliph's diplomas legitimated the authority of Sunnī rulers, authorized the processes of Muslim law in their territories, and validated contracts including contracts of marriage. The extinction of the caliphate with the killing of al-Mustaʿṣim in 656/1258 thus created a juristic vacuum. Baybars was not the first to try to rectify the situation. A refugee ʿAbbasid prince, Abu'l-ʿAbbās Aḥmad, had been flitting restlessly about the Fertile Crescent since the taking of Baghdad, and Kutuz had made contact with him. After the accession of Baybars, Abu'l-ʿAbbās had set out for Egypt, but was anticipated by another ʿAbbasid pretender, whose credentials were approved by a commission of Egyptian jurists, and who on 13 Rajab 659/13 June 1261 was solemnly installed as caliph with the throne-name of al-Mustanṣir. Baybars took the oath of allegiance (*bayʿa*) traditionally sworn to the head of the Muslim community. In return he was invested by the caliph not merely with Egypt and Syria, which he actually ruled, but also with Diyār Bakr and the Euphrates provinces (i.e. the eastern Fertile Crescent, at that time under Hülegü), the Ḥijāz and the Yemen, together with all future conquests. The diploma of investiture was in effect the announcement and authorization of a programme of expansion. This was emphasized in a later passage, which dwelt on the obligation of the Holy War and the duty of maintaining the fortresses and the fleet. The diploma also implied that Baybars was not just the sultan of Egypt and Syria but the universal sultan of Islam, the deputy of the universal caliph.

Al-Mustanṣir's caliphate was brief. A few weeks later he accompanied the sultan to Damascus, whence he and the three sons of Badr al-Dīn Lu'lu' were sent with a small force to recover their lost dominions. It was a forlorn hope; the only one to have even limited success was al-Ṣāliḥ Ismāʿīl, who regained Mosul for a short time. While al-Mustanṣir was on the way, he met his kinsman and rival, Abu'l-ʿAbbās Aḥmad, who in the meantime had been at the court of al-Barlī. He had been recognized as caliph by al-Barlī, who sought thereby to legitimate his own position. The two ʿAbbasids joined forces, and advanced down the Euphrates. About 40 miles from Baghdad they were confronted by a Mongol army, and defeated (23 Muḥarram 660/18 December 1261). Al-Mustanṣir was among the slain, and his head was promenaded around Baghdad. His kinsman succeeded in escaping, and made his way to Cairo, where he too, after due investigation of his pedigree, was installed as caliph with the throne-name of al-Ḥākim. More fortunate than his predecessor, al-Ḥākim was to reign (but never to rule) for over forty years, and was to be succeeded in the caliphate by his descendants until the Ottoman conquest.

The new caliph was immediately useful to Baybars in connection with an important diplomatic development. The harmony which had existed among the descendants of Chingiz Khan, the rulers of the vast Mongol empire, ended with the death of the Great Khan Möngke in 657/1259. A civil war ensued between two of his brothers, Arıgh Böke and Qubilai (the Kubla Khan of Coleridge's poem), and this ended with the victory of the latter. Of the western Mongol rulers, Hülegü, the *ilkhan* of Persia and the eastern Fertile Crescent, supported Qubilai, while Berke Khan of the Golden Horde (whose dominions extended over the Kıpchak steppe) was a partisan of Arıgh Böke. The defeat of his candidate left Berke isolated in the face of Hülegü; he was also (uniquely among the Mongol rulers of the time) a Muslim. For both these reasons, he was anxious for an alliance with Baybars, who headed the only Muslim power which had successfully resisted Hülegü. In 660/1262 he ordered contingents of Mongol tribesmen of the Golden Horde, who had been serving with Hülegü, to return home or join the Mamluk forces. Many of them moved into Syria and Egypt, where they settled. These immigrants were known as the Wāfidiyya.

Baybars equally welcomed an alliance, both because of its strategic value against Hülegü, and because Berke controlled the Kıpchak steppe, the principal recruiting-ground at that time for Mamluks. The caliph as the nominal head of the *Umma* and the kinsman of the Prophet played an important, if symbolic, part in the negotiations by giving audience to Berke's ambassadors. An embassy returning to Berke in Ramaḍān 661/July 1263 took princely gifts, including a copy of the Qur'ān supposedly transcribed by the Caliph ʿUthmān. The ambassadors were invested with the *futuwwa*, a name originally given to associations of young men, which had been re-formed as a courtly organization by the Caliph al-Nāṣir, and was now revived as an instrument of diplomacy by Baybars. The sultan ordered Berke's name to be inserted (although after his own) in the *khuṭba* – a unique sign of diplomatic recognition. Berke died in 665/1266. Although his successor, Möngke Temür, was not a Muslim, the common interest of the Golden Horde and the Mamluks in opposing the *ilkhans* kept their *entente* in being.

The continuing danger from Hülegü and, after his death in 663/1265, from Abaqa, his son and successor, dominated Baybars's Syrian policy. Once the early separatist movements had been overcome, he had two principal aims: to retain control of the essential frontier fortresses, and to prevent any potential threat from the Frankish states. Two frontier towns were of great strategic importance. The first of these was al-Karak in Transjordan. Its lord, al-Mughīth ʿUmar, remained the most independent of the Ayyubids, and his great castle dominated the routes from Damascus to Egypt and the Ḥijāz. His downfall was brought about by politic treachery. At Baybars's invitation, he came to the sultan's encampment by Mount Tabor in Jumādā I 661/April 1263. He was immediately arrested, and brought before a tribunal of jurists, headed by the chief judge of Damascus. Evidence was produced of his correspondence with the Mongols. He was dispatched to Egypt under escort, and in the following month his sons and troops surrendered al-Karak to the sultan. The great fortress was to play an important part in the later history of the Mamluk sultanate, both as a stronghold and a place of exile. In the north, al-Bīra on the left bank of the Euphrates was a bridgehead into Mongol-held territory, and a bastion to protect northern Syria. On al-Barlī's withdrawal it was incorporated into Baybars's dominions. The town was besieged in 663/1265 by the Mongols, perhaps in collusion with the Franks. Baybars advanced into Syria, and sent forward a relieving expedition. While passing through Palestine, he learnt that the enemy had withdrawn, and thereupon he turned his operations against the Latin kingdom.

The Frankish states were by this time in a condition of increasing weakness. During his four years in the kingdom, Louis IX had done much to raise its morale and to rally its energies. After his departure in 1254 the kingdom was again leaderless. The nominal king, Conradin of Hohenstaufen, the grandson of the Emperor Frederick II, was a baby and an absentee. Behind the façade of the feudal constitution, the substance of power was held in the towns by the Italian communes, in the countryside by the military orders – groups which were not only mutually hostile but were riven by internal struggles of Venetians against Genoese, Templars against Hospitallers. The principality of Antioch and the county of Tripoli were now united in the person of Bohemond VI (1252–75), who was married to the daughter of King Hethoum I of Lesser Armenia. The defeat of the Mongols at ʿAyn Jālūt was a serious reverse for the rulers of Lesser Armenia and Antioch–Tripoli, who had been their partisans.

The condition of coexistence which had generally subsisted between the Frankish and Muslim states in the time of the later Ayyubids was now replaced by a phase of increasing aggression on the part of the Mamluk sultans. Other factors than the possibility of collaboration between Franks and Mongols contributed to this. St Louis's campaign in Egypt, although unsuccessful, had shown that there was still the possibility of a crusade from Europe. The Mamluk regime, which had begun in the resistance to the French Crusaders, presented itself as embodying the spirit of the *jihād* as its public pronouncements, made through the mouth of the caliph, bore witness. Almost every year Baybars led an expedition into Syria, and his successive hammer-blows fell upon the Frankish states. In 661/1263, after the arrest of al-Mughīth ʿUmar, he razed the church at Nazareth, and raided up to the walls of Acre. When in 663/1265 he knew that al-Bīra had been relieved, he marched against the coastal town of Palestine. Caesarea, Haifa and Arsūf were captured and forthwith demolished, so that they should not serve as bases for any force of Crusaders from overseas. In Shawwāl 664/July 1266 the great inland fortress of Ṣafad, dominating the routes through

Galilee, was taken from the Templars. Unlike the coastal strongholds, Ṣafad was carefully restored, Baybars himself participating in the work. It was provided with a Muslim garrison, and became one of the provincial capitals of Mamluk Syria. The same year saw a thrust into Lesser Armenia, the expedition being commanded by al-Manṣūr Muḥammad of Ḥamāh. A heavy defeat was inflicted on the Armenians, and their capital, Sīs, was devastated. This was a punitive raid on a grand scale, and it ended the political importance of Lesser Armenia. Subsequent years saw the further erosion of the Frankish states. In Jumādā II 666/March 1268, Jaffa was captured and demolished. The Templars' castle of Belfort (Shaqīf Arnūn), overlooking the lower valley of the River Leontes, was taken and, like Ṣafad, garrisoned by its new master. The events of this year culminated in the capture of Antioch, which fell on 4 Ramaḍān 666/18 May 1268, after 171 years of rule by the house of Hauteville. This marked the end of the political and economic greatness of the city.

Baybars was now at the height of his power. In 667/1269 he felt secure enough to pay a semi-secret visit to the Ḥijāz. There he visited Mecca and Medina, making the Pilgrimage – a pious duty and at the same time a means of asserting his suzerainty over the Arab rulers of the two Holy Cities. In 668/1270 came the fear of another crusade led by Louis IX, and Baybars thereupon demolished the remaining fortifications of Ascalon lest it should be used as a base. But Louis died of plague outside Tunis, and in 669/1271 Baybars made his last great campaign against the Frankish states. Ḥiṣn al-Akrād (Crac des Chevaliers) was taken from the Hospitallers. It was perhaps the strongest of all the Crusaders' castles, and it was refortified by Baybars. Tripoli now seemed in danger, but unexpectedly the sultan offered Bohemond a truce. The reason was the arrival in Palestine of the last army of Crusaders. It was commanded by the Lord Edward, soon to be King Edward I of England, who hoped to break Mamluk power in Syria by combined operations with the *ilkhan*. The scheme proved impractical, and Edward's forces were too few to be effective on their own. In September 1272, having narrowly escaped death at the dagger of an Assassin, he set sail from Acre.

Towards the end of his reign, Baybars attempted to break the military deadlock with the *ilkhan*'s Mongols by an initiative in a new direction. Since the battle of Köse Dagh, the sultanate of Rūm had been a Mongol protectorate. As early as 660/1262, Baybars had been invited to intervene in Anatolia by ʿIzz al-Dīn Kay-Kāvūs II, one of two brothers who were rivals for the throne of Rūm (see below, pp. 173–4). He was at this time an exile in Constantinople, and offered

Baybars half of his lands – an offer he was in no position to fulfil, and the negotiations petered out. In these years the effective ruler in the Rūm sultanate was a regent, Muʿīn al-Dīn Süleymān, usually known by his title of office as the *Pervāne*. He had been in touch with Baybars since 670/1272, but it was not until 675/1277 that a full-scale Mamluk expedition to Anatolia was mounted. Hoping for the collaboration of the *Pervāne* and the Turcomans against the Mongols, Baybars led his forces northwards. The Mongols were heavily defeated in the frontier territory of Elbistan (Abulustayn) in Dhu'l-Qaʿda 675/April 1277. The Mamluks advanced to the Seljuk capital of Kayseri, where Baybars was enthroned as sultan of Rūm. But the *Pervāne* did not come in as expected, local support for the Mamluks was doubtful and the *Ilkhan* Abaqa was on the march. Baybars therefore withdrew from the most transitory of his conquests, leaving the *Pervāne* and lesser collaborators to Abaqa's revenge. He made his way back to Damascus, where after thirteen days of sickness he died on 27 Muḥarram 676/30 June 1277. The college-mosque of the Ẓāhiriyya (now the Syrian National Library) holds his tomb.

It has been said that Baybars was a second Saladin, and certainly his biographer Ibn ʿAbd al-Ẓāhir was at pains to present his master as the true heir of the Ayyubids, and to show him as equalling, if not surpassing, his great predecessor. Saladin and Baybars had some things in common. Both were aliens to the mass of their subjects, one a Kurd, the other a Kıpchak Turk; but Saladin, whose family came from old Islamic territory, was the more fully assimilated to the culture of his dominions. Baybars was to the end a Turkish warrior-chief, a recent convert playing very successfully the roles of a Muslim sultan and fighter in the Holy War. As a soldier he excelled Saladin; he was more single-minded in his military objectives, as in yearly campaign after yearly campaign he brought the great fortresses and towns of the Frankish states into his possession. Although he spent so much of his time in the field, he had also the instincts of an administrator. As his reaction to Sanjar al-Ḥalabī showed, he would not tolerate a partition of the sultanate, and unlike Saladin he left to his successors a centralized kingdom, which retained its unity until the Ottoman conquest. Baybars also took the decisive step in the transfer of administrative control to a hierarchy of Mamluk amirs, and the structure so established was to last as long as the Mamluk sultanate.

It is not easy to see in Baybars the human touches which are characteristic of Saladin. Both men grew up in a hard school, where friendship was precarious and misjudgement perilous, but at least the son and nephew of Nūr al-Dīn's magnates started his career under more favourable auspices than the Turkish military slave. On several occasions Baybars showed a resolute and ruthless determination in pursuing his aims. He was twice a regicide through his participation in the murders of al-Muʿaẓẓam Tūrān-Shāh and Kutuz – and in the latter case he was the originator of the conspiracy. His treacherous seizure of al-Mughīth ʿUmar excited the disapproval of his Mamluk peers, and some of his contemporaries apparently suspected that he had sent the Caliph al-Mustanṣir with a small army deliberately to his doom. In his two most ambitious plans he failed. His last campaign into Anatolia brought him only a transient and nominal sovereignty over Rūm. His purpose, systematically pursued over a long period, to make the sultanate hereditary in his family was defeated within three years of his death, when his comrade Kalavun usurped the throne from his sons. Nevertheless, Baybars's reign was one of outstanding achievement, and the masterful sultan was a worthy contemporary and opponent of Edward I.

NOTE

1. Ibn ʿAbd al-Ẓāhir, *al-Rawḍ al-zāhir fī sīrat al-Malik al-Ẓāhir*, ed. ʿAbd al-ʿAzīz al-Khuwayṭir, al-Riyāḍ [1396/1976], 74. English version P. M. Holt.

CHAPTER TWELVE

The Establishment of the Kalavunid Dynasty 1277–1293

Many years before he died, Baybars had taken steps to ensure the succession of his son, al-Malik al-Saʿīd Muḥammad Baraka Khān, whose name, the arabicized form of Berke Khan, was not taken from Baybars's ally, the chief of the Golden Horde, but from the Khwarazmian warrior whose daughter Baybars had married. In 660/1262, when Baraka Khān was about two years old, he had been publicly recognized as heir apparent, and on 13 Shawwāl 662/8 August 1264 he was appointed joint sultan. During his father's lifetime, his authority remained nominal.

When Baybars died in Damascus, Bilik al-Khāzindār, his Mamluk and chief minister as vicegerent in Egypt, secretly sent word to Baraka Khān, and concealed the sultan's death until the army had been brought back to Cairo. By this means Bilik secured a quiet and undisputed succession, but he had not gained the gratitude of the new ruler. A few weeks later Bilik died, and the chroniclers report rumours that he was poisoned – one indeed gives circumstantial and probably fictional details of his murder by the queen-mother. He was succeeded as vicegerent by Aksungur al-Fāriqānī, who had been one of Baybars's most trusted servants. But, as had happened before with al-Muʿaẓẓam Tūrān-Shāh, the new sultan had his own household, the *khāṣṣakiyya* (in effect, the Mamluks of the Privy Chamber), and neither he nor they were anxious to leave power in the hands of the older generation. Aksungur was arrested and thrown into prison, where he died. His post went to a school-friend of the sultan, a Mongol named Küvendik al-Sāqī (i.e. the Cup-bearer). About the same time, two other magnates were arrested, Sungur al-Ashqar and Baysarı, both veterans of the Baḥriyya. When the sultan's maternal uncle dared to plead for them, he too was arrested. After this show of strength, all three were released but it was clear that a new master ruled.

In Dhu'l-Qaʿda 677/March 1279, Baraka Khān led his forces to Damascus, whence he sent an expedition to Lesser Armenia. Its commanders were Baysarı and another veteran of the Baḥriyya, Sayf al-Din Kalavun al-Alfī, Baraka Khān's father-in-law. During their absence, the rift between the old and the new Mamluks increased, and rather surprisingly Küvendik sided with the Ẓāhiriyya (i.e. the household of al-Ẓāhir Baybars) against the *khāṣṣakiyya* and the young sultan. When the expeditionary force returned in Rabīʿ I 678/August 1279, Küvendik warned Kalavun and Baysarı of the dangerous shift of power at court, and a crisis ensued. The veterans demanded that the sultan dismiss the *khāṣṣakiyya*, and confirm the assignments and appointments of the amirs. Baraka Khān sent his mother to negotiate but no real agreement was possible, and the rebels slipped away by night to secure possession of Cairo. The sultan sent his mother and his treasure to al-Karak and set out for his capital, but on the way he was abanḍoned by nearly all his supporters. He managed to gain entry to the Citadel, only to find himself besieged there. He was enabled to surrender on terms negotiated by the Caliph al-Ḥākim. In Rabīʿ II 678/August 1279, he came down from the Citadel, and abdicated. He was allowed to go to al-Karak, where he kept royal state, and recruited many Mamluks.

The new sultan was Baraka Khān's half-brother, a seven-year-old boy named Salāmish (the arabicized form of the Mongolian, Sülemish), who was entitled al-Malik al-ʿĀdil. Clearly he was no more than a figurehead, playing the same part that al-Ashraf Mūsā had done for Aybeg, and the real power was held by Kalavun, who had emerged as the leader of the victorious faction, and was now appointed *atābak* and administrator of the kingdom. He was already planning to take the throne but circumstances were not yet propitious. The Ẓāhiriyya, who formed the bulk of the Egyptian forces, might revolt at the exclusion of Baybars's sons from the throne, and there was the possibility of opposition from Kalavun's own *khushdāshiyya*, the Baḥriyya of al-Ṣāliḥ Ayyūb. Within a few weeks the situation had changed in his favour. Of his leading colleagues, Baysarı had refused the sultanate on the abdication of Baraka Khān, while Sungur al-Ashqar had gone off to Damascus as governor. The amirs and the *khāṣṣakiyya* were prepared to be compliant, having experienced Kalavun's bountiful patronage. There was, therefore, no opposition when on 21 Rajab 678/27 November 1279, he proposed that the state required a ruler of mature years. Al-ʿĀdil was thereupon deposed, and sent to al-Karak to join his brother. Kalavun then became sultan with the title of al-Mālik al-Manṣūr.

Like Baybars, the new sultan was a Kıpchak Turk by origin. He was born about the year 619/1222 but was not brought in as a Mamluk until he was in his late twenties; for this reason, it is said, he never learnt to speak Arabic properly. His first master, a member of al-Kāmil's household, paid for him the high price of 1,000 dinars (in Arabic, *alf dīnār*), whence he obtained his *nisba* of al-Alfī. On his master's death, Kalavun passed into the household of al-Ṣāliḥ Ayyūb during the last year of the sultan's life. He was one of the Baḥriyya who fled to Syria when Aybeg murdered Aktay al-Jamadār, and in the reign of Baybars he was an important amir. The marriage of Baraka Khān to his daughter gives an indication of his standing and Baybars's appreciation of his political significance.

When Kalavun usurped the throne, his position was still precarious, and he carried out a purge of the Ẓāhiriyya, appointing his own Mamluks, the Manṣūriyya, as governors of provinces and castellans of fortresses. The most serious challenge came, however, from his own *khushdāsh*, Sungur al-Ashqar, with whom he is said to have plotted the usurpation. Sungur as governor of Damascus acted exactly as Sanjar al-Ḥalabī had done twenty years previously. He refused to swear allegiance to Kalavun, declared himself sultan with the title of al-Malik al-Kāmil, and sent a force to Gaza to guard the frontier against an attack from Egypt. Fighting began in Muḥarram 679/May 1280, and in the following month Sungur was worsted in a battle outside Gaza against an Egyptian force under the command (ironically enough) of Sanjar al-Ḥalabī. He sought refuge with his ally, the Arab chief of Āl Faḍl, ʿĪsā b. Muhannā, and ultimately established himself in Ṣahyūn, formerly the Crusader castle of Saone, in the mountains east of Latakia, to which he had sent his family and treasure. He and his servants retained control of a group of north Syrian strongholds, from which they could defy the sultan.

The position of the family of Baybars in Transjordan must also have caused some anxiety to Kalavun. Baraka Khān as lord of al-Karak was joined by his brothers, Salāmish and Khaḍir, the latter named after Baybars's soothsayer. With his treasure and his Mamluk household, he proceeded to build up a faction of supporters. His death in Dhu'l-Qaʿda 678/March 1280 came very conveniently for Kalavun, and naturally rumours of poison spread. Al-Karak was, however, conferred on Khaḍir, who assumed the royal title of al-Malik al-Masʿūd. He retained a good deal of power until early 685/1286, when the castle capitulated to an army sent by Kalavun. Khaḍir and Salāmish were honourably brought to Cairo, and later, after Kalavun's death, exiled to Constantinople, where Salāmish died in 690/1291. Five years later, the Sultan al-Manṣūr Lachın recalled Khaḍir and his family to Egypt at the request of his wife, a daughter of Baybars. On his return Khaḍir made the Pilgrimage, and he died ten years later in 708/1308–9. A last descendant of Baybars, a great-grandson of Salāmish died in 893/1488.

A greater threat to Kalavun was constituted by the Mongols under *Ilkhan* Abaqa, who since his accession in 663/1265 had been endeavouring to break the Mamluk hold over Syria. He established contact with the papacy and the rulers of Western Europe but his diplomatic initiatives were fruitless. The usurpation of Kalavun and the separatist movement of Sungur al-Ashqar, reproducing as they did the situation at the start of Baybars's reign, offered Abaqa an opportunity for intervention in Syria – at one time, in fact, Sungur appears to have been in touch with the *ilkhan.* Küvendik who was accused of heading a conspiracy of Mamluks of Mongol origin against the sultan, was drowned in Lake Tiberias in Muḥarram 680/May 1281. But in Rabīʿ I 680/June 1281, Kalavun, who had brought his army to Damascus, made terms with Sungur, who gave up his royal title (and hence his pretensions to independence) but kept his northern castles. He joined forces with the sultan, and on 14 Rajab 680/29 October 1281 the long-planned Mongol invasion of Syria was halted at the second battle of Ḥimṣ. The Mongols, supported by their Armenian allies and commanded by Abaqa's brother, were utterly routed. Abaqa's intention to lead an avenging army into Syria the following year was frustrated by his death from delirium tremens in Dhu'l-Ḥijja 680/April 1282. He was succeeded by his brother Tegüder, who was a Muslim, and on his conversion had taken the name of Aḥmad.

The temporary ending of the Mongol threat and the reconciliation with Sungur al-Ashqar left Kalavun free to continue Baybars's *jihād* against the Frankish states, and this was the principal occupation of the remaining years of his reign. The political weakness of the Latin kingdom was becoming ever more obvious. The crown was disputed by two claimants, Hugh III of Lusignan, king of Cyprus, and Mary of Antioch, who in 1277 sold her rights to Charles of Anjou, king of Sicily, the formidable brother of Louis IX. Within the Latin kingdom, his Angevin party was supported by Acre, Sidon and the Templars, while the Lusignans were backed by Tyre and Beirut. This was the situation at Kalavun's accession, and the fragmentation of the Latin kingdom is shown in the several treaties concluded by the sultan (see below, pp. 156–8). One in Muḥarram 681/April 1282 was with William of Beaujeu, the Master of the Temple (and incidentally a cousin of Charles of Anjou); another in Rabīʿ I 682/June 1283 was with the Frankish authorities in Acre, viz. Odo Poilechien, the deputy of Charles of

Anjou's regent, William of Beaujeu, and Nicholas Lorgne, the Master of the Hospital; a third in Jumādā I 684/July 1285 with King Hugh's sister, the Lady Margaret of Tyre. When this last treaty was made both Hugh and Charles were dead, the Angevin claim had lapsed and Hugh's son, Henry II of Cyprus, was recognized as king of Jerusalem. His coronation in the cathedral of Tyre in 1286 was the last great court occasion for the Frankish chivalry of Outremer.

Kalavun began his operations against the Frankish states in Ṣafar 684/April 1285, when he led an army against al-Marqab (Margat), the last stronghold of the Hospitallers, south of Latakia. It surrendered in the following month, and like the inland castles taken by Baybars, it was reinstated as a Mamluk fortress. The coastal stronghold of Maraqiyya (Maraclea) in the same district, on the other hand, was demolished. Four years later, Kalavun set out on an expedition against Tripoli. Bohemond VII, the last reigning count of the house of Hauteville, had died in 1287, since when Tripoli had been held by Bartolomeo Embriaco, whose family, of Genoese origin, were lords of Jubayl. His position was challenged by Bohemond's sister, and the Venetians looked askance at the increase of Genoese influence in Tripoli. In this confused situation, envoys, perhaps sent by the Venetians, invited Kalavun to intervene. The city fell to him on 4 Rabīʿ II 688/27 April 1289. Like the other coastal towns retaken by the Muslims, Tripoli was demolished. Three of the four Frankish capitals in Outremer had now fallen. Only Acre remained, and it was Kalavun's ambition to capture this city also. A pretext came to hand in the summer of 689/1290, when a rabble of Italian Crusaders rioted in the streets of Acre, and killed many Muslims and innocent bystanders. By the beginning of November the Egyptian army was ready to march, but the sultan fell ill and died in his tent outside Cairo on 6 Dhu'l-Qaʿda 689/10 November 1290.

Like Baybars before him, Kalavun intended to make the sultanate hereditary. As early as 679/1280, he had proclaimed his son ʿAlī heir to the throne with the title of al-Malik al-Ṣāliḥ. In the following year, ʿAlī ruled on Kalavun's behalf during his absence on campaign, and his name was associated with that of his father as a party to treaties. In a treaty with the king of Lesser Armenia in 684/1285 another name appears, that of a second son, Khalīl, who is styled al-Malik al-Ashraf. Then in the summer of 687/1288, al-Ṣāliḥ ʿAlī died, to his father's deep distress, and al-Ashraf Khalīl was appointed joint sultan in his place. It seems that Kalavun never entirely trusted his second son. He repeatedly refused to sign the diploma of his appointment, saying to his secretary, "I will not set Khalīl over the Muslims."

Nevertheless when the end came, al-Ashraf Khalīl succeeded quietly to his father's throne, and in 690/1291 he took up the interrupted project of the campaign against Acre. It has been described by one of the participants, the young Ayyubid prince of Ḥamāh, Ismāʿīl Abu'l-Fidā', a junior officer at the time. This is his account:

The Sultan al-Malik al-Ashraf marched on Acre with the Egyptian forces. He sent to order the Syrian forces to come, and bring the mangonels with them. So al-Malik al-Muẓaffar, the lord of Ḥamāh, and his uncle al-Malik al-Afḍal, with all the Ḥamāh contingent went to Ḥiṣn al-Akrād [Crac des Chevaliers]. There we took delivery of a great mangonel called "al-Manṣūrī", which made a hundred cart-loads. They were distributed among the Ḥamāh contingent, and one cart was put in my charge. . . . Our journey with the carts was late in the winter season, and we had rain and snowstorms between Ḥiṣn al-Akrād and Damascus. We suffered great hardship thereby because of the drawing of the carts, the oxen being weak and dying from the cold. Because of the carts we took a month from Ḥiṣn al-Akrād to Acre – usually about an eight days' journey for horses. . . . The descent of the Muslim armies upon it [Acre] was in the early part of Jumādā I of this year [May 1291], and severe fighting developed. The Franks did not close most of their gates but left them open and fought in them. The contingent from Ḥamāh was stationed at the head of the right wing, as was their custom, so we were beside the sea, with the sea on our right as we faced Acre. Ships with timber vaulting covered with ox-hides came to us firing arrows and quarrels. There was fighting in front of us from the direction of the city, and on our right from the sea. They brought up a ship carrying a mangonel which fired on us and our tents from the direction of the sea. This caused us distress until one night there was a violent storm of wind, so that the vessel was tossed on the waves and the mangonel it was carrying broke. It was smashed to pieces and never set up again. During the siege, the Franks came out by night, surprised the troops and put the sentries to flight. They got through to the tents and became entangled in the ropes. One of their knights fell into an amir's latrine and was killed there. The troops rallied against them and the Franks fell back routed to the town. . . . The troops tightened their grip on Acre until God Most High granted them its conquest by the sword on Friday, 17 Jumādā II [17 June]. When the Muslims stormed it, some of its inhabitants took flight in ships. Inside the town were a number of towers holding out like citadels. A great mass of Franks entered them and fortified themselves. The Muslims slew, and took an uncountable amount of booty from Acre. Then the sultan demanded the surrender of all who were holding out in the towers, and not one held back. The sultan gave the command and they were beheaded around Acre to the last man. Then at his command the city of Acre was demolished and razed to the ground.[1]

The sultan's forces went on to take the remaining Frankish footholds on the coast – Tyre, Sidon, Beirut and Haifa, together with the last two Templar castles of Anṭarṭūs (Tortosa) and ʿAthlīth. So in a little under two centuries ended the history of Outremer. On 9 Shaʿbān/7 August, Khalīl returned to Cairo, and made a state entry into his capital as the final victor in the long struggle with the Crusaders. He sent word of his triumph to the king of Lesser Armenia, Hethoum II, in a letter indicating his intention of continuing the *jihād* in that direction. This he did in the following year, when in Rajab 691/June 1292 he captured Qalʿat al-Rūm on the upper Euphrates, an enclave in Muslim territory (originally part of the county of Edessa) which was the patriarchal see of the Armenian Church. Khalīl again returned in triumph to an illuminated Cairo, and when he mustered his forces for another campaign in the next year, an Armenian embassy hastened to make terms with him. The three fortresses of Behesni, Marʿash and Tall Ḥamdūn near Adana were surrendered to the sultan. The Armenian kingdom was now being eroded in much the same way as the Frankish states with which it had been so closely connected.

The career of al-Ashraf Khalīl, although apparently so successful, was nevertheless soon to be brought to a disastrous end by regicide. The seeds of the trouble had been sown before his accession. Kalavun had sought to strengthen his position against the dominant Turkish military element by a new Mamluk recruitment – this time of Circassians from the eastern coastlands of the Black Sea. This new force was known as the Burjiyya from their barracks in the towers (Arabic sing., *burj*) of the Citadel of Cairo. The recruitment of Circassians was continued by Khalīl, and this development alarmed the Turkish Mamluks. Several of their magnates suffered at his hands, including Sungur al-Ashqar, who died in prison in 691/1292. A Turk, Baydara al-Manṣūrī, was appointed vicegerent in Egypt but the sultan's confidence was given to a Syrian Arab, Ibn al-Salʿūs, who became *wazīr* in Muḥarram 690/1291. He had originally been a merchant, but on coming to Cairo in Kalavun's time he gained Khalīl's favour. Under Ibn al-Salʿūs the wazirate, which had lost much of its importance under the later Ayyubids and early Mamluks, regained its old pre-eminence as a great office of state. When he went up to the Citadel for an audience of the sultan, the dignitaries waited at his door and accompanied him in procession, headed by the four chief judges. Towards the Mamluk magnates he displayed an arrogant lack of etiquette, and he particularly delighted in thwarting the vicegerent Baydara. Counting upon the sultan's unswerving support, Ibn al-Salʿūs made enemies for both his master and himself.

Matters came to a head in Muḥarram 693/December 1293. The sultan had crossed the Nile to Giza for hunting, and in an outburst of anger he struck Baydara on the head, and publicly insulted him. The vicegerent had already built up a faction of Turkish malcontents, among them the sultan's sword-bearer, Lachın al-Manṣurī. Shortly afterwards, when Khalīl rode out with only a small escort, Lachın warned Baydara that his opportunity had come. The conspirators gathered quickly, and overpowered Khalīl, who was killed on the spot.

Baydara and his companions then went back to the royal tent, where (following the precedent set by Baybars after the murder of Kutuz) he sat in the sultan's seat, and received the allegiance of the amirs. At the same time he assumed a royal title, probably that of al-Malik al-Awḥad.

When the news of the coup reached Cairo, panic filled the city. The shops were shut and the streets deserted except for sturdy beggars intent on loot. But about 1,500 Circassian Mamluks of the dead sultan's household, the Ashrafiyya, set out to obtain revenge for their master, defeated Baydara in a brief engagement and cut off his head. They were joined by deserters from Baydara's faction, notably the Amir Kitbogha al-Manṣūrī, who himself soon afterwards usurped the sultanate. Lachın al-Manṣūrī (another future usurper) absconded in Cairo. When the victorious Ashrafiyya returned to Giza, the Turkish governor of the Citadel of Cairo, Sanjar al-Shujāʿī al-Manṣūrī, at first prevented their crossing the Nile. Sanjar was Baydara's stepfather, and had probably been privy to the conspiracy against the sultan. A compromise was reached. Khalīl's half-brother Muḥammad, who had barely reached the ninth lunar anniversary of his birth, was enthroned with the title of al-Malik al-Nāṣir. The Kalavunid dynasty thus survived, although in little more than name, while the great offices of state were shared out among the Mamluk magnates. Kitbogha became vicegerent, Sanjar al-Shujāʿī *wazīr* and administrator of the realm. Ibn al-Salʿūs, who had lost his royal protector and had no military household, was arrested and tortured to death. The episode which had occurred was in a sense a recurrence of the traditional antagonism between Mamluk veterans and the household of a new ruler; it was, however, now complicated by the ethnic rivalry between Turks and Circassians.

NOTE

1. P. M. Holt (tr), *The memoirs of a Syrian prince*, Wiesbaden 1983, 16–17.

CHAPTER THIRTEEN

The Reign of al-Nāṣir Muḥammad (1)

The Usurpations 1293–1310

The child who was enthroned as al-Malik al-Nāṣir Muḥammad in Muḥarram 693/December 1293 was still sultan of Egypt and Syria when he died nearly half a century later in Dhu'l-Ḥijja 741/June 1341. His long reign was interrupted by two periods of usurpation from 694/1294 to 698/1299, and from 708/1309 to 709/1310 respectively, and it was not until his second restoration in Shawwāl 709/March 1310, when he was in his twenty-fifth year, that his effective rule began.

When al-Nāṣir Muḥammad was first installed as a compromise candidate, there seemed to be no reason why his nominal sultanate should be any more durable than those of the earlier stopgaps such as al-Ashraf Mūsā and Salāmish. That he succeeded in regaining and holding the throne was due partly to the factional divisions of the magnates, partly to the continuing loyalty of the populace of Cairo to the house of Kalavun, and (in the months leading up to and following his second restoration) to his own early maturity as a skilful, determined and ruthless politician.

The settlement between the factions at the time of al-Nāṣir Muḥammad's accession had set up a ruling duumvirate of Kitbogha and Sanjar al-Shujāʿī, between whom a struggle for power quickly developed. Kitbogha built up a group of clients and allies among the Turkish amirs, while Sanjar, although himself a Turk, bought the support of the Circassian Burjiyya, the more numerous party. The breach between the two leaders came in Ṣafar 693/January 1294, ostensibly over an accusation by Sanjar that Kitbogha was concealing Lachın al-Manṣūrī, who was obnoxious to the Ashrafiyya for his part in the killing of their masters. A plot by Sanjar to have Kitbogha taken miscarried, and he and his supporters found themselves pent up in the Citadel by their opponents. As Sanjar's chances of success diminished, his following gradually melted away. He fell into the hands of Kitbogha's faction, and was beheaded.

Kitbogha was now master of the situation. His first aim was to break the strength of the Burjiyya, which he did by imprisoning some, and by expelling many of them from their stronghold in the Citadel. Next he brought Lachın out of hiding, and had him received by the sultan at the festival at the end of Ramaḍān (25 August 1294). In resentment at this, the Ashrafiyya revolted, and were ruthlessly put down. The way was now open to Kitbogha to take the final step, to which he was urged by Lachın. On 12 Muḥarram 694/3 December 1294, an assembly composed of the caliph, the judges and the amirs concurred in the deposition of al-Nāṣir Muḥammad and the enthronement of Kitbogha with the title of al-Malik al-ʿĀdil. The deposed child was kept in the Citadel, and was not allowed to make any public appearance.

Unlike his predecessors, Kitbogha was not a Turk but a Mongol, nor had he entered Kalavun's Mamluk household by purchase but as a prisoner of war, having been captured (when he was about fifteen years old) at the first battle of Ḥimṣ in 659/1260. Once on the throne, he appointed Lachın as his vicegerent. His reign coincided with the peaceful immigration into Syria of Mongol refugees from the *Ilkhan* Ghazan, rather like the entry of the Wāfidiyya in the time of Baybars (see above, p. 94). The immigrants were Oirat tribesmen with their families. The chiefs were brought to Cairo, and welcomed by the sultan in late Rabīʿ II 695/February–March 1296, and the tribesmen were settled mostly in the coastlands of Palestine, where their presence would act as a deterrent to Frankish raiders. Kitbogha may have reckoned that the arrival of these Mongols would strengthen his own position. If so, he was wrong, since to the entrenched Turks and Circassians the newcomers appeared as a threat and a challenge.

Kitbogha's authority thus rested on unsure foundations. In Muḥarram 696/November 1296, when he was returning to Egypt after a royal progress to Ḥimṣ and Damascus, he was surprised by a group of conspirators headed by Lachın, who sought his life. He succeeded in escaping to Damascus but was unable to offer resistance to Lachın, who was recognized as sultan. Kitbogha's life was spared, and he died as governor of Ḥamāh in 702/1303.

In this way Lachın obtained the throne by usurpation from a usurper. However, the conspirators who installed him in power endeavoured to impose terms on him, much as the amirs had done on the accession of Baybars. They swore allegiance on condition that he remained first among equals rather than an autocratic monarch, and that he did not promote his own Mamluks to the disadvantage of the veterans. The latter had, of course, been the crucial issue in successive coups from the time of al-Muʿaẓẓam Tūrān-Shāh; the former point indicates the tension which existed throughout the Mamluk sultanate between the concept of autocratic monarchy and that of the oligarchy of magnates. This accession-compact, an embryonic contractual sovereignty, was to prove ineffectual as a safeguard against arbitrary rule, although the precedent was later to be followed on several occasions.

Although at first Lachın (who assumed the royal title of al-Malik al-Manṣūr) rewarded his fellow-conspirators with high office, a rift quickly opened. His *khushdāsh* Karasungur al-Manṣūrī, who had been appointed vicegerent, was removed from office in Dhu'l-Qaʿda 696/ September 1297, and the post was given to the sultan's own Mamluk and his closest associate, Mengütemir. The leading magnates were ousted, and the boy al-Nāṣir Muḥammad (who might become a figurehead for malcontents) was packed off to al-Karak. The sultan, aided by Mengütemir, also put through an important financial reform to secure his position against the magnates. The principal financial support of the military establishment in Egypt was the land-revenue, which was assigned in *iqṭāʿ* (see above, pp. 68–69, 75). Saladin's fiscal settlement (*al-rawk al-Ṣalāḥī*) was apparently still the basis of the system over a century later. Under it the sultan's fisc (*khāṣṣ*) received one-sixth of the assignments, the amirs five-twelfths and the *Ḥalqa* (in Saladin's time, the royal bodyguard) also five-twelfths. With the decline of the *Ḥalqa* and the emergence from the time of al-Ṣāliḥ Ayyūb onwards of the sultan's Mamluk household as the principal military force, this distribution had become unrealistic, and Lachın intended to safeguard himself at the expense both of the amirs and of the *Ḥalqa*. A new cadastral survey of Egypt and a redistribution of assignments, known as *al-rawk al-Ḥuṣāmī* (from the sultan's personal honorific of Ḥusām al-Dīn) were pushed forward in a few weeks between Jumādā I and Rajab 697/February–April 1298. Although the sultan's fisc assignment was left at one-sixth, the amirs and the *Ḥalqa* together were cut to eleven twenty-fourths, thus leaving a surplus of nine twenty-fourths from which Lachın could recruit and maintain a new guard. The reform was inevitably most unpopular with the magnates, who found their share of the assignments reduced by almost half, and Mengütemir, who played a prominent part in the proceedings, attracted a good deal of odium.

The opponents of Mengütemir and of the sultan who protected him coalesced into a conspiratorial group in the months following the *rawk*. The leaders were two men who had earlier supported Lachın against Kitbogha – Ṭughjī and Kurjī, both probably from the Ashrafiyya. Kurjī commanded the young Mamluks whom Lachın himself had recruited, and in this position (like Aktay al-Jamadār among the Baḥriyya) he had more immediate authority over them than the sultan himself. Another former member of Lachın's faction who now plotted against him was Salār, who may have been a Turk but was probably an Oirat. Closely connected with him was another senior amir, Baybars al-Jāshnikīr, i.e. "the Taster" (Persian, *chāshnīgīr*), so named from his court office. He was a Circassian from the Burjiyya. The sultan and Mengütemir were warned of the plot, and Salār urged his comrades to act at once, saying, "Have him for dinner before he has you for breakfast." On the night of 10 Rabīʿ II 698/15 January 1299 they struck. Kurjī murdered Lachın as he rose to pray the night-prayer, and soon afterwards Mengütemir was also done to death. The two leading conspirators, however, gained nothing from the deed. Their ambition stirred the opposition of the other magnates, and both lost their lives. Again a stopgap sultan was needed. Al-Nāṣir Muḥammad (now aged fourteen) was recalled and again enthroned in Jumādā I 698/February 1299.

The nominal second sultanate of al-Nāṣir Muḥammad was actually a duumvirate of Salār and Baybars al-Jāshnikīr, who held the offices of vicegerent in Egypt and high steward (*ustadār*) respectively. Their relationship was not entirely harmonious since each became the patron of a Mamluk faction, Salār of the Turks, and Baybars of his Circassian fellow-countrymen. But the former group were a declining force, while the latter were increasing in numbers and power.

It was in these years that the Mongols of the ilkhanate presented for the last time a serious challenge to the Mamluks. Since 694/1295 the *ilkhan* had been Ghazan, a convert to Islam from the time of his accession. The common religion of the Mongol and Mamluk rulers had, however, no effect upon their relations. Shortly before Lachın's fall, the governor of Damascus, Kıpchak al-Manṣūrī, defected to Ghazan together with a number of his Mamluks and amirs. Ghazan received them with favour, since an important defector from his own side, Sülemish, the commander-in-chief in Anatolia, was equally warmly welcomed in Cairo. In Rahīʿ I 699/December 1299, the Mongol forces crossed the Euphrates into Syria, while the Mamluks with al-Nāṣir Muḥammad advanced to Ḥimṣ, the scene of two earlier victories. On this occasion the decisive battle, fought in the vicinity of Wādi'l-Khāzindār ended in the rout of the Mamluks. Damascus surrendered, and the *khuṭba* was recited there in Ghazan's name. But the *ilkhan* did not attempt a permanent occupation of Syria, still less the pursuit of the sultan into Egypt. In Jumādā I 699/February 1300 he left Damascus, having appointed Kıpchak as the governor. The Mongol garrison soon withdrew, followed by Kıpchak, and in Rajab 699/April 1300 the *khuṭba* was again recited in the name of al-Nāṣir Muḥammad. Kıpchak and his companions were caught and sent to the sultan, who pardoned them.

Another Mongol invasion took place in the winter of 700/1300–1, but on this occasion no confrontation occurred, since abnormally heavy rain and snow frustrated both armies. In 702/1303 Ghazan undertook his last campaign against Syria. He himself stopped at the Euphrates, and the command passed to his general, Qutlugh-Shāh, who had played a leading part in the two previous campaigns. The Mongols advanced to the vicinity of Damascus, and met the Mamluk army headed by Baybars, Salār and the sultan at Shaqḥab. Although a Mongol charge swept away the Mamluk right wing, the centre and the left held firm, and succeeded in encircling the Mongols. The next day (4 Ramaḍān 702/22 April 1303) the Mamluks allowed the Mongols to pass through their lines, and then hunted them down. Ghazan himself died in the following year (703/1304).

As al-Nāṣir Muḥammad grew to maturity, he became increasingly impatient of the control of Baybars and Salār. In Muḥarram 707/July 1307 he planned to use his household of young Mamluks to overthrow them, but the two amirs had wind of the plot, and for a time it looked as if they would depose him. The rumour of this produced a violent reaction in Cairo, and Baybars and Salār staged a formal reconciliation with the sultan. He was, however, still trying to escape from their tutelage, and in Ramaḍān 708/February 1309 he announced his intention of making the Pilgrimage. The two amirs were not sorry to see him go, and his departure provided an opportunity for Baybars and his Circassian *khushdāshiyya* to establish their ascendancy. Al-Nāṣir Muḥammad and his retinue went no further than al-Karak. There he expelled the governor from the fortress, which he garrisoned with his own Mamluks. He may have written to inform the duumvirate in Cairo of his abdication; at any rate they announced that the throne was vacant. On 23 Shawwāl 708/5 April 1309, the Burjiyya demonstrated their strength by imposing their patron, Baybars al-Jāshnikīr, as sultan, although the magnates had offered the throne to Salār. Baybars assumed the title of al-Malik al-Muẓaffar, while Salār was reappointed as vicegerent.

Meanwhile al-Nāṣir Muḥammad was using al-Karak as a base from which to regain the sultanate. Of the governors, only one, Akkush al-Afram in Damascus, was a Circassian and a partisan of Baybars. It was not difficult for al-Nāṣir Muḥammad to concert plans with three others – Karasungur al-Manṣūrī of Aleppo, Kıpchak al-Manṣūrī of Ḥamāh (the former governor of Damascus and defector to Ghazan) and Esendemir of Tripoli. After one false start he advanced to Damascus

(Shaʿbān 709/January 1310). Thence he set out for Egypt, accompanied by all the Syrian governors. Baybars's power was crumbling. A low Nile, dearth and pestilence had inauspiciously characterized his reign; there was deep mistrust between himself and Salār, and his troops were deserting to al-Nāṣir Muḥammad. He tried to bolster his authority with a diploma from the Caliph al-Mustakfī, which elicited from his general the jeering comment, "Tell him he's stupid. Nobody takes any notice of the caliph." Finally he fled from the Citadel, insulted and stoned by the mob.

Salār stayed behind, and ordered the password to be given in the name of al-Nāṣir Muḥammad. The restored sultan entered Cairo without meeting resistance. On 2 Shawwāl 709/5 March 1310 he was enthroned in the Citadel in the presence of the caliph, the chief judges, the amirs and the officers of state. At this first court, the magnates had a foretaste of the quality of their ruler. When the caliph came forward to greet him, al-Nāṣir Muḥammad, remembering the recent diploma in Baybars's favour, demanded, "Why are you here to greet a rebel? Was I a rebel? Is Baybars a scion of the ʿAbbasids?" Whereupon the countenance of the caliph fell, and he was reduced to silence.

Al-Nāṣir Muḥammad's first task was to secure his position. Although Baybars had abdicated, he was still at large with a retinue of Mamluks, and he hoped to escape to Arabia. He was finally taken near Gaza and brought to Cairo, where he was strangled in the sultan's presence on the night of 15 Dhu'l-Qaʿda 709/15 April 1310. His reign forms an ironic contrast with that of his namesake, al-Ẓāhir Baybars, the effective founder of the Mamluk sultanate. Salār seemed by well-timed compliance to be better placed than his former confederate. He offered a large gift of Mamluks, horses, camels and textiles to the sultan, and on the day after al-Nāṣir Muḥammad's enthronement, he resigned his amirate and the vicegerency. He was allowed to retire to al-Shawbak, but he was too dangerous to be left in that remote stronghold. In Rabīʿ I 710/August 1310 he was brought back under duress to Cairo. Once there, he was arrested, compelled to disclose his hidden treasure and starved to death in the Citadel.

Baybars and Salār were only the most conspicuous victims of the purge which al-Nāṣir Muḥammad carried out in the two years following his restoration. There were numerous arrests of amirs and Mamluks, including those belonging to the households of Baybars and Salār. At the same time the sultan was promoting members of his own household, the Nāṣiriyya. In the month of his enthronement, he arrested twenty-two veteran amirs, and raised thirty-two of his own Mamluks to the amirate. Among them was a former Mamluk of

Lachın, Tengiz al-Ḥusāmī, who was to play a great part in the history of the reign. The new amirs rode in a procession through illuminated streets, and scattered largesse as they went. Another great creation of amirs took place two years later, when the sultan promoted forty-six men in one day. In this way al-Nāṣir Muḥammad shifted the base of his regime from the old military establishment to the more reliable members of his own Mamluk household.

After the elimination of Baybars and Salār, the most prominent members of this old establishment were the Syrian governors who had enabled al-Nāṣir Muḥammad to regain his throne. He could not feel safe as long as these kingmakers remained in office, but he began by rewarding them for their aid. Karasungur was promoted to Damascus, Kıpchak to Aleppo and Esendemir to Ḥamāh. Akkush al-Afram, compromised by events, was pardoned but demoted to the inferior governorship of Tripoli. Then in 710/1310 Kıpchak died, and Esendemir was promoted to Aleppo. Soon afterwards he was arrested and taken to Cairo, leaving only Karasungur of the three kingmakers. He realized the danger of his position, and in Dhu'l-Ḥijja 710/May 1311 he obtained a transfer to Aleppo, where he would be further away from the sultan. A year later, accompanied by Akkush al-Afram, he fled to the *Ilkhan* Öljeitü, who in the following winter (712/1312–13) launched an abortive invasion of Syria on their behalf. This was the last Mongol enterprise against the Mamluks. After Karasungur's flight, the sultan appointed Tengiz al-Ḥusāmī as governor of Damascus, and soon afterwards another of his household, Arghun al-Dawādār, became vicegerent in Egypt. Al-Nāṣir Muḥammad was now firmly in the saddle. The success with which he had carried out the delicate operation of substituting his own Mamluks for the entrenched veterans of previous royal households, the test of a new sultan from the time of al-Muʿaẓẓam Tūrān-Shāh, was an indication of his political ability.

CHAPTER FOURTEEN

The Reign of al-Nāṣir Muḥammad (2)

The Autocracy 1310–1341

The situation of al-Nāṣir Muḥammad on his second restoration in 709/1310 offered him particular opportunities which he was not slow to exploit. For the first time since the inception of the Mamluk sultanate sixty years before, there was no danger from an external enemy. The Frankish states had ceased to exist, and the unsuccessful Mongol invasion of Syria in the winter of 712/1312–13 demonstrated that the *ilkhan*, even in alliance with powerful Mamluk malcontents, was no more to be feared. Thus for nearly thirty years al-Nāṣir Muḥammad was free to concentrate on the internal problems of his realm. The passing of the external danger in itself subtly altered his relations with the Mamluk magnates. They traditionally regarded the sultan as essentially a war-leader and the first among equals, but it was al-Nāṣir Muḥammad's achievement to establish a firm autocratic monarchy in time of peace. He also sought, like al-Ẓāhir Baybars and his own father, to ensure hereditary succession to the sultanate. In this he was in appearance remarkably successful: his sons, grandsons and great-grandsons reigned without interruption by a usurper until 784/1382, but his autocratic rule perished with him. Almost without exception the later Kalavunids were puppet sultans, in whose name the faction-ridden Mamluk magnates held power.

The change in the preoccupations of the Mamluk sultan is shown by the fact that al-Nāṣir Muḥammad, unlike his great predecessors al-Ẓāhir Baybars and Kalavun, spent very little time in Syria. Instead of mounting a campaign there almost every year, al-Nāṣir Muḥammad delegated the effective control of the region to Tengiz al-Ḥusāmī. A couple of years after his appointment to Damascus in 712/1312, Tengiz became in effect govenor-general of Syria, when the governors of Aleppo, Ḥamāh, Ḥimṣ, Tripoli and Ṣafad were instructed to communicate with the sultan only through him. This subordination was unpopular, and the governor of Ṣafad, who demurred, was disgraced and sent in chains to Egypt. How long this measure of centralization continued is not clear, but in the summer of 739/1338, when Tengiz was visiting Cairo (as he did frequently), the sultan issued a diploma formally conferring the governor-generalship of Syria on him. At this time Tengiz was at the height of his power and favour with al-Nāṣir Muḥammad. One of his daughters was married to the sultan, and had borne him a son, while during this same visit al-Nāṣir Muḥammad had arranged for two of his daughters to marry two of Tengiz's sons. But such pre-eminence was dangerous. It aroused the envy of the other amirs, and those in the personal entourage of the sultan no doubt fed his suspicions after Tengiz had gone back to Syria. By the summer of 740/1340 the two men were at odds. Tengiz prepared to flee the realm, while the sultan mobilized an expeditionary force against him. In the end Tengiz was captured in Damascus, and brought to Egypt (Muḥarram 741/July 1340), where he was put to death. The enormous wealth he had accumulated was seized and disposed of by his enemies.

Other aspects of al-Nāṣir Muḥammad's rule in Syria appear in his relations with the Ayyubids and the tribal chiefs. The last of the Ayyubid ruling princes had been al-Muẓaffar Maḥmūd, the lord of Ḥamāh, who died in 698/1299. There had been a dispute over the succession, so a Mamluk governor, Karasungur al-Manṣūrī (later as governor of Aleppo to be one of al-Nāṣir Muḥammad's supporters), was installed there. In the following year, he was succeeded by the ex-sultan al-ʿĀdil Kitbogha. On Kitbogha's death in 702/1303, a cousin of al-Muẓaffar Maḥmūd named al-Malik al-Mu'ayyad Ismāʿīl Abu'l-Fidā' (whose account of the fall of Acre is quoted above, p. 104), tried unsuccessfully to obtain the governorship. He was on good terms with al-Nāṣir Muḥammad, who in 710/1310, shortly after his restoration, gave Abu'l-Fidā' the appointment that he desired. Thereafter Abu'l-Fidā' played a minor but consistently loyal part in Syrian affairs. In 712/1312 he received a diploma from the sultan granting him the kingdom of Ḥamāh, Maʿarrat al-Nuʿmān and Baʿrīn, a sizeable tract of central Syria. Then in 720/1320 he received the unique honour of the title and insignia of a sultan, and rode in state through Cairo. In fact he was nothing more than a favoured vassal, but the episode is the last flicker of Ayyubid rule in Syria. On his death in 732/1331, he was succeeded as sultan of Ḥamāh by his son, al-Afḍal Muḥammad, but after al-Nāṣir Muḥammad's death, this last Ayyubid lost his throne. He was compensated with a high amirate in Damascus (which he held for only a few days before he died), and Ḥamāh passed finally under direct Mamluk rule.

The most important nomadic Arab tribe in Syria at this time was Āl Faḍl, which occupied a strategic position on the desert frontier between Mamluk territory and the ilkhanate. The tribe made an important contribution to the Mamluk military economy as providers of horses. The sultan had informers in every tribal group, who told him where good steeds were to be found, and he made considerable grants of assignments to the tribesmen in recompense for their services. Al-Nāṣir Muḥammad's interest was not merely that of a fancier of blood stock; his security depended on maintaining a numerous and efficient household of Mamluk troopers. He inaugurated a special office of the royal stables, which kept registers of the horses and stable-lads, and he also maintained a stud.

Al-Nāṣir Muḥammad's security is reflected in the fact that on three occasions (in 712/1313, 719/1320 and 732/1332) he made the Pilgrimage. The only previous Mamluk sultan to have done so was al-Ẓāhir Baybars in 667/1269, and he had gone there almost by stealth, while al-Nāṣir Muḥammad's second and third Pilgrimages were state visits to the Ḥijāz. He travelled in comfort, even having portable vegetable-gardens carried in frames on the backs of camels. On reaching Mecca, the sultan behaved (we are told) in a most edifying manner. Invited to ride round the Kaʿba for the ritual circumambulations, he exclaimed piously, "Who am I to liken myself to the Prophet (God's blessing and peace be on him)? By God, I will go round only as the people go round." He washed with his own hands not only the Kaʿba but also the garments of pilgrims, who called down blessings on his head. As these two acts are also reported of al-Ẓāhir Baybars, one cannot be certain whether al-Nāṣir Muḥammad was imitating his predecessor or whether these are appropriate anecdotes without any historical foundation.

The province of Damascus was the scene of an important experiment in 713/1313–14, when commissioners appointed by the sultan and accompanied by members of the Egyptian army office carried out a cadastral survey, in the light of which the assignments in the province were redistributed, while a surplus was transferred to the royal fisc. This *rawk* in southern Syria was the pilot scheme for a similar operation in Egypt, where the political implications were delicate and dangerous, as Lachın's attempted reform had shown. The sultan's object was indeed primarily political – to diminish the extensive assignments in the hands of partisans of al-Muẓaffar Baybars, Salār and the Burjiyya, assignments which he feared to withdraw outright. The *rawk* was directed by a civil servant, the head of the army office, and bodies of Mamluk commissioners were sent to the various Egyptian provinces. In every village they carried out an inquisition into revenue and acreage, followed by a survey. This operation lasted for two and a half months, at the end of which the commissioners made their returns in writing. The financial officials then carried out a redistribution of assignments under the sultan's direction. The share of the royal fisc was raised from one-sixth (as it had been under the Ṣalāḥī and Ḥusāmī *rawks*) to five-twelfths, while the remaining seven-twelfths went to the maintenance of the amirs and the troopers of the *Ḥalqa*.

The distribution of the warrants entitling their holders to *iqṭā's* lasted through the whole of Muḥarram 716/26 March–24 April 1316. It was carried out in full court, held in the new audience-hall which the sultan had built in the Citadel – a domed chamber with a marble pavement and pillars from Upper Egypt. In the centre was al-Nāṣir Muḥammad's ebony and ivory throne, on which he sat surrounded by his great officers and magnates, while each day two amirs of the first rank paraded before him with their men. Each of these high amirs theoretically maintained a household of 100 Mamluk retainers, and commanded 1,000 troopers of the *Ḥalqa*. After questioning each amir about his origins and military service, the sultan handed him a warrant, apparently taken at random – although it was observed that if the courtiers were heard to praise an amir, he received a poor *iqṭā'*. Then the sultan's own household, the Royal Mamluks, were similarly paraded, questioned and given their warrants. One of them, finding that his revenue had been cut by half, dared to return and protest that there had been a mistake. "Oh no," said the sultan, "the mistake was in your previous assignment."

At the end about 200 warrants remained undistributed, and al-Nāṣir Muḥammad was able to make other economies. At the same time he won popularity by abolishing a wide range of taxes on corn and other commodities. His fisc did not suffer greatly thereby since these sources of revenue had mainly been granted to assignment-holders, whose economic strength relative to that of the sultan was thus reduced. The Nāṣirī *rawk* in Egypt and Syria (where it was extended in 717/1317 to the province of Tripoli, and in 725/1325 to that of Aleppo) created a firm financial basis for al-Nāṣir Muḥammad's autocracy.

The affluence of the royal fisc after the Nāṣirī *rawk* is reflected in the new importance of the civilian supervisor of this department. Two of them played a leading part in affairs, and were for several years close intimates of the sultan. Both of them were ultimately disgraced, and came to terrible and untimely ends. The first of them, Karīm al-Dīn al-Kabīr, was from a Christian family. He became a clerk in the service of al-Muẓaffar Baybars, and was converted to Islam. On al-Nāṣir Muḥammad's restoration, Karīm al-Dīn made his peace by paying a fine, and was appointed supervisor of the fisc (*nāẓir al-khāṣṣ*). His tenure of office lasted until 723/1323, but his influence was shaken two years previously when a series of fires in Cairo led to rumours that Christians were responsible. A period of repression ensued, in which the sumptuary regulations (usually a dead letter) were enforced, and Christians were expelled from the offices of the sultan and the amirs. Some Christians disguised themselves as Jews, who were not victims of this wave of persecution, others accepted Islam. At this point Karīm al-Dīn went off to Alexandria to enforce the regulations on his former co-religionists, and thereby win popular approval. But his position was crumbling. In Ṣafar 722/March 1322 the Royal Mamluks demonstrated against him because their pay was two months overdue. He still had the sultan's support, but in Rabīʿ II 723/April 1323 the blow suddenly fell. He was arrested, and for two months he was held in his house, and stripped of his great possessions. After banishment, first to al-Shawbak, then to Jerusalem, he was sent to Aswān where he was found strangled with his own turban.

The second of the two great supervisors of the fisc, al-Nashw, was also a Christian by origin and a clerk by profession. In 731/1331 he became a Muslim, and took the name of Sharaf al-Dīn ʿAbd al-Wahhāb. A few weeks later he obtained a post in the household of the sultan's son, Enik. This brought him into close touch with al-Nāṣir Muḥammad, who had selected him for the post, and in Rajab 732/April 1332 he was appointed supervisor of the fisc. In this position he worked unremittingly to increase the sultan's revenue, thereby incurring intense unpopularity with the common people, who accused him of oppression, and with the merchants, from whom he obtained money by compelling them to purchase commodities at arbitrarily fixed prices, a device known as *ṭarḥ* or *rimāya*. These groups were, however, politically impotent. Al-Nashw retained the sultan's confidence and support until the summer of 740/1339, when he projected measures which would harm the financial reserves of the amirs. They were in a position to resist him, and three of the sultan's favourite Mamluks urged him to arrest al-Nashw, who was seized with his two brothers in Ṣafar 740/August 1339. Immediately a popular demonstration backed by the amirs took place below the Citadel. The vast wealth of the supervisor was sequestrated, and he was put to death. His house was demolished, and the site ploughed up to discover any hidden treasure.

While Karīm al-Dīn and al-Nashw played a leading part in the financial administration, their position was always insecure. They were marginal to court politics, in which the great Mamluk amirs formed a constant factor. Four in particular acquired influence with the sultan. Arghun al-Nāṣirī was vicegerent in Egypt from 712/1312 to 727/1326, after which no further appointment to the office seems to have been made – a fact which is itself indicative of al-Nāṣir Muḥammad's determination to rule personally. In 726/1326 he had made the Pilgrimage with his son, and during his absence an enemy, the civilian supervisor of the army office (*nāẓir al-jaysh*), had gained the sultan's ear. When he returned, he was arrested and held for a time. Shortly afterwards he was sent off as governor of Aleppo, a kind of honourable exile. It was there that he died in 731/1330. In the middle years of the reign, the sultan's favourite was Bektemir the Cup-bearer, al-Nashw's original patron, who had been a Mamluk of al-Muẓaffar Baybars. Bektemir's influence was at its zenith in Ṣafar 732/November 1331, when the sultan's son Enik married his daughter. A few months later, Bektemir and his son accompanied al-Nāṣir Muḥammad on his third Pilgrimage. On the way the sultan learned that they were plotting against him. For a time there seemed some danger of his being overthrown. Al-Nāṣir Muḥammad handled the affair with his accustomed skill, and on the return journey Bektemir and his son died within two days of each other. The sultan was inevitably suspected of having poisoned them.

In the last years of the reign, two other Mamluks came to the fore, both members of the sultan's own Nāṣiriyya household. The first, Qawṣūn, had come to Egypt as a free man (i.e. not a Mamluk) with a daughter of the khan of the Golden Horde who was to be a bride of the sultan. He caught the sultan's eye, was formally purchased as a Mamluk (the price being sent home to his brother), and embarked on a highly successful career, during which he married one of the sultan's daughters. The other, Beshtek, owed his prosperity to his succeeding to the estate of Bektemir the Cup-bearer, whose widow he married.

These were the two most influential Mamluks at court, and their mutual rivalry was one of the problems of the ageing sultan. Another was the succession. In Ṣafar 732/November 1331, just before Enik's marriage to Bektemir's daughter, al-Nāṣir Muḥammad had convoked the magnates, judges and caliph to give formal recognition to Enik as his heir apparent. He changed his mind at the last minute, and appointed him only to an amirate. Another son, Abū Bakr, received a similar appointment in Rabīʿ I 735/November 1334. In Dhu'l-Ḥijja 740/June 1340 the sultan convoked the amirs to swear allegiance to himself and to Abū Bakr after him (or, according to another account, to his heirs), and in Rabīʿ II 714/October 1340 Enik died after a long illness. Then on 10

Dhu'l-Ḥijja 741/27 May 1341 al-Nāṣir Muḥammad himself was taken ill during the prayers on the Feast of Sacrifices. It was soon known or suspected that he was dying. The magnates at court began to send their families and wealth down from the Citadel into Cairo, where disturbances began in the streets. Tension grew between Qawṣūn and Beshtek, and they carried their disputes even into the presence of the dying sultan. On 18 Dhu'l-Ḥijja/4 June al-Nāṣir Muḥammad nominated Abū Bakr to succeed him. Three days later the sultan died.

CHAPTER FIFTEEN

The Later Kalavunids and the Circassian Succession 1341–1399

Although descendants of al-Nāṣir Muḥammad reigned for over forty years after his death, none of the later Kalavunids succeeded in maintaining the autocracy which he had created. The very fact that there were twelve sultans in less than half a century is an indication of their weakness. They mostly came to the throne as young and inexperienced men, sometimes mere children. Al-Ashraf Küchük (Turkish, "the little one") was not more than seven, perhaps under five, on his accession, and his tutor guided his hand to sign state papers. For the most part, the later Kalavunids were figureheads, behind whom the great amirs managed the state, and struggled for power and the control of the royal fisc.

The reconciliation of Beshtek and Qawṣūn, and the settlement of the succession imposed by al-Nāṣir Muḥammad on his deathbed, did not long endure. The nominated heir, al-Manṣūr Abū Bakr, was about twenty when he became sultan. He had no taste for rule, and was a shadowy figure compared to the Mamluk magnates who held the great offices. The rivalry between Qawṣūn and Beshtek ended with the arrest of the latter, and the seizure of his property. This occurred within three weeks of Abū Bakr's accession. Qawṣūn was now ruler in all but name. Six weeks later he deposed Abū Bakr, and installed the child Küchük as sultan – a more docile figure. The deposed sultan and seven of his brothers were packed off to exile in Upper Egypt, where Abū Bakr was shortly afterwards killed.

One son of al-Nāṣir Muḥammad, and he a grown man, escaped the clutches of Qawṣūn. This was Aḥmad, who had lived at al-Karak since he was ten, and who had acquired a fondness for the ways of the desert Arabs. Al-Nāṣir Muḥammad when dying had specifically excluded him from the succession, but at this juncture a faction in his name grew up among the amirs, who had become alarmed at the fate of Beshtek and al-Manṣūr Abū Bakr. In Rajab-Sha'bān 742/January 1342 Qawṣūn was overthrown, and his puppet, Küchük, dethroned. Aḥmad was invited to come to Cairo and assume the sultanate. He was installed in Shawwāl 742/March 1342 with the title of al-Malik al-Nāṣir, but he gave little satisfaction to the partisans who had brought him in. His brusque and peremptory manner, still more his reliance upon his own entourage from al-Karak, offended and alienated the magnates in Cairo. In Dhu'l-Ḥijja 742/May 1342 he returned to al-Karak, taking with him the two chief officials of the administration, the secretary and the supervisor of the army office and the fisc. On his refusal to return to the capital, the amirs deposed him in Muḥarram 743/June 1342, and installed his brother, al-Ṣāliḥ Ismā'īl, as sultan. Thus in barely more than twelve months from the death of al-Nāṣir Muḥammad, three of his sons had reigned and suffered deposition at the hands of the magnates.

The accession of al-Ṣāliḥ Ismā'īl gave some hope of greater stability. Although young (he was about seventeen), he bore a reputation for piety, and his relations with the magnates were formalized in a mutual exchange of oaths, by which the sultan undertook not to harm anyone or to arrest any Mamluk who had not committed a fault. This was the device of the accession-compact, which had not been employed since the coup of al-Manṣūr Lachın in 696/1296. The amirs perhaps insisted upon it because at this time a rival centre of power appeared in the sultan's kinsmen and domestic officers. His stepfather, Arghun al-'Alā'ī, accumulated a number of functions which made him regent, and a great deal of influence was enjoyed by the sultan's tutor (*lala*), a eunuch named 'Anbar al-Saḥartī, who had his own Mamluk household.

Al-Ṣāliḥ Ismā'īl's position at the beginning of his reign was weakened by the existence of his two predecessors in the sultanate: al-Nāṣir Aḥmad in his distant lordship of al-Karak, and al-Ashraf Küchük, who had returned to his mother's care in the women's quarters. The first was not easily dealt with. He refused to surrender the regalia and treasure he had taken with him, and only after seven fruitless expeditions was al-Karak at last taken, and the ex-sultan captured and killed. He was put to death in Rabī' II 745/August 1344 by a secret messenger from the sultan without the knowledge of the amirs. Al-Ashraf Küchük and his mother, meanwhile, were victims of the hatred felt by the new sultan's mother, who ascribed al-Ṣāliḥ Ismā'īl's ill-health to her rival's sorcery. The little ex-sultan was murdered. In Rabī' I 746/July 1345 al-Ṣāliḥ Ismā'īl took to his bed, and he died in the following month. Arghun al-'Alā'ī had already been at work to secure his own position by purchasing support for his other royal stepson, al-Ṣāliḥ Ismā'īl's full brother, Sha'bān.

Sha'bān was duly enthroned in Rabī' II 746/August 1345 with the title of al-Malik al-Kāmil. Once again the swearing of mutual oaths by the sultan and the magnates indicated an accession-compact. As on previous occasions, this lacked sanctions, and the sultan quickly alienated all his possible supporters: the great amirs in Cairo, the governors in Syria, even his own domestic officers. A revolt broke out in Jumādā II 747/September 1346, and al-Kāmil Sha'bān was captured and put to death. Arghun al-'Alā'ī, who had stood by him to the last, fell from power, and was sent to Alexandria, where he too died.

The sultan who was enthroned by the victorious faction was another son of al-Nāṣir Muḥammad, who reigned as al-Muẓaffar Ḥājjī. His life had been in considerable danger in al-Kāmil Sha'bān's last days. Again an accession-compact was sworn but the domestics of the sultan continued to be, as in the two previous reigns, a rival power-centre to the Mamluk establishment. This led to a crisis in the palace in 748/1347. At its centre was a Black slave-girl, Ittifāq the Lutanist, who had been a favourite of the last two sultans, and who was lawfully (but secretly) married to Ḥājjī. Under pressure from the magnates, communicated to the sultan through the amirs of the Privy Chamber (*khāṣṣakiyya*), Ittifāq and another of his women were expelled from the Citadel with nothing but the clothes they stood up in. Ittifāq lost the jewelled head-dress which three sultans had competed to adorn, and which was worth over 100,000 dinars. The magnates resented Ḥājjī's extravagance and neglect of his royal duties but they gained little by their harsh measures. Deprived of feminine company, the sultan took to pigeon-fancying. In Ramaḍān 748/December 1347 matters came to a head, when Ḥājjī was confronted by a group of Circassian conspirators. They were alarmed at the downfall and death of a fellow-countryman, who had formerly been the all-powerful favourite of the sultan. Al-Muẓaffar Ḥājjī went out in battle-order against his enemies, but on the outskirts of Cairo he was abandoned by his forces, taken and put to death.

With the overthrow of al-Muẓaffar Ḥājjī, this episode of harem politics comes to an end, and henceforward until the supersession of the Kalavunid dynasty power was normally held by the Mamluk amirs. At the start there was an attempt to institutionalize this development. Ḥājjī's successor was his eleven-year-old half-brother, who reigned as al-Nāṣir Ḥasan. It is significant that there was no suggestion of an accession-compact at his enthronement but only a covenant of loyalty (*ḥilf*) by the amirs. Nine of the magnates formed a council of regency – an expedient only previously employed on the first restoration of al-Nāṣir Muḥammad in 698/1299. As on that occasion, it lacked reality as the amirs competed for power. Two brothers, Beybogha Urus and Manjak al-Yūsufī, emerged as the real rulers of Egypt until in Shawwāl 571/December 1350, al-Nāṣir Ḥasan took advantage of Beybogha's absence on Pilgrimage to arrest Manjak. But the sultan lacked an effective base of power against the magnates, who in Jumādā II 752/August 1351 deposed him. They enthroned his half-brother, Ṣāliḥ, who took the royal title of al-Malik al-Ṣāliḥ. He was then about eighteen years of age, and was the son of al-Nāṣir Muḥammad by the daughter of Tengiz-Ḥusāmī. It was during this reign of al-Nāṣir Ḥasan that the Black Death struck Egypt and Syria (1347–9), a visitation which combined with the political instability of the period to bring about the decline of the Mamluk sultanate.

The reign of al-Ṣāliḥ Ṣāliḥ was purely nominal, three of the Mamluk magnates being in control of affairs. On his deposition in consequence of a factional struggle, al-Nāṣir Ḥasan was restored after making an accession-compact (Shawwāl 755/October 1354). For nearly four years the most powerful man in the kingdom was the Amir Sarghıtmısh, originally a Mamluk of al-Nāṣir Muḥammad's household. In Ramaḍān 759/August 1358 he plotted to overthrow the sultan and make himself ruler. The coup was anticipated by al-Nāṣir Ḥasan, and in a fight in Cairo the Royal Mamluks were victorious. Once he had rid himself of Sarghıtmısh, the sultan tried to create a firm power-base. This he did partly in the usual fashion by placing his own Mamluks in key positions (chief among the beneficiaries being a certain Yalbogha al-ʿUmarī), partly by the new expedient of promoting *awlād al-nās* (i.e. descendants of Mamluks) to office. For such men to hold important military or administrative posts was almost unprecedented, and the sultan justified the innovation by saying, "These people are reliable and under my flag. They go where I tell them, and when I want to remove them from office, I can do so easily. Also they treat my subjects kindly, and understand the regulations."

Following this policy, al-Nāṣir Ḥasan appointed *awlād al-nās* as governors of Damascus, Aleppo and Ṣafad, and also as castellans of most of the Syrian strongholds. A chronicler notes that in consequence of this, no rebel appeared in Syria during his reign.[1] In addition, he gave ten amirates of the highest rank (out of a normal establishment of twenty-four) to eight *awlād al-nās* and two of his own sons. Many other *awlād al-nās* were appointed to the lower amirates. Besides all this, the sultan granted jurisdictional powers to his eunuchs, such as had been enjoyed in the previous decade by ʿAnbar al-Saḥartī, and conferred great assignments on women. The sultan's actions inevitably aroused the mistrust of the Mamluk establishment, and the ambitious Yalbogha al-ʿUmarī emerged as the leader of a faction. Once again as in his dealings with Sarghıtmısh, the sultan tried to anticipate a coup, but this time he failed. His supporters were beaten in a fight, and he himself was captured and put to death by Yalbogha (Jumādā I 762/March 1361). The killing by a Mamluk of the master in whose household he had been brought up was a felony most unparalleled in the history of the Mamluk sultanate. So ended the second reign of the only son of al-Nāṣir Muḥammad who showed something of his father's political capacity.

Yalbogha secured his own ascendancy by installing a young sultan and assuming the regency. The nominal ruler was a boy of perhaps sixteen years, a son of al-Muẓaffar Ḥājjī, who reigned as al-Manṣūr Muḥammad. A little over two years later, in Shaʿbān 746/May 1363, the magnates deposed him because, we are told, of his improper and profligate behaviour. Thereafter he was detained in the Citadel, presumably in tolerable comfort since he lived until 801/1398. One of his daughters married the father of Ibn Taghrībirdī, a major chronicler of the Mamluk sultanate.

Al-Manṣūr Muḥammad was succeeded as sultan by his cousin, al-Ashraf Shaʿbān, whose father, Ḥusayn, a son of al-Nāṣir Muḥammad, had never held the sultanate. The new sultan was about ten years old, and was thus effectively under the domination of Yalbogha al-ʿUmarī. During Yalbogha's regency an episode occurred which might be called the last Egyptian Crusade, when in Muḥarram 767/October 1365 Alexandria was briefly occupied by a force under Peter I of Lusignan, king of Cyprus and titular king of Jerusalem. Peter's intention may have been like that of his predecessors in the previous century, to strike at the centre of Muslim power in the eastern Mediterranean as a means to the reconquest of the kingdom of Jerusalem. More probably, it seems, his primary purpose was commercial – to hold Alexandria and so profit from its transit-trade, or failing that to destroy the port and so eliminate it as a competitor.[2] Whether religious or commercial in its objectives, the Crusade had been long prepared, and Peter himself spent over two years in Western Europe recruiting support for his expedition.

The coming of the invaders to Alexandria is thus described by the ninth/fifteenth-century chronicler, al-Maqrīzī:

> For some months the Alexandrians had been aware of the Franks' intention to raid them, and the governor of Alexandria, the Amir Ṣalāḥ al-Dīn Khalīl b. ʿArrām, had accordingly written to the sultan and the Amir Yalbogha, but the government had shown no interest in their affairs. Ibn ʿArrām went on Pilgrimages, appointing as his deputy in Alexandria the Amir Jangharā, an amir of Twenty. The season came for the arrival of the Venetian ships from the Franks,

and a number of sails on the sea became visible to the coastguard. Then in the early morning of Wednesday, 21 [Muḥarram/8 October], eight galleys arrived at the harbour followed by between seventy and eighty craft, both galleys and warships. The Muslims closed the gate of the city, and mounted the wall with their weapons. A group went outside to keep the night-watch. Early on Thursday morning they went forth to seek the enemy, but all the day, and the night of [i.e. before] Friday, the Franks did not move against them. In the early morning of Friday, groups of the nomad Arabs of the Buḥayra and others passed in the direction of the lighthouse. A number of Franks had disembarked with their horses by night, and concealed themselves among the tombs outside the city. When a good number of Muslims, both Arabs and townspeople, had joined together by the lighthouse, a galley sailed against them towards the sea of the Chain until it was near the wall. The Muslims attacked it vigorously, killing a number of Franks aboard it, and a company of the Muslims achieved martyrdom. The townspeople went out to them, forming two divisions. One division passed with the Arabs towards the lighthouse, and the other remained to fight the Franks in the galley. Traders and youths went out for amusement, taking no notice of the enemy.

Thereupon the Franks sounded the trumpet, and those in concealment made a knavish charge on the Muslims. The Franks discharged arrows from the ships. The Muslims were routed, and the Franks followed them up with the sword. The rest of them disembarked on the shore, and captured it without opposition. They brought their ships up to the walls. A great number of the Muslims achieved martyrdom, and a company of them perished in the crush in getting through the gate. The walls were left without defenders, so the Franks erected ladders, and climbed the wall. They made their way to the arsenal and burnt its contents, throwing fire into it. They passed on to the Gate of the Thorn-tree, and hung a crucifix on it. The people were crowded together at the Rosetta Gate. They burnt it down, and made their way out, leaving the city and its contents open to the Franks. The Amir Jangharā took what was in the treasury, and led away fifty Frankish merchants, whom he had imprisoned. He and the people in general set off for Damanhūr. On Friday forenoon, the king of Cyprus (whose name was King Peter, the son of King Hugh) entered and passed through the city on horseback, and the Franks took the people with the sword. They plundered everything they found, taking many prisoners and captives, and burning many places. The number of those who perished in the crush at the Rosetta Gate was beyond counting. The Franks made proclamation of their religion. They were joined by the Christians of Alexandria, who showed them the dwellings of the rich people. They took what was in them. So they continued, killing, taking prisoners and captives, plundering and burning from the forenoon of Friday to the early morning of Sunday. Then they ended hostilities, went with the captives and loot to their ships, and stayed on board until Thursday, 28 [Muḥarram/15 October]. They then set sail with five thousand captives, after having stayed for eight days.

They were of several contingents: twenty-four Venetian galleys, two Genoese galleys, ten galleys belonging to the people of Rhodes, with the French in five galleys, and the rest of the galleys belonging to the people of Cyprus.[3]

Yalbogha and the sultan had assembled a relieving force in Cairo, and were advancing towards Alexandria when they received the news that the Franks had withdrawn. A series of retaliatory measures followed. The Franks in Egypt and Syria were arrested, and the wealth of the native Christians was distrained to ransom the Muslim prisoners. Preparations were made for naval defence. Yalbogha started to build a fleet, ordering timber and craftsmen to be sent from Syria, and he carried out a muster of sailors and (apparently) gunners to man the ships. The governorship of Alexandria was raised in rank. The prosperity of the city had suffered a severe blow, but over four centuries were to pass before another Frankish invader in the person of Napoleon Bonaparte captured Alexandria.

Yalbogha's regency lasted until Rabīʿ II 768/December 1366, when al-Ashraf Shaʿbān, now old enough to take a hand in politics, gave his patronage to a faction of malcontent Mamluks. Fighting ensued, in which Yalbogha was deserted by his followers, captured and put to death. Thereafter the sultan ruled as well as reigned for over ten years. Then in 778/1377 he decided to make the Pilgrimage – an indication that he felt firmly in control. It was a fatal error. When the royal caravan reached al-ʿAqaba, a general insurrection of the Mamluks took place. The sultan fled, and hid in Cairo. His refuge was betrayed, and he was taken and killed (Dhu'l-Qaʿda 778/March 1377).

The Kalavunid dynasty was now approaching its end. The oligarchy of magnates, although unstable and prone to faction, controlled the state. The nominal sultan, al-Manṣūr ʿAlī, was a seven-year-old boy, a son of al-Ashraf Shaʿbān, and when he died four years later, he was succeeded by his brother, al-Ṣāliḥ Ḥājjī, who was about nine years of age (Ṣafar 783/May 1381).

These years witnessed the rise of the man who was soon to usurp the throne, and establish the second succession of Mamluk sultans, Barkuk the Circassian. It is indicative of the decline of the military resources of the later Kalavunid sultans that he was not a Royal Mamluk but came from the household of Yalbogha al-ʿUmarī, to which he had been recruited about the year 764/1363–4. He joined in the revolt which overthrew al-Ashraf Shaʿbān, and in the ensuing time of troubles, he rose rapidly. In 779/1378 he became *atābak al-ʿasākir* in Egypt – a title which had come to signify essentially the senior amir. At first he shared power with another Mamluk of Yalbogha's household, whom, however, he ousted in 782/1380. A little later, now supreme in the state, he brought his old father, Anaṣ, and others of his kinsfolk to settle in Egypt. He would have taken the throne on the death of al-Manṣūr ʿAlī had it not been for the opposition of other magnates. After the accession of al-Ṣāliḥ Ḥājjī, his partisans canvassed the great amirs, and Barkuk was able to usurp the sultanate in Ramaḍān 784/November 1382. He assumed the title of al-Malik al-Ẓāhir – probably a deliberate echo of Baybars.

On his accession Barkuk was surrounded by powerful amirs, many of them his *khushdāshiyya* from Yalbogha's household, and some of senior standing to himself. His position was thus precarious, and his summons to his kinsfolk may have been an attempt to construct a power-base outside the Mamluk establishment. If so, it proved abortive. A threat to his rule appeared in the early months of 791/1389 in Syria, where a revolt was fomented by the governor of Malatya in the borderlands of Anatolia, Mintash, who came from the household of al-Ashraf Shaʿbān, and the governor of Aleppo, another Yalbogha, a *khushdāsh* of Barkuk's. This alliance gained control of Syria. As Mintash and Yalbogha al-Nāṣirī advanced on Egypt, Barkuk absconded, and in Jumādā II 791/June 1389 Ḥājjī was restored as sultan with a significant change of title. He was now al-Malik al-Manṣūr – "the Divinely Aided King".

The coalition of Yalbogha and Mintash did not last long. After a faction-fight in Cairo around the Citadel, Mintash overthrew Yalbogha, and was appointed *atābak al-ʿasākir* in Egypt and administrator of the kingdom. Barkuk, who had been caught and sent to al-Karak, found supporters there, and built up a faction. An expedition headed by the restored sultan and Mintash was defeated at Shaqḥab in Muḥarram 792/January 1390, and Ḥājjī was captured. Meanwhile Barkuk's Mamluks in Cairo regained control of the Citadel. Barkuk returned to Cairo, and was reinstated as sultan (Ṣafar 792/February 1390).

Ḥājjī, deposed for a second time, was given quarters in the Citadel, where he survived until 814/1412 – long after Barkuk himself had died. For some years Barkuk used to invite Ḥājjī to his drinking-parties, when the ex-sultan would get tipsy, and address his successor without due respect. At this Barkuk would smile, and say to Ḥājjī's companions, "Take my lord Amīr Ḥājj home." He would go off jeering and cursing, and next morning would apologize to Barkuk for his behaviour of the night before. Barkuk found Ḥājjī a troublesome neighbour. He was given to beating his slave-girls, and Barkuk, disturbed by their cries, would send to ask him to forbear. Ḥājjī then thought of concealing his sadistic propensity by ordering his domestic band to strike up, and drown the screams of the victim. Barkuk learnt of this from his womenfolk, and it became his practice, whenever he heard Ḥājjī's band, to put in a plea.

Ḥājjī was far less of a danger to Barkuk than was Mintash, who remained at large and under arms in Syria until Ramaḍān 795/July 1393. When he was captured and put to death, his head was paraded around the cities of the sultanate from Aleppo to Cairo. In the meantime Barkuk was replacing his over-mighty *khushdāshiyya* with Mamluks from his own household, so that when the ninth *Hijrī* century began on 13 September 1398, all save two of the Syrian governors and the great officers in Egypt had personal bonds of loyalty to him. Peaceful as the later years of his reign were, they were overshadowed by the conquests of Timur Leng (Tamerlane), who was creating a new Turco-Mongol empire from his homeland in Central Asia. Nevertheless the Mamluk sultanate, although threatened, was spared invasion for the time being. In Shawwāl 801/June 1399 Barkuk died, having arranged for the succession of his son Faraj. Events were to show that neither he nor any other of the Circassian Mamluk sultans was to found a dynasty.

NOTES

1. Ibn Taghrībirdī, *al-Nujūm al-zāhira fī mulūk Miṣr wa'l-Qāhira*, x, Cairo n.d., 317.
2. P. W. Edbury, "The crusading policy of King Peter I of Cyprus, 1359–1369", in P. M. Holt (ed.), *The eastern Mediterranean lands in the period of the Crusades*, Warminster [1977], 90–105.
3. Al-Maqrīzī, *Kitāb al-sulūk li-ma'rifat duwal al-mulūk*, III, pt 1, ed. Said A. F. Ashour, Cairo 1970, 105–7. English version P. M. Holt.

CHAPTER SIXTEEN

Egypt and Nubia to the late Fourteenth Century

The southern boundary of Egypt until modern times was the natural frontier formed by the First Cataract of the Nile, a few miles upstream of Aswān. Beyond this point lay the territory of the Nubians, whose settlements were thinly strung out along the river banks, wherever cultivation was possible. Politically they formed two kingdoms. The more northerly, al-Maqurra, had its capital at Dongola[1] and it extended to a region called al-Abwāb (i.e. the Gates), probably south of the confluence of the Atbara and the Nile. Upstream of al-Abwāb lay the southern kingdom of ʿAlwa with its capital of Sōba on the Blue Nile. The people (or at least the rulers) of both kingdoms had been converted to Christianity in the century before the Arab conquest of Egypt. The eastern deserts and hills between the Nile valley and the Red Sea were the home of nomadic tribesmen, the Beja, who spoke a Hamitic language, were still pagan, and were independent of control by either Egypt or Nubia. The Red Sea itself was a Muslim lake, and ports on the African coast were important entrepôts for international trade. Between the fifth/eleventh and the eighth/fourteenth centuries, ʿAydhāb (now a deserted site north of Port Sudan) was busy with merchants and pilgrims passing between Upper Egypt and the Ḥijāz.

To the Muslim rulers of Egypt, the Nubians constituted a permanent problem. They and the Beja endangered Upper Egypt by their raids. It is therefore not surprising that soon after the Arab conquest of Egypt, the Muslim governor, ʿAbdallāh b. Saʿd b. Abī Sarḥ, led an expedition into Nubia, which reached and besieged Dongola (31/561–2). That, however, was the limit of his success. His long line of communications through very difficult territory, and the effective resistance of the Nubians, whose archers were renowned for their accuracy, made a military conquest impossible. Christian Nubia and Muslim Egypt thereupon settled down to several centuries of more or less peaceful coexistence.

The two sectors of the Nile valley, whatever their political and religious differences, were bound together by trading relations. Nubia was the source (or perhaps the channel) which supplied Egypt with its Black slaves, the *Sūdān* of medieval writers. They were, as we have seen (above, p. 12), an important component of the Fatimid army. There thus developed, perhaps in continuation of the practice of pre-Islamic Egypt, a barter trade in which the Nubians annually delivered a fixed quota of 360 slaves, and received in return corn and other provisions. The existence of this trade is known to us only from Arabic Muslim sources, where it is represented as a tribute imposed on the defeated Nubians by ʿAbdallāh b. Saʿd, and recorded in a treaty, the particulars of which are reported in increasing and suspicious detail with the passage of time. The annual transaction was known in Arabic as the *baqṭ*, almost certainly a loan-word from the Latin *pactum* by way of hellenistic Greek. As time went on, and Islamic legal concepts hardened, the *baqṭ* and the status of Nubia as neither *dār al-Islām* nor *dār al-ḥarb* (see below, p. 155) became increasingly troublesome to Muslim jurists.

With lapses and interruptions the barter trade went on for centuries, not always to the profit of the Muslims – the Caliph al-Muʿtaṣim, when investigating a breakdown in the arrangements (*c.* 218/833), discovered that the annual balance had been in favour of the Nubians. Meanwhile, although no further attempts were made to conquer Nubia, developments were taking place which were to undermine the stability of the northern kingdom. The Egyptian frontier with Nubia, ill defined except on the Nile, could not be held as an impermeable barrier against visitors and immigrants from the north. The attempt was indeed made: Ibn Sulaym al-Aswānī, who went as a Fatimid envoy to Dongola in the later part of the fourth/tenth century, described the reach of the Nile above the Second Cataract (a narrow and barren region) as being a closed military district, where unauthorized intruders were liable to the death-penalty. But although the Nile might be held in this way, the desert could not, and the discovery of gold and emeralds in the eastern desert had, as early as the third/ninth century, stimulated Arab migration to the Land of the Mines (*Bilād al-Maʿdin*), where there evolved a frontier society in which adventurers flourished. These Arab immigrants encountered not Nubians but Beja, and by the mid-fourth/tenth century intermarriage had produced a mixed people who dominated the region. Their chief won the favour of the Fatimid Caliph al-Ḥākim in 397/1007 by capturing Abū Rakwa, a dangerous rebel, for which service he received the honorific of Kanz al-Dawla, "The Treasure of the State". The title was inherited by his successors, Banu'l-Kanz, who were rulers of a marcher-principality between the territories effectively controlled by the rulers of Egypt and al-Maqurra. The modern representatives of Banuʿl-Kanz are a tribal group, the Kunūz, in the far north of the Sudan.

A presage of coming danger to the Nubian kingdom accompanied the rise of Saladin to power in Egypt. When the Black troops (i.e. the *Sūdān*), the principal support of the Fatimid caliphate in its last days, were put down in 564/1169 by Saladin's brother, Shams al-Dīn Tūrān-Shāh (see above, p. 50), a remnant of them joined forces with some Nubians to attack and loot Aswān but were defeated in battle by the reigning Kanz al-Dawla, reinforced by a contingent sent by Saladin. The danger of an invasion from Nubia remained, and in Jumādā I 568/December 1172–January 1173 Saladin sent an expeditionary force under the command of Tūrān-Shāh, which occupied the great fortress of Ibrīm between the First and Second Cataracts. Tūrān-Shāh made no attempt to keep this stronghold, although the main purpose of his expedition may have been to find a place of refuge for the Ayyubids if they were attacked by Nūr al-Dīn. He granted Ibrīm in *iqṭāʿ* to one of his Kurdish officers named Ibrāhīm, who with a company of time-expired men turned the place into a nest of robbers. Two years later, Ibrāhīm and some of his comrades were drowned on a raid, and the rest of the gang hastily evacuated Ibrīm, which was reoccupied by the Nubians.

This was the only major conflict of the Ayyubid period, but with the establishment of the Mamluk sultanate in the middle of the seventh/thirteenth century, the kings of Dongola found themselves face to face with an aggressive and efficient military power ruling a centralized state. The early Mamluk sultans had three principal objects in their Nubian policy: to obtain the continuance of the *baqṭ*, which had probably lapsed in the troubled period when the new regime was establishing itself; to secure the southern frontier of Egypt, a region which was the special responsibility of the governor of Qūṣ, and in which Banu'l-Kanz played an important part; and to ensure safe passage for pilgrims, traders, and others by the desert-route from Qūṣ to ʿAydhāb. The commercial importance of ʿAydhāb had been a development of the Fatimid period, when it served as an entrepôt for goods from India. In the later fifth/eleventh century, and particularly after the establishment of the Latin kingdom of Jerusalem, it served pilgrims going from Egypt to the Holy Cities. Although it was sacked by Reynald of Châtillon in 578/1173, its prosperity revived after this setback. Its governor was appointed from Egypt, but its revenues were shared with the chief of the local Beja tribe, the Ḥadāriba. Further down the coast another town, Suakin (Sawākin), also participated in the Red Sea trade.

The pattern of Mamluk relations with Nubia was established in the reign of al-Ẓāhir Baybars. A Nubian embassy in 667/1268–9 brought a letter reporting that the blind king of Dongola, Abu'l-ʿIzz Murtashkar, had been deposed and imprisoned by his sister's son, David (Dāwūd). The sons of Murtashkar had been exiled to al-Abwāb, which seems to have been (in this period at least) an autonomous marcher-lordship between al-Maqurra and ʿAlwa. The embassy brought a present to the sultan, who responded with a demand for the *baqṭ*. Then in Muḥarram 671/August 1272 King David's Nubians raided ʿAydhāb, despoiling and killing merchants from Aden and Egypt. They also killed the two chief port officials, the governor and the supervisor of customs. Such a challenge to the ruler of Egypt could not be ignored. The immediate response was a punitive raid into Nubia by the governor of Qūṣ. In Ṣafar 671/September 1272 he penetrated upstream beyond Aswān and Ibrīm (which he stormed and burnt) to within twenty days' journey of Dongola.

Then in 674/1276 Baybars seized what appeared to be an opportunity to bring Nubia under effective control. A disgruntled nephew of King David named Shakanda arrived at the sultan's court, claiming the throne of Nubia. Baybars organized an expedition to support the pretender. A force of 300 horsemen commanded by two Mamluk amirs left Cairo on 1 Shaʿbān 674/20 January 1276, and reached Dongola on 13 Shawwāl/31 March. King David and his brother came out to fight, but the Nubians were defeated with great slaughter, and many captives were taken to be sold as slaves. The king crossed the Nile, and fled southwards. Abandoning his mother, sister and niece, he made his way to al-Abwāb. The Mamluks pursued him for three days; then they returned to Dongola, where Shakanda was installed as king. At this point Baybars endeavoured radically to alter the status of al-Muqurra in regard to Egypt. Hitherto Nubia had been treated as an independent kingdom. Now at his enthronement Shakanda took an oath as the sultan's governor, and undertook to deliver to him half of the annual revenue of the kingdom. Most significant of the change of status was the imposition of a poll-tax of one dinar annually upon each adult male. This was the canonical *jizya*, and the Christian Nubians were thus assimilated in law to the *dhimmīs* in the sultan's dominions. In addition, the Land of the Mountain (*Bilād al-Jabal*) with its strongholds of al-Daw and Ibrīm, i.e. the marcher-territory immediately upstream of Aswān, was annexed to the sultan's fisc, and placed under one of King David's enemies. The work completed, the Mamluk expedition returned, reaching Cairo on 5 Dhu'l-Ḥijja/21 May. There ensued a great sale of enslaved Nubians. The captive members of the royal family were lodged in the towers of the Citadel, where they were soon joined by David himself – betrayed by the lord of al-Abwāb. The sultan's *wazīr* was instructed to recruit staff to deal with the tribute and other revenue from the subjugated kingdom, and to provide Dongola with artisans, cultivators and merchants from Qūṣ.

In the event this scheme for the incorporation of al-Maqurra into the sultanate quickly failed – and indeed a similar project was only to be realized by Muḥammad ʿAlī Pasha, five and a half centuries later. Attempts to control Nubia through a puppet ruler were, however, a recurrent feature of Mamluk policy for another 100 years. Nubian pretenders were never lacking. Kalavun, who tried to isolate Dongola by sending his envoys to Adur, ruler of al-Abwāb, launched two successive expeditions against King Shamāmūn, and installed rulers whom they had brought in their baggage. Their reigns were short. Once the Mamluk armies had withdrawn, Shamāmūn came back to Dongola. After the greater of the two expeditions, he wrote to the sultan asking pardon, and promising an increased *baqṭ* (688–9/1289–90). Kalavun, now nearing his end, and preoccupied with his intended campaign against Acre, thereupon formally confirmed Shamāmūn in office.

The first decades after the death of Kalavun seemed to show that nothing much had changed in Mamluk–Nubian relations or in the condition of al-Maqurra itself. During al-Ashraf Khalīl's short reign (probably in Ṣafar 691/January–February 1292), an embassy arrived from a king of the Nubians whose name appears to have been Ay or Ayāy. Shamāmūn must have been ousted: there is no further mention of him. The envoys, who included the king's brother and the governor of the Land of the Mountain, brought a conciliatory message to explain that the *baqṭ* had not been sent because of the spoliation of the land by Muslim invaders and Adur of al-Abwāb. A gift including slaves and camels was sent in lieu of the *baqṭ*. A few years later, in 704/1305, King Ayāy himself came to Cairo with a similar gift and a request for military assistance. The organization of an expedition was delegated to the governor of Qūṣ, and the force was constituted from second- and third-rate troops from the Wāfidiyya, the *Ḥalqa*, the garrison of Upper Egypt and Arab tribesmen. The expedition seems to have been needed for general police duties rather than to suppress a pretender; at least we are told that it went back to Qūṣ after nine months spent in fighting the Blacks.

By 711/1311–12 Ayāy had been killed and succeeded by his brother,

Karanbas, who duly visited Cairo early in al-Nāṣir Muḥammad's third reign. Five years later, however, the sultan decided to depose him in favour of a pretender, Barshanbū, the son of King David's sister. The choice was significant: Barshanbū, a resident at the sultan's court, was a convert to Islam. On hearing of the sultan's intention, Karanbas sent a remarkable envoy to Cairo. This was the reigning Kanz al-Dawla, a great chief in his own right, a Muslim, and the son of Karanbas's sister. In effect Karanbas was putting forward an alternative Muslim candidate for the Nubian throne, one whom he himself would find more congenial than the sultan's protégé. The move failed. Kanz al-Dawla was imprisoned, the Mamluk army reached Dongola, and Karanbas and his brother were captured. Barshanbū became king, and established Islam as the state religion by opening a mosque in his palace at Dongola on 16 Rabīʿ I 717/29 May 1317. Barshanbū (or Sayf al-Dīn ʿAbdallāh al-Nāṣir, as he styled himself) was soon overthrown by Kanz al-Dawla, whom the sultan had released. Al-Nāṣir Muḥammad was, however, unwilling to leave Kanz al-Dawla as ruler of al-Maqurra, and twice sent an expedition against him – on the second occasion (in 723–4/1323–4) to reinstate Karanbas. But like Shamāmūn before him, Kanz al-Dawla was irrepressible, and once the Mamluk force had gone he ousted the sultan's nominee.

At the same time as the expedition to install Barshanbū, another Mamluk force was sent to punish the nomads of the desert of ʿAydhāb, who had attacked and robbed an embassy from the Yemen as well as some merchants. A squadron of 500 horsemen left Cairo for Qūṣ, whence they advanced into the eastern desert in Muḥarram 717/March 1317. They reached ʿAydhāb, and then went on to Suakin. Thence they made a remarkable overland journey which brought them to the River Atbara and al-Abwāb. On the way they encountered and defeated a horde of Beja tribesmen. From al-Abwāb, the furthest point up the Nile reached by any Mamluk force, they returned by way of Dongola to Qūṣ and Cairo, where they arrived in Jumādā II 717/August 1317.

The last recorded Mamluk expedition into Nubia occurred half a century later, when the young al-Ashraf Shaʿbān was sultan. The whole frontier region from the Red Sea coast at ʿAydhāb and Suakin to the Nile at Aswān was dominated and despoiled by Banu'l-Kanz in alliance with the Arab tribe of ʿIkrima. Mamluk intervention was invoked after the king of Dongola had been killed, and his throne taken by his sister's son assisted by Arab tribesmen. The usurper held Dongola, but his opponents established themselves in the fortress of al-Daw and sent envoys to ask the sultan's help. A considerable expeditionary force of some 3,000 horsemen was sent out in Rabīʿ I 767/December 1365. The chiefs of Banu'l-Kanz were summoned to Qūṣ, and duly made their submission. The force proceeded upstream, joined forces with the Nubian king and carried out a punitive raid on the Arabs. No attempt was made to restore the town of Dongola, exposed as it was to the raids of the nomads. The king kept al-Daw as his residence, while his nephew, the recent usurper, held Ibrīm. This is almost the last we hear of the shattered kingdom, although in Muḥarram 800/September 1397 a Nubian king with the Muslim name of Nāṣir al-Dīn arrived at the court of Barkuk to ask for help against his usurping cousin, and the governor of Aswān was ordered to assist him.

In the century that had elapsed since al-Ẓāhir Baybars sent the first Mamluk army to Dongola, political authority in al-Maqurra had crumbled, while no sultan in Cairo could impose permanent and effective control over this remote region. With the breakdown of the defences of the kingdom, there was a renewed movement southwards of the Arabs. A few years before he became sultan, Barkuk introduced an important new factor into Upper Egypt by transferring thither a fraction of an arabized Berber tribe called Hawwāra. They balanced and later supplanted Banu'l-Kanz, and dominated the region until the eighteenth century. The situation in Nubia at the end of the eighth/fourteenth century was summarily described by the contemporary historian Ibn Khaldūn in these words:

> Then the clans of the Juhayna Arabs spread over their country, and settled in it, ruling it and filling it with ruin and decay. The kings of the Nubians set about holding them back, but lacked strength. Then they proceeded to win them over by marriage-alliances, so that their kingdom broke up, and it passed to some of the offspring of Juhayna through their mothers, according to the custom of the barbarians by which possession goes to the sister and the sister's son. So their kingdom was torn to pieces, and the Juhayna nomads took possession of their land. They have no means of imposing royal control over the damage which could be stopped by the submission of one to another, and they are faction-ridden up to the present. No trace of sovereignty remains in their land, but now they are wandering bedouin who follow the rainfall like the bedouin nomads. No trace of sovereignty remains in their land, because the tincture of Arab nomadism has changed them through mixture and union.[2]

With the domination of the Arabs came the ascendancy of Islam, and Christianity withered in the former kingdom of al-Maqurra. Only further south did it survive until the overthrow of the kingdom of ʿAlwa in the early tenth/sixteenth century.

NOTES

1. The reference is to Old Dongola on the right bank of the Nile, not to the later Dongola, founded in the nineteenth century, which is on the left bank about 70 miles further north.
2. Ibn Khaldūn, *Kitāb al-ʿibar*, v, [Beirut n.d.], 922–3; cited in P. M. Holt and M. W. Daly, *The history of the Sudan*, London [1979], 23.

CHAPTER SEVENTEEN

Institutions of the Mamluk Sultanate

POLITICAL AND MILITARY INSTITUTIONS

Although the Mamluk sultanate was historically and geographically the successor to the Ayyubid confederacy, and although there was some continuity of institutions between the two polities, there were certain important differences. The most fundamental of these was the nature of the ruling group. During the first half of the seventh/thirteenth century, Egypt and Muslim Syria were ruled by the Ayyubid clan. Its members quarrelled and conspired among themselves, but they were undisturbed by usurpers from outside the clan until al-Muʿaẓẓam Tūrān-Shāh was murdered by the Mamluks in 648/1250. Even then a shred of legitimacy was preserved for a while in Egypt by the recognition as sultan, first of all of al-Ṣāliḥ Ayyūb's widow, Shajar al-Durr, then of the infant Ayyubid, al-Ashraf Mūsā. The repercussions of the Mamluk coup in Egypt rather strengthened the Ayyubid regime in Syria, since it enabled al-Nāṣir Yūsuf of Aleppo to become lord of Damascus, and thereby assured him a paramountcy in the region which was only ended by the Mongol invasion.

The Mamluk sultanate was very different. Its basic and essential institution was the military household of *mamlūks*, warriors recruited in their early youth as slaves beyond the frontier of *dār al-Islām*. Purchased, trained as horse-soldiers, converted to Islam and finally emancipated, the *mamlūks* of a given master (*ustādh*) shared a close bond of loyalty to him and to each other. Loyalty to the *ustādh*, however, rarely extended after his death to his sons. On the other hand, the group-loyalty (*khushdāshiyya*) of the *mamlūks* persisted, although it was counterbalanced by the personal ambition of individuals. These domestic loyalties easily developed into political bonds. Mamluk households became factions which supported their masters in the contest for high office, even the sultanate itself. The political history of the Mamluk sultanate (and subsequently of Ottoman Egypt) is dominated by the struggle of factions originating in this way.

There was a further significant factor. The Baḥriyya, the original military household of al-Ṣāliḥ Ayyūb, and those of the earliest Mamluk sultans had been recruited chiefly from Kıpchak Turks, whose homeland at that period was in southern Russia and the Crimea. The Mongol impact on this region in the middle decades of the seventh/thirteenth century had uprooted its inhabitants, and thereby stimulated the flow of military slaves to the lands of the Islamic Near East. As an ethnically homogeneous group, the Mamluks viewed alien warriors with resentment. The immigration of Mongols from the lands of the *ilkhan* (the Wāfidiyya, as they were designated) was welcomed by the Mamluk sultans, especially al-Ẓāhir Baybars, but the immigrants were not easy to assimilate to the military system. The Wāfidiyya were, however, a transient phenomenon. Of much greater and lasting importance was the change in recruitment from Turks to Circassians, begun by Kalavun to form his Burjiyya garrison in the Citadel of Cairo. Turkish and Circassian Mamluks confronted one another in the struggle for power as long as the Kalavunid dynasty survived. The usurpation of the sultanate by the Circassian Barkuk marked the final ascendancy of his ethnic group. The working of this ethnic factor in politics was demonstrated earlier in the century in the brief and unsuccessful usurpations which interrupted the reign of al-Nāṣir Muḥammad. The first usurper, al-ʿĀdil Kitbogha, a Mongol, was himself ousted by al-Manṣūr Lachın, almost certainly a Turk. The third usurper, al-Muẓaffar Baybars, was the first, and for over seventy years the only, Circassian ruler.

The principal Mamluk household was normally that of the sultan himself. It provided him not only with a well-trained military force but also with the staff of his palace service. The inner circle of his attendants was formed by the *khāṣṣakiyya*, a term approximately equivalent to the men of the Privy Chamber. They were the most favourably placed both to influence him and to obtain appointment to the great offices at court and in the provinces. The recruitment and training of a household of Mamluks was necessarily a slow process, and it is significant that the four most successful sultans down to the end of the eighth/fourteenth century, al-Ẓāhir Baybars, Kalavun, al-Nāṣir Muḥammad and Barkuk, all began their effective reigns with an existing military power-base. That of Baybars was furnished at the outset by his comrades of the Baḥriyya, whom he had rallied and led in exile, and whose prospects depended on his patronage. Kalavun as a leading amir during the reign of Baybars had the opportunity to recruit a Mamluk household before he usurped the sultanate, as had Barkuk a century later. Al-Nāṣir Muḥammad had time to build up a military household during the period of tutelage in his first and second reigns. On the other hand, the sons of Baybars and the Kalavunids after al-Nāṣir Muḥammad seem usually to have had little chance either before or during their brief reigns to make an effective recruitment of Mamluks. Al-Nāṣir Ḥasan attempted during his second reign (755–62/1354–61) to base his power not only on Mamluks but on their free-born descendants, who were known as *awlād al-nās*, "the sons of the People", but this was a unique and unsuccessful experiment.

The role of a household of Royal Mamluks as a political faction was exemplified in recurrent succession crises, when an incoming sultan sought to place his own Mamluks in the key positions held by the military household of his predecessor. The Mamluk sultanate itself originated in such a crisis, when members of al-Ṣāliḥ Ayyūb's Baḥriyya, provoked by envy and resentment at the appointments made by al-Muʿaẓẓam Tūrān-Shāh, murdered him and usurped the sultanate. Relations between the same Baḥriyya and the Muʿizziyya, the household of al-Muʿizz Aybeg, were a major political factor in the reign of that sultan, and subsequently led to the murder of Kutuz (a Muʿizzī) by Baybars with the consequent triumph of the Baḥriyya. A similar jealousy between veteran and new households led to the murder of Kalavun's son and successor, al-Ashraf Khalīl. The polarization of the Royal Mamluks continued under the Circassian sultans in the ninth/fifteenth century, when the members of the household of the reigning sultan were known as the *ajlāb* or *julbān*, and those of his predecessors as *qarāniṣ* or *qarāniṣa*. The *qarāniṣ*, however, only formed a united group against the *julbān*; if at any time they were composed of the veterans of two or more former sultans, they would compete among themselves for power and place. There was thus an inbuilt political weakness at the centre of the Mamluk sultanate.

The characteristic and distinguishing feature of Mamluk military society was that it was composed almost wholly of first-generation immigrants, newly converted to Islam. *Awlād al-nās*, their sons and later descendants, had wealth and privilege but rarely held military or political offices of any significance. One need not assume that there was a formal law of exclusion; rather it would seem that with new recruits always available, they were simply passed over. In the Ottoman period, when sources of recruitment were drying up, the sons of Mamluks played a more prominent part in the military households, which turned into patronage systems. During the Mamluk sultanate, however, *awlād al-nās*, brought up from birth as Muslims among Arabic-speakers, and bearing an Arabic (not a Turkish or Mongol) name, were rapidly assimilated into the ancient culture, of which their forebears were the barbarian protectors and rulers. Not a few of them made contributions to that culture; e.g. three of the principal chroniclers, Ibn al-Dawādārī (*fl.* 776/1335) and Ibn Ṭūlūn (880–953/1473–1546) in Syria, and Ibn Taghrībirdī (d. 874/1470) in Egypt.

One exception (on the whole more apparent than real) to the general rule that high office was not open to *awlād al-nās* was the sultanate. From 648/1250 to 784/1382 seven sultans were Mamluks, seventeen *awlād al-nās*. This reflects an inherent ambiguity in the Mamluk sultanate. The early sultans were primarily war-leaders, virtually chiefs of a synthetic Turkish tribe, constituted on the soil of Egypt and Syria by the Mamluks. As such, and except on the battlefield, their position in regard to their comrades was that of first among equals. This is exemplified in a remark attributed to Kutuz on his usurpation of the throne from al-Manṣūr ʿAlī b. Aybeg in 657/1259. Speaking to the amirs, he declared, "My only aim is that we should combine to fight the Mongols, and this cannot be attained without a king. If we go out and defeat this enemy, the matter will pass to you – install in the sultanate whom you will." The implication is that the sultanate was elective with the Mamluk amirs constituting an informal electoral college.

This concept persisted throughout the period of the Mamluk sultanate: a sultan was always inaugurated with the consent, and sometimes on the initiative, of the magnates. At times of factional strife – as after the murder of al-Ashraf Khalīl (693/1293), and frequently in the last decades of the Kalavunid dynasty after the death of al-Nāṣir Muḥammad (741/1341) – this notional "electoral college" was contracted in practice to the leaders of the dominant faction. The electors sometimes took the opportunity of requiring the new sultan to undertake certain obligations, intended to secure their position against the new military household. Al-Ẓāhir Baybars had to give such an undertaking to his comrades of the Baḥriyya before they would enter into a covenant (*ḥilf*) to recognize him as sultan after the murder of Kutuz. Lachın's usurpation (696/1296) was signalized by a similar agreement with the magnates, by which he undertook to remain first among equals, and to renounce the absolute discretion which characterized traditional Islamic sovereignty. Other accession-compacts were made by later sultans but they lacked any constitutional sanction. They were a relic of Mamluk quasi-tribalism rather than a nascent concept of contractual sovereignty.

Although the powerful early sultans, Aybeg, Kutuz, al-Ẓāhir Baybars and Kalavun, were essentially barbarian chiefs and recent converts, they were also heirs to the old traditions of Islamic monarchy, and it is in this sometimes misleading context that they are set by contemporary biographers and chroniclers. So presented, the Turkish war-leader became a champion in the *jihād*, and his services to Islam in this and other respects (such as the establishment of pious foundations for mosques and schools) made his authority legitimate. A crucial step in the process of legitimation was taken by al-Ẓāhir Baybars in 659/1261, when an ʿAbbasid refugee after the fall of Baghdad to the Mongols was installed as caliph in Cairo, and duly granted Baybars a diploma of investiture as sultan. The ʿAbbasid caliphs' formal investiture of successive sultans was an essential item in the accession-observances.

The inauguration ceremony as it became established in the eighth/fourteenth century is thus described by al-Maqrīzī, writing in the next century:

> It was also a custom that whenever a descendant of al-Malik al-Nāṣir Muḥammad b. Kalavun succeeded to the kingdom that the amirs would attend at his residence in the Citadel, and he would be invested with the black caliphal robe with a green gown underneath and a round black turban. He would be girded with the golden Arab sword, and, mounting the royal steed, he would proceed with the amirs before him, and with the saddle-cover in front, while the criers shouted and the royal flutes were blown; the halberdiers escorting him as he passed from Bāb al-Nuḥās to the steps of this hall [i.e. the Palace of Justice]. Then he would dismount, go up to the throne, and take his seat on it; and the amirs would kiss the ground before him. Then they would approach him, and kiss his hand in order of precedence, then the commanders of the *Ḥalqa*. When they had finished, the judges and the caliph would attend. Robes of honour would be conferred on the caliph. He would sit with the sultan on the throne, and invest the sultan with the kingdom in the presence of the judges and the amirs as witnesses. Then he and the judges would depart, and a banquet would be held for the amirs. When they had all finished eating, the sultan would rise and go to his private apartment, and the amirs would depart.[1]

The black robe and turban referred to were the ʿAbbasid livery, and indicated the nominal dependence of the sultan on the caliph. The carrying of a jewelled saddle-cover in procession as an emblem of sovereignty was a usage that went back to Ayyubid and Seljukid precedents. The royal ride from Bāb al-Nuḥās to the Palace of Justice was between two points in the Citadel; at an earlier date a sultan on his accession would ride through the city of Cairo and up to the Citadel.

The transmutation of the warrior-chief into the Muslim ruler must have strengthened the propensity of the Mamluk sultans to make their position hereditary. The succession of Aybeg's son, al-Manṣūr ʿAlī, was the consequence of factional politics – the determination of the Muʿizziyya to secure their ascendancy. Al-Ẓāhir Baybars, however, sought deliberately to establish a hereditary sultanate by nominating his infant son, al-Saʿīd Muḥammad Baraka Khān, as his heir in 660/1262, and as joint sultan (when aged about four) in 662/1264. This attempt failed in a couple of years after Baybars's death, but it was tried with greater success by the usurper Kalavun, whose dynasty reigned (with three brief intervals of usurpation) for over a century until the last Kalavunid was finally ousted by Barkuk in 792/1390.

There was an inherent tension between the elective and hereditary concepts of the sultanate, and it is significant that the hereditary succession of the Kalavunids only became established from the third reign of al-Nāṣir Muḥammad. This corresponds to a shift in the essential functions of the sultan. The early sultans had ruled over an embattled state, of which Syria had been a bastion liable to attack from the Mongols and Crusaders. The conquest of Acre and the last Frankish mainland territories in 690/1291, together with the ending of the Mongol threat in the opening years of the next century, made it less important to have a sultan who could lead his army in the field but still indispensable to have one who could serve as the real or nominal mainspring of government. It was in these circumstances that al-Nāṣir Muḥammad was able in his third reign (709–41/1310–41) to establish a more autocratic personal rule than any of the earlier sultans had exercised. But an autocrat was not always necessary. Even a child such as al-Ashraf Küchük under the tutelage of the Mamluk magnates might be an acceptable puppet ruler.

After the sultanate had been usurped by Barkuk, he tried to secure its continuance in his family by laying down from his death-bed an order of succession for his sons. From start to finish, however, the house of Barkuk reigned for only thirty years, and hereditary succession never took root during the Circassian Mamluk sultanate. A recurrent pattern of events is observable. The death of a usurping sultan is followed by the accession of his son, who during a brief reign serves as a stopgap (and formal linchpin of government) until the throne is again usurped by one of the magnates. But succession by usurpation was not a career open to every Mamluk: after Barkuk, all the successful usurpers came from the military households of previous sultans. The two great "royal nurseries" in this sense were the households of Barkuk himself and of Kayitbay, each of which provided five sultans apart from the sultans' own sons.

The sultan's residence was in the Citadel of Cairo (Qalʿat al-Jabal), which had been begun by Saladin, and was completed in its original form by al-Kāmil. This was a strongly fortified complex of buildings comprising barracks, halls of public audience and the private apartments of the ruler and his family. An elaborate court organization with household departments and officers bore a resemblance to that of the Fatimids, although it may be doubted if there was any continuity between the two. There was perhaps a deliberate imitation of the Seljukids in the court nomenclature; e.g. the Fatimid armoury had been designated by the purely Arabic term *khizānat al-silāḥ*, its Mamluk counterpart was known by the Arabo-Persian hybrid *silāḥkhānāh*, while the term *ṭashtkhānāh* (in Seljukid times the royal pantry) was revived for the sultan's wardrobe. One important difference between the Fatimid and Mamluk courts was the much diminished role of eunuchs in the latter. Eunuchs, however, staffed the barrack-schools, where Mamluk recruits were housed and trained. There they formed a hierarchy headed by a great officer entitled *muqaddam al-mamālīk al-sulṭāniyya*, "the prefect of the Royal Mamluks", who apparently had a prototype in a eunuch responsible for the Fatimid soldiery called *zamm al-rijāl*.

The old tradition that the ruler should make himself accessible to his subjects and hear their complaints, institutionalized by Nūr al-Dīn through the establishment of *dār al-ʿadl*, was continued in a highly formal manner by the Mamluk sultans. Court was held in the great hall of the Palace of Justice in the Citadel. The hall had originally been built by Kalavun. His son, al-Nāṣir Muḥammad, demolished and rebuilt it more magnificently. Al-Maqrīzī has described the manner of holding court:

It was the custom of the sultan to sit in this hall at daybreak on Mondays and Thursdays throughout the year, except for the month of Ramaḍān, when he would not hold these sittings. Such a session was solely for the [redress of] wrongs. It was held in full court, to which generally the ambassadors of rulers were summoned.

When he sat for the [redress of] wrongs, he would take his seat upon a chair which would almost allow his foot to touch the ground when he was seated. It was set up beside the elevated seat which was the royal throne, the seat of the sultanate. It was at first the usage for the chief judges of the four *madhhabs* to take their seats on his right, the senior of them being the Shāfiʿī, who was next to the sultan, then beside the Shāfiʿī the Ḥanafī, then the Mālikī, then the Ḥanbalī. Beside the Ḥanbalī was the agent of the treasury, then the supervisor of the *ḥisba* in Cairo. On the left of the sultan sat the secretary, in front of him the supervisor of the army, and the corps of writers (known as the clerks of the bench and the writers of the bench) completing the circle. If the *wazīr* was one of the Men of the Pens, he was between the sultan and the secretary; if the *wazīr* was one of the Men of the Swords, he would stand apart from the rest of the officials. If there was a vicegerent, he would stand with the officials. Behind the sultan to his right and left stood two ranks of the sword-bearers, the pages of the Wardrobe, and the pages of the Privy Chamber. At a distance of fifteen cubits to his right and left sat the elderly and venerable great amirs of a Hundred, who were called the amirs of the council. Next below them were the great amirs and the officials, who were standing, and the rest of the amirs, who were standing behind the amirs of the council. Standing behind this circle surrounding the sultan were the chamberlains and the *dawādārs* to offer the petitions of the people, and to summon the ambassadors, plaintiffs and those submitting their needs and wants.

The secretary and the writers of the bench read the petitions to the sultan, and if necessary he would take the advice of the judges on what related to legal matters and religious jurisdiction. In matters relating to the army, if the petitions involved amirs holding assignments, the supervisor of the army would read them. If he needed to take advice concerning the army, he would confer with the chamberlain and the clerk of the army. Otherwise the sultan would command as he thought fit.[2]

Perhaps it was as a result of the formality of this *maẓālim* procedure that another extra-canonical jurisdiction developed in the first half of the ninth/fifteenth century, when the chamberlain (*ḥājib*), a military officer, extended his functions from the hearing of soldiers' disputes to those of ordinary subjects – to the detriment of the *Sharīʿa* courts.

As in other Islamic military polities, governmental functions were carried out by a partnership between the Men of the Swords and the Men of the Pens, the military rulers and the chancery and treasury officials; the former being Turkish-speaking immigrants, the latter indigenous Arabic-speakers. Under the Mamluk sultanate, there was an increased militarization of the administration in comparison with the Ayyubid system. The *wazīr* (usually a civilian, as under the Ayyubids) declined in importance. Before the end of the seventh/thirteenth century he had lost his administrative powers to a great Mamluk officer, the vicegerent in Egypt (*nāʾib al-salṭana biʾl-diyār al-Miṣriyya*), and his confidential secretarial functions to a new civilian official, the secretary (*kātib al-sirr*), originally the head chancery clerk (*ṣāḥib dīwān al-inshāʾ*). His fiscal powers were whittled away in consequence of changes in the eighth/fourteenth century, so that al-Maqrīzī, writing in the first half of the following century, said of the *wazīr*, "If he is a civilian, he is no more than a head clerk, who frequents the door of the steward by night and day, and acts according to his commands and prohibitions."[3]

The increasing elaboration of the governmental system is reflected in the rapid emergence of a body of great Mamluk officers of the royal household and state. Some of their offices were ancient, some had previously been held by civilians, but from the time of al-Ẓāhir Baybars with the trend towards militarization, the definition of functions, and the ranking in a hierarchy are clearly discernible. At the head of the great officers was the vicegerent, who (like the *wazīr* under previous regimes) held plenary power by delegation from the sultan. Most of the other great officers were concerned, at least in appearance, with the royal household or the personal service of the sultan; e.g. the sword-bearer (*amīr silāḥ*), the constable (*amīr akhūr*) in charge of the royal stables, the bearer of the royal inkwell (*dawādār*), the chamberlain (*ḥājib*) and the steward (*ustādār*, i.e. *ustādh al-dār al-ʿāliya*, "the master of the high household"). The appearance was, however, misleading as some of the domestic officers acquired public functions. The *dawādār* rose in rank, became the channel of communication between the sultan and his chancery, and further extended his power under the Circassian sultans. The extension of the chamberlain's jurisdiction has already been mentioned. The steward acquired financial responsibilities such as had formerly been held by the *wazīr* when Barkuk put him in charge of two new personal treasuries. As time went on, each of the great officers built up a personal staff, and became in effect the head of a department.

Early in the Mamluk sultanate, the old Seljukid office of *atabeg* reappeared, usually in the form of *atābak al-ʿasākir*, i.e. the *atabeg* of the armies, whose function it was to command the forces if the sultan could not do so, being a woman or a child. The first Mamluk holder of this office was Aybeg, who indeed acted, if only briefly, like a Seljukid *atabeg* by serving as regent to a prince of the royal house, the Ayyubid al-Ashraf Mūsā, and by marrying the widow of his former master, Shajar al-Durr. Subsequently *atābaks* (sometimes with the additional title of *mudabbir al-mamlaka*, i.e. administrator of the kingdom) were appointed as protectors to infant sultans down to the time of the later Kalavunids, when the title became synonymous with *al-amīr al-kabīr*, i.e. the senior *amīr*. The title of *atābak* also came to be held by amirs in the Syrian provinces.

The two great departments of state were the chancery (*dīwān al-inshāʾ*) and the army department (*dīwān al-jaysh*). The promotion of the chief chancery clerk to the new office of confidential secretary to the sultan has already been mentioned. The chancery staff comprised two categories of clerks: *kuttāb al-dast*, the clerks of the bench, who attended on the sultan in his public audiences to minute his responses to petitions, and *kuttāb al-darj*, the clerks of the roll, who prepared the decrees and other formal instruments to which the sultan's instructions gave rise. The army department, in spite of its name, was purely civilian in its personnel, and was responsible for the financial administration of the soldiery. As in the Ayyubid period, the troops were maintained by *iqṭāʿs*, but the Mamluk system differed in two important respects. In the first place, only in the most exceptional circumstances was an *iqṭāʿ* allowed to become hereditary; this was the obvious consequence of the continuous recruitment of new Mamluks. The transfer and resumption of *iqṭāʿs* were common occurrences, and a Mamluk might hold several different *iqṭā'^s* successively in the course of his career. In the second place, the grant of *iqṭā'^s* was strictly centralized. With only minor exceptions, grants originated in the army department in Cairo, and passed to the chancery, where a patent (*manshūr*) was prepared for the sultan's signature.

The valuation and distribution of the *iqṭā'^s* in the early Mamluk sultanate were probably substantially as they had been in the Ayyubid period, going back to the fiscal reform made by Saladin in 572/1176 (*al-rawk al-Ṣalāḥī*). One-sixth of the cultivable land of Egypt formed the royal fisc (*al-khāṣṣ al-sulṭānī*), five-twelfths provided for the maintenance of the amirs and the remaining five-twelfths for the troopers of the *Ḥalqa*. This distribution became obsolete as the Baḥriyya, originally part of al-Ṣāliḥ Ayyūb's *Ḥalqa*, emerged from this matrix to acquire military and political predominance. To reform the distribution, and at the same time to strengthen his own position against the Mamluk magnates, al-Manṣūr Lachın carried out a cadastral survey and reassignment of *iqṭā'^s* in 697/1298 (*al-rawk al-Ḥusāmī*). Under this allotment, the amirs and *Ḥalqa* together received only a share of eleven twenty-fourths, while the balance saved of nine twenty-fourths was intended by the sultan to be used for the recruitment of a new military force. This attempted reform caused the overthrow of Lachın, and was never implemented.

Early in his third reign, in 715–16/1315–16, al-Nāṣir Muḥammad carried out a successful reform (*al-rawk al-Nāṣirī*), which provided the financial base of his autocracy. Henceforward five-twelfths of the cultivable land of Egypt was set aside for the fisc, while the remaining seven-twelfths provided for the amirs, soldiery and other *muqṭa'^s*. The great increase in the fisc turned the department responsible for its administration (*dīwān al-khāṣṣ*) into the principal treasury of the sultanate, while the ancient state treasury (*bayt al-māl*) sank into insignificance. The supervisor of the fisc (*nāẓir al-khāṣṣ*), who might be a Copt or a convert to Islam, became one of the most important administrative officials. The instability of the four decades after al-Nāṣir Muḥammad's death, with the magnates struggling among themselves to appoint and dominate feeble sultans, was probably due as much to financial as to political causes, since to control the sultan meant to have the disposal of his fisc.

The establishment of the Mamluk sultanate was followed by a systematization of the military organization as well as of the administrative and financial branches of government. Mamluk troopers, purchased, trained and emancipated by the sultan and the amirs, formed the core of the army. The *Ḥalqa* sank into a unit of secondary importance, recruited almost wholly from free-born Muslims, who lacked the discipline and loyalties which a Mamluk acquired through his training. *Awlād al-nās* entered the *Ḥalqa* as a matter of course – indeed towards the end of the Mamluk sultanate the first term superseded the second. The decline of the *Ḥalqa* was, however, a gradual process, and some indication of its size and importance under the early Mamluk sultans is given by the title of the highest-ranking amirs – *amīr mi'a wa-muqaddam alf*, i.e. the commander of a military household of 100 horsemen and of 1,000 troopers of the *Ḥalqa*. The notional establishment was of 24 amirs of this rank, hence of 24,000 troopers in the *Ḥalqa*, but no reliance can be placed on either figure. Below the amirs of a Hundred were two other ranks of officers. The first of these were the commanders of a military household of 40 horsemen (sing., *amīr arbaʿīn*), usually entitled *amīr ṭablkhānāh*, because they like their superiors were entitled to a military band (*ṭablkhānāh*) of drums, trumpets and flutes, which played before their houses in the evenings. The lowest regular officer was the commander of a military household of 10 horsemen (*amīr ʿashara*). The inferior rank of commander of 5 horsemen (*amīr khamsa*), in effect a half-pay officer, was chiefly held by sons of deceased amirs, who were of course *awlād al-nās*.

Although there was thus a hierarchy of ranks and titles, which provided a *cursus honorum* such as had been lacking under the Ayyubids, this did not imply a chain of command. The Mamluk field army, like that of the Ayyubids, consisted of a number of contingents supporting the sultan's military household. The centralization of the *iqṭaʿ* system, the substitution of provincial governorships for autonomous principalities, and to some extent the Mamluk loyalty of the amirs towards a sultan who was their *ustādh* or *khushdāsh*, were all factors which tended to make the Mamluk army a more united and formidable fighting force than its Ayyubid predecessor. Improvement in organization was not, however, matched by innovations in military technique. With the passing of the external threat to Syria and Egypt, even the traditional training came to be neglected. The cavalry exercises encouraged by the early sultans, and the hippodromes (Arabic sing., *maydān*) they built, fell into disuse. The last effective Kalavunid, al-Ashraf Shaʿbān (764–78/1363–77), encouraged cavalry training, but the decline continued under the Circassian sultans in the following century. On the eve of the overthrow of the Mamluk sultanate, Kansawh al-Ghawrī attempted to revive the old training, and to bring in the use of cannon and firearms, in which the Ottomans had long been proficient. It was too late, and his defeat by Selīm the Grim at Marj Dābiq in 922/1516 bore witness both to the military obsolescence of the Mamluk sultanate, and to the inveterate factionalism which was its political weakness (see below, p. 200).

The terminology of the period made a distinction between the two regions of the Mamluk sultanate: *al-diyār al-Miṣriyya*, "the Egyptian homelands", and *al-mamālik al-Shāmiyya*, "the Syrian kingdoms", since the Syrian provinces largely corresponded to the former Ayyubid principalities. After the completion of the reconquest of the Frankish states, there were six Syrian provinces with their capitals at Damascus, Aleppo, Ḥamāh, al-Karak, Tripoli and Ṣafad, the last two being formed out of territory reconquered by the Mamluks. Damascus and Aleppo, the two great provinces of southern and northern Syria respectively, far outstripped the others in importance, and of these two Damascus was pre-eminent. The governor (*nā'*ib, literally "deputy") of Damascus ranked equally with the vicegerent in Egypt, but whereas the vicegerent bore the title of *al-nā'ib al-kāfil*, indicating that he enjoyed a general delegation of the sultan's powers, the governor of Damascus was styled *malik al-umarā'*, "the king of the amirs", a title used also in the Seljuk sultanate of Rūm. In the ninth/ fifteenth century, it came to be applied to the other Syrian governors.

The governor of Damascus maintained an almost royal state, which was publicly demonstrated every Monday and Thursday, when he entered the city in a formal procession, went to the citadel, and thence to his residence. There he held court as if in the presence of the sultan, who was symbolized by an empty throne draped with yellow satin (yellow being the Mamluk colour as it had been of the Ayyubids before them), on which lay the *namjāh* (Persian, *nīmchah*), a small sword, one of the royal insignia. Surrounded by his military, civil and judicial officers, the governor would hear the petitions submitted to him. He would then hold a banquet for his military officers, and subsequently meet his secretary and the head of the provincial army department to deal with the petitions. Similar procedures were followed in Aleppo, Tripoli and Ḥamāh, but there the symbolic empty throne had no place.

Although the Syrian governors seemed like kinglets in their provinces, they were closely subjected to a number of controls. Their tenure of office depended on the arbitrary will of the sultan, so that even the great Tengiz al-Ḥusāmī, after nearly thirty years of service as governor of Damascus, was disgraced and put to death. The knowledge of the precariousness of their positions as much as ambition may have moved Sanjar al-Ḥalabī and Sungur al-Ashqar to proclaim themselves sultans in Damascus at the start of the reigns of al-Ẓāhir Baybars and Kalavun respectively (see above, pp. 91, 101). Other controls were of an administrative nature. In both the appointment of provincial officials and the grant of *iqṭā'ṣ*, the governor's powers were severely limited. Although, for example, warrants for *iqṭā's* could originate with the governor of Damascus, they had to pass to Cairo, where the resulting patent received the sultan's signature. Several of the principal officials in Damascus were appointed directly by the sultan. Among them were the governor of the citadel, the great chamberlain (who was empowered to arrest the governor at the sultan's command, and then to serve as acting governor) and the secretary, who was the head of the provincial chancery, and acted as a spy on the governor himself. In addition, a number of appointments to the subprovinces were retained by the sultan, e.g. the subgovernorships of Gaza (a key to the approach to Egypt), Maṣyāf (a stronghold in the Syrian highlands, formerly held by the Assassins) and the Holy City of Jerusalem. The Mamluk sultan and his administration thus exercised far more control over the governors in Syria than the Ayyubid sultan in Egypt had done over his princely kinsmen.

RELIGIOUS INSTITUTIONS

The religious institutions of Egypt and Syria under the Mamluk sultans were substantially what they had been under the Ayyubids. Al-Ẓāhir Baybars, however, made two important innovations which survived until the Ottoman conquest. The first of these was his establishment of the 'Abbasid caliphate in Cairo. The significance of this for his internal position and external policy is indicated elsewhere (see pp. 92–4 ff), but it must be stressed that the caliphs of Cairo rarely played a political role of any significance. A writer of the ninth/fifteenth century, Khalīl al-Ẓāhirī, after stating that God has made the caliph ruler over all the land of Islam, and listing his high prerogatives, descends to the reality of his time with the words, "he is required to occupy himself with scholarship, and to have a library. If the sultan travels on business, he is to accompany him for the benefit of the Muslims."[4]

Baybars's second innovation, one of more practical importance for his Muslim subjects, was a reform of the Islamic judiciary. Under his predecessors there had been one chief judge (*qāḍī al-quḍāt*) in Cairo, a jurist who administered the *Sharī'a* according to the Shāfi'ī *madhhab*. In 663/1264 the chief judge fell foul of one of the Mamluk magnates, who accused him of being dilatory in handling cases dealt with under the other *madhhabs*. Matters came to a head during a session in *dār al-'adl*, when Baybars found the judge less compliant than he expected. Thereupon three other chief judges were appointed to deal with cases brought under the Ḥanafī, Mālikī and Ḥanbalī *madhhabs* respectively, and a similar reform was carried out in Damascus.

Baybars's awareness of the political implications of religious institutions appears also in developments connected with the Pilgrimage. These enabled him to demonstrate his suzerainty over the Holy Cities, where at first his chief competitor was the Rasulid ruler of the Yemen, al-Muẓaffar Yūsuf (647–94/1250–95). The object of their rivalry was the right to provide the *kiswa*, i.e. the curtain veiling the exterior of the Kaʿba. The presentation of the *kiswa* had been the prerogative of the ʿAbbasid caliphs but had been usurped by other rulers in the decline of the caliphate. In 661/1263 a *kiswa* was manufactured in Egypt (a chronicler significantly says "as usual"), and sent to Mecca with an escort of eminent pilgrims including officials, judges, jurists and Ṣūfīs, after having been paraded around Cairo. This was more than an ordinary religious delegation: it was a demonstration of Baybars's claim to a special status in Mecca. He sent timber and craftsmen to repair the sanctuary, and when the sultan's representative reached Mecca, he received the key of the Kaʿba in symbolic recognition of Baybars's overlordship. The same point was made in another way in the same year, when the ambassadors of Berke Khan were informed that their master's name would be recited after that of Baybars in the *khuṭba* in Mecca, Medina and Jerusalem.

In 664/1266 there was a curious innovation when, apparently for the first time, the *maḥmil* accompanied the Egyptian Pilgrimage caravan. The *maḥmil* was an empty covered litter, mounted on a specially selected camel. Thereafter it was sent annually by the Mamluk sultans and their successors in Egypt down to the reign of King Fu'ād in 1926. It is not clear what the *maḥmil* was originally intended to signify, and at first it attracted little notice from the chroniclers, but it came to be regarded as the essential token of sovereignty over Mecca. At about the same time as the introduction of the *maḥmil*, Baybars assumed the style of "Servitor of the Two August Sanctuaries" (*khādim al-ḥaramayn al-sharīfayn*), which continued to be used by his successors until it was appropriated by Selīm the Grim on the Ottoman conquest of Egypt. In this as in some other ways, Kalavun completed what Baybars had begun. In 681/1282 Abū Numayy, the ruling *sharīf* of Mecca, made a sworn profession of obedience to the sultan. He undertook that the sultan's *kiswa* only should hang on the Kaʿba, that the sultan's banners should be given precedence, and that the sultan's name alone should be recited in the *khuṭba* and placed on coins. The Mamluk sultanate thus established its hold over the religious centre of Islam.

The Mamluk sultans, like earlier rulers in Egypt and Syria, gave their patronage to Ṣūfīs, and founded convents for them. A bizarre instance of relations between a sultan and a Ṣūfī occurred in the reign of al-Ẓāhir Baybars. Shaykh Khaḍir al-Mihrānī, a Ṣūfī of Kurdish origin, who had a disreputable early career, foretold Baybars's reign, and in 661/1263 joined the retinue of the sultan, whom he served as a soothsayer rather than a spiritual director. For some years his influence was enormous, and one of Baybars's sons was named after him. The sultan endowed convents for him in Cairo, Jerusalem, Damascus, Baʿlabakk, Ḥamāh and Ḥimṣ, and allowed him to expropriate a synagogue in Damascus and churches in Jerusalem and Alexandria. In the end, Bilik al-Khāzindār, Baybars's Mamluk minister, threatened by Khaḍir's malevolence, brought about his downfall. He was imprisoned in the Citadel of Cairo, where he made his last prophecy:

When the sultan went to Anatolia [675/1277], one of his comrades had a meeting with Shaykh Khaḍir and asked him about the outcome of the expedition for the sultan. He informed him that he would be victorious; then he would return to Damascus and die there "twenty days after my death". And so it fell out.[5]

The greatest of the Mamluk patrons of Sufism was, as might be expected, the magnificent and wealthy al-Nāṣir Muḥammad, who founded the royal *khānaqāh* near Siryāqūs, north of Cairo. Its building in the year 725/1325 is described by the chronicler Ibn Taghribirdī:

Then the sultan went out to Siryāqūs, and with him a number of engineers. He appointed a site at about a league from Siryāqūs for the building of a convent. It contained a hundred cells for a hundred Ṣūfīs. Beside it was a mosque where the *khuṭba* was recited, a guest-house, a bath and a kitchen. Aksungur was commissioned as controller of works to recruit the labourers. [The sultan] also assigned the palaces of Siryāqūs for the amirs and the pages of the Privy Chamber. He returned, and the work went on zealously so that it was completed in forty days. Then the sultan thought it necessary to cut a canal from Cairo to end at Siryāqūs, provided with water-wheels and plots for cultivation, so that during the high Nile boats could pass with cereals, etc. to the palaces in Siryāqūs.[6]

Less than a century and a half later, Ibn Taghrībirdī visited the plundered ruins of the palaces.

While Ṣūfī beliefs and practices were popular in every stratum of Muslim society from the sultan and his court downwards, the older orthodoxy resting on the Qur'ān and the Traditions of the Prophet remained the touchstone of Sunnī Islam. It found an outstanding and rigorous defender during this period in the jurist and theologian Ibn Taymiyya (661–728/1263–1328). He came from a scholarly family belonging to the Ḥanbalī *madhhab*, the strictest of the four Sunnī legal systems. He was brought as a child to Damascus, when his family were in flight from the Mongols (667/1269), and he spent most of his life in Syria. Throughout his career, he showed himself a champion of the

Faith as he conceived it against its external and internal enemies. He preached the *jihād* against Lesser Armenia in 697/1298, and against the Mongols in 700/1300. Twice, in 699/1300 and 704/1305, he took part in expeditions into the mountains of Kisrawān (in modern Lebanon), the home of the bellicose Druze hillmen.

An incident in Damascus showed his opposition to *bid'a*, i.e. unscriptural innovation in religion. Al-Maqrīzī reports that in 704/1305:

> Taqı al-Dīn Aḥmad Ibn Taymiyya clashed with the people of Damascus about the rock in the mosque of al-Nāranj near the oratory of Damascus, and [the belief] that the mark on it was the footprint of the Prophet, and [he asserted] that the practice of the people in seeking a blessing from it, and kissing it, was not permissible. He went with stonemasons, and broke up the rock on 16 Rajab [12 February 1305], and the people resented his action.[7]

At a different level, he was involved in polemics with Ṣūfī leaders and with Sunnī jurists and theologians who did not share his views. The controversies he aroused led to his involvement with the political authorities in Syria, and to more than one term of imprisonment. He died a prisoner in the Citadel of Cairo. Although his following was never numerous in his own time, his writings have exerted a lasting influence. They were the inspiration of Muḥammad b. 'Abd al-Wahhāb (1703–92), the founder of the Wahhābī movement for the purification of Islam, and the co-founder of the Sa'udi state in Arabia.

In addition to the numerous mosques, *madrasas* and Ṣūfī convents that were established by Mamluk sultans and magnates, a foundation of a different but related kind should be noted. This was the great hospital in Cairo, al-Māristān (from the Persian, *bīmāristān*) al-Manṣūrī, built by Kalavun in 683/1284. He was following the example of several previous rulers, notably Nūr al-Dīn, who had founded hospitals in Aleppo, Damascus and al-Raqqa, and Aḥmad b. Ṭūlūn and Saladin, who had done the same in Cairo, The Māristān formed part of a complex of institutions which included the founder's domed tomb-chamber, a *madrasa* and a school for orphans. Altogether they received an annual revenue of nearly one million dirhams from *waqfs* in Egypt. The hospital was thus essentially a religious foundation like its counterparts in medieval Europe.

NOTES

1. Al-Maqrīzī, *Kitāb al-mawā'iẓ wa'l-i'tibār bi-dhikr al-khiṭaṭ wa'l-āthār*, II, Beirut n.d. [repr. of edn of Būlāq, 1270/1853], 209. English version P. M. Holt.

2. *Ibid.*, II, 208–9.
3. *Ibid.*, II, 223.
4. Khalīl al-Ẓāhirī, *Kitāb zubdat kashf al-mamālik wa-bayān al-ṭuruq wa'l-masālik*, ed. Paul Ravaisse, Paris 1894, 90. English version P. M. Holt.
5. 'Izz al-Dīn Ibn Shaddād, *Ta'rīkh al-Malik al-Ẓāhir*, ed. Ahmad Hutait, Wiesbaden 1403/1983, 273. English version P. M. Holt.
6. Ibn Taghrībirdī, *al-Nujūm al-zāhira fī mulūk Miṣr wa'l Qāhira*, IX, Cairo n.d., 79–80. English version P. M. Holt.
7. Al-Maqrīzī, *al-Sulūk*, II, pt 1, ed. M. Mustafa Ziada, Cairo 1971, 8–9. English version P. M. Holt.

CHAPTER EIGHTEEN

Diplomatic and Commercial Relations of the Mamluk Sultanate

The period which began with the First Crusade and the foundation of the Frankish states saw increasingly close relations between the Muslim rulers in the Near East and Christendom. The formal hostility between the representatives of Islam and Christianity, expressed in the ideology of the *jihād* on the one side, of the crusade on the other, was only one aspect of the dealings between the two groups, to both of which practical commercial needs and political considerations were of immediate importance. The basic concept of Islamic international law, the division of the world into two warring communities, the Muslims in *dār al-Islām* and the infidels in *dār al-ḥarb*, while never abandoned in theory, was sufficiently modified in practice to allow of peaceful contacts and diplomatic relations. Hence, although no permanent settlement with a Christian power could be contemplated by the jurists, a truce (*hudna*) for a period of up to ten years was permissible, and such an agreement might be renewed on its lapse. In fact it was only with the neighbours of Muslim rulers that a *hudna* was no more than a precarious armistice.

The Christian powers with which the Muslim rulers had diplomatic relations fall into three groups. First came the four Frankish states established after the First Crusade, together with the neighbouring and closely associated kingdom of Lesser Armenia in Cilicia. All these were in territory formerly held by the Muslims. Secondly, there was the Byzantine empire. Thirdly, there were the remoter states of western Europe, among which the Italian republics (especially Venice and Genoa) and the kingdom of Aragon were of particular significance. Occasionally because of unusual contingencies, there were negotiations with other Western rulers, as for example between al-Kāmil and the

Emperor Frederick II (see above, pp. 64–5), but these resulted from no long-term political or economic factors.

The history of relations between the Frankish and Muslim states provides many examples of peaceful coexistence, and indeed of more or less formal alliances against local rivals. It is not, however, until late in the seventh/thirteenth century, when the Mamluk sultans were pressing hard on the remnants of the Frankish states, that we have much detailed information about the procedure in negotiations and the diplomatic instruments which were the outcome. In this late period the enfeebled Frankish states took the initiative, hoping thereby to avert invasion and conquest. Negotiations were carried out at the sultan's court, and a truce would be drafted jointly by a Muslim and a Frankish clerk. The final Arabic text adhered closely to the Frankish draft. This was insisted on by the Franks although the clumsy phraseology distressed the clerks of the sultan's chancery, who regarded the composition of state papers as a challenge to their skill in rhetoric.

The resulting instrument was attested by the oath of the sultan or his representative, and an embassy consisting of a senior amir and a high chancery official was sent to obtain the Frankish ruler's oath in ratification of the truce. On such occasions both parties stood on their dignity. Baybars, when receiving a delegation from Acre in 659/1261, deferred his reply, and spoke harshly to the envoys. Ten years later (669/1271) a truce was negotiated with Bohemond VI of Tripoli, the titular prince of Antioch, which Baybars had taken in 666/1268. The envoys sent to receive the oath of ratification were the *Atābak* Fāris al-Dīn Aktay al-Mustaʿrib and Ibn ʿAbd al-Ẓāhir, the head of chancery. The proceedings began with the reading of the truce, but at once Bohemond objected because he was styled "count" and not "prince". It seemed likely that the conclusion of the truce would be indefinitely delayed but Baybars, who was present in disguise as a sword-bearer, gave the *atābak* a gentle kick. The hint was sufficient: Bohemond was accorded his princely title, and the truce was duly ratified.

The texts are extant of several truces concluded in the reigns of Baybars and Kalavun with one or other of the authorities which held power in the Frankish states at that time. The most comprehensive was that negotiated between Kalavun and Acre in 682/1283. There was then no king resident in the Latin kingdom – indeed the throne was in dispute between Hugh III of Cyprus and Charles of Anjou. The Frankish party to the truce is therefore described in the preamble as "the authorities in the kingdom of Acre", and these are listed: Charles of Anjou's representative and the grand masters of the Templars, the Hospitallers and the Teutonic Order. There are five other treaties between these sultans and authorities within the Latin kingdom, and one between Kalavun and Bohemond VII of Tripoli in 680/1281.

The truces follow a common form, and display some general characteristics. They open with the names and titles of the two contracting parties, the duration of the truce (i.e. ten years) and the date of its commencement. Usually at this point the two parties' territories are specified in detail; perhaps to show an ironic contrast but quite possibly because of a desire for pettifogging accuracy. In the provisions which follow a principal aim is to secure the sultan's dominions and to put the Franks at a disadvantage: thus the construction or restoration of Frankish fortifications is forbidden, and the Frankish authorities are required to give the sultan warning of preparations in Europe for a crusade. Other clauses deal with the policing of border areas, compensation for theft or homicide and the extradition of fugitives. The situation on the borders was complicated by the existence of *munāṣafāt*, i.e. districts of which the revenue, and hence to some extent the administration, were shared between both parties to the truce. They amounted to condominia. In the early days of the Frankish states, *munāṣafāt* had been created to the disadvantage of the Muslims, e.g. in the Biqāʿ, the produce of which was divided in 503/1109–10. The device was now employed by the Mamluk sultans to whittle away Frankish authority in the border districts. The truces usually guaranteed the security of travellers and merchants, and provided for the lawful disposal of property from shipwrecks. They almost always assured the continuing validity of the truce throughout its full specified period, and sometimes allowed forty days of grace after the lapse of a truce so that strangers might return home. Some texts of the oaths of ratification are also extant. They are elaborate productions, especially the Christian oath, breach of which incurred the penalty of thirty pilgrimages to Jerusalem and the release of 1,000 Muslim captives.

In the procedure of negotiation and the form, the truces between the Mamluk sultans and the Frankish states are bilateral treaties, explicit in their terms and specific in their details. But as between two such disparate powers, they were necessarily unequal treaties, and the question is unavoidable as to whether Baybars and Kalavun negotiated and concluded them in good faith. The evidence is that they did not. Baybars's truce with the Hospitallers "for the period of ten consecutive years, ten months, ten days and ten hours beginning on Monday, 4 Ramaḍān, AH 665" (i.e. 29 May 1267) contains an explicit provision against premature abrogation. Nevertheless Ibn ʿAbd al-Ẓāhir, Baybars's court biographer, states that it was provided that the sultan might abrogate the truce at will. In 689/1290 Kalavun wished to denounce the ten-year truce which he had concluded with the authorities in Acre seven years earlier. His chancery was set to work to manufacture a *casus belli* out of a riot in Acre in which some Muslims had been killed. Ibn ʿAbd al-Ẓāhir, as head of chancery, could not find that the truce had been infringed but his nephew, Shāfiʿ b. ʿAlī, declared, "We serve the purpose of our lord the sultan", and (as he himself has recorded) he succeeded in providing an interpretation of one or two clauses which would justify Kalavun in going to war.

The kingdom of Lesser Armenia on the north-western frontier of Syria had a similar history to that of the Frankish states. It developed in territory which had been Muslim, but was retaken by the Byzantines in the second half of the fourth/tenth century. It received considerable numbers of immigrants from the Armenian homeland between Lake Van and the Caucasus. With the collapse of the Byzantine frontier in Anatolia after the battle of Manzikert in 463/1071, Armenian chiefs dominated Cilicia and the territories lying eastwards, as far as and beyond the upper Euphrates. They facilitated the passage of the First Crusade, although one of their number, Toros, lost his lordship of Edessa (and his life) to Baldwin of Boulogne. In the following century two great Armenian families, the Roupenids and the Hethoumids, contended for Cilicia, and the ascendancy of the former was confirmed when its head, Leo II, was crowned in Tarsus in 1198. The kingdom of Lesser Armenia thus came formally into being. In 1226, Leo's daughter married Hethoum I, and the rival dynasties were thus united. The Hethoumid kings were allied in marriage to the princes of Antioch, and followed a policy of submission to, and co-operation with, the Mongols. Like the Frankish states, Lesser Armenia found itself in a vulnerable position after the defeat of the Mongols at ʿAyn Jālūt in 658/1260. A Mamluk campaign in 664/1266 resulted in the defeat of the Armenians, and the capture of King Hethoum's son, Leo. Peace was concluded, and the prince released, only in 666/1268, when by a treaty (the text of which has not survived) Hethoum surrendered six fortresses to Baybars. The treaty was drafted in Antioch immediately after the Mamluk capture of the city.

The prince succeeded to the throne as Leo III in 1269. He supported the Mongols when the *Ilkhan* Abaqa invaded Syria to be defeated at the second battle of Ḥimṣ (Rajab 680/October 1281). Again, a treaty was difficult to obtain, and the king sought the mediation of the commander of the Templars in Lesser Armenia. The resulting truce, which was to run for ten years, ten months, ten days and ten hours from 1 Rabīʿ II 684/ July 1285, resembled in its general structure and terms the settlements concluded with the Frankish states. The security of the territories of the two rulers, freedom of passage for merchants and others, arrangements for the repatriation of fugitives, and police matters are thus covered. There are, however, two unusual provisions. First, King Leo was to release all Muslim merchants and prisoners, while Kalavun was to set free the Armenian ambassadors who had gone to Cairo when Leo first attempted to negotiate. Secondly, an annual tallage (*qaṭīʿa*) was imposed. It consisted of 500,000 Armenian silver dirhams, payable in advance, 25 horses, 25 mules, and 10,000 horseshoes with nails – in all, a substantial contribution to both the financial and military resources of the sultanate.

The early Mamluk period witnessed an important development of relations with the restored Byzantine empire. Michael VIII Palaeologus (1259–82), the emperor of Nicaea, recaptured Constantinople from the last Latin emperor in 1261, the year after Baybars's accession to the sultanate. It was important for Baybars to have a good understanding with the ruler who controlled the passage between the Black Sea and the Mediterranean, since *mamlūks* were brought by that route from the territory of the Golden Horde to Egypt. The alternative land-route across eastern Anatolia to Syria, by which Baybars himself had come in 640/1242–3, was now controlled by the hostile ilkhanate. But the enmity between the *Ilkhan* Hülegü and Berke Khan of the Golden Horde encouraged Baybars to secure his line of communications with the latter as a potential ally. Mamluk–Byzantine relations were thus chiefly significant in the context of Mamluk–Mongol relations. The story opened with a request from Michael VIII that Baybars should send him the Egyptian Melkite patriarch, apparently on the occasion of the reconquest of Constantinople. A delegation was dispatched, including not only the patriarch and other clerics but also a Mamluk envoy, the Amir Fāris al-Dīn Akkush al-Masʿūdī. The emperor rode round the liberated capital with Akkush, and pointed out an ancient mosque, founded in the Umayyad period, which he was restoring – a gesture which gratified Baybars.

Michael also sent Baybars a letter containing a sworn undertaking to give the sultan aid if needed. This marked the entry of the two rulers into treaty relations, and the opening of the straits to dealers in *mamlūks*. Baybars forthwith sent off a second and more formal embassy, regularly composed of a military officer and a civilian jurist. With it he sent presents, which included a giraffe (indicating the extension of Baybar's power into Nubia) and a number of Mongol prisoners. Both this mission and the clerical delegation with Akkush seem to have returned at the same time in Shaʿbān 660/July 1262. An embassy from the emperor followed, accompanied by envoys sent by ʿIzz al-Dīn Kay-

Kāvūs, the refugee Seljukid sultan of Rūm, who had been ousted in 659/1261 (see below, p. 174). To gain Baybars's military support, Kay-Kāvūs promised him and half of his kingdom – a visionary offer, which he was never able to fulfil.

In the meantime, Baybars was moving towards the establishment of diplomatic relations with Berke himself. As a Mamluk the son of an unknown father, originating from the lands of the Golden Horde, Baybars was at a disadvantage in approaching Berke, a descendant of the world conqueror Chingiz Khan. Both rulers were, however, converts to Islam, and here Baybars had a trump-card to play in the refugee ʿAbbasid who had been installed as the Caliph al-Ḥākim in Muḥarram 661/November 1262. As nominal head of the universal Islamic community, the caliph conferred legitimacy on the sultan, and served him as a useful mouthpiece in his negotiations with Berke. The embassy from Baybars travelled by way of Constantinople, whence it was sent on by Michael VIII with his own mission to Berke. It returned to Cairo in Dhu'l-Qaʿda 662/September 1264 with an account of the curiosities of protocol at the Mongol court.

Already before their return, an embassy from Berke had arrived in Cairo to ask for Baybars's help against Hülegü. It is probably significant that at the same time envoys arrived from Michael VIII, Kay-Kāvūs and Genoa, which had important trading interests in the Black Sea. Berke's ambassadors were received with signal honours, and once again the Caliph al-Ḥākim was assigned a leading part in court ceremonial. The ambassadors attended the Friday prayer on 28 Shaʿbān 661/July 1263, and heard the caliph recite their ruler's name in the *khuṭba*. Then on 4 Ramaḍān/12 July, an interesting ceremony took place. About half a century before the fall of Baghdad to the Mongols, the Caliph al-Nāṣir (578–622/1180–1225) had reformed and brought under his own patronage an amorphous and heterogeneous movement (originally a young men's association) known as the *futuwwa*. Baybars revived this on his restoration of the caliphate, and was invested as an initiate by al-Ḥākim's predecessor, the Caliph al-Mustanṣir. Al-Ḥākim himself was now somewhat hastily invested, so that he in turn could initiate Berke's ambassadors. Shortly afterwards they started back, accompanied by an embassy from Baybars, the members of which were of superior standing to his earlier envoys. The military member was the experienced Fāris al-Dīn Akkush al-Masʿūdī, while the civilian was no ordinary jurist but a kinsman of the caliph who had come to Cairo with Kay-Kāvūs's ambassadors.

On the way to the Golden Horde, the ambassadors encountered an unexpected delay, being detained in Byzantine territory by order of

Michael VIII. The emperor found himself in a delicate situation, since their arrival had coincided with an embassy from Hülegü, with whom he was negotiating a reinsurance treay. When the delay became known, Baybars denounced the emperor, and procured his excommunication by the Egyptian clergy, while Berke sent an army into Byzantine territory. On its withdrawal (possibly through the mediation of Akkush), the ambassador was allowed to continue his journey alone – his eminent colleague had earlier returned to Egypt. Akkush, however, found no welcome at Berke's court. Kay-Kāvūs, who had lost Michael's support when the emperor reached an agreement with the *ilkhan*, was now a refugee with Berke, and intrigued against Akkush. The gifts of rare animals and other treasures which Baybars had sent with the embassy had been lost or spoilt during the long delay on the journey. Akkush had a sour reception from Berke, and was disgraced by Baybars when he got back to Egypt in Jumādā II 665/March 1267.

By this time Berke was dead, and his successor, Möngke Temür, was not a Muslim. Nevertheless in spite of occasional tension, military, political and commercial interests continued to link the Mamluk sultanate with the Byzantine empire and the Golden Horde. Shortly before his death, Berke sent an embassy which was detained on the way by Michael VIII. Baybars reacted vigorously; the emperor responded with a sworn undertaking, and sent the embassy on. It reached Egypt in 667/1268–9, and returned with letters urging Möngke Temür to continue his predecessor's hostile policy towards the ilkhanate. The emperor, as before, was anxious to be on good terms with the sultan and with the rival Mongol rulers. He explained that he had held the embassy because of Berke's death and Möngke Temür's accession – presumably to see how matters developed in the Golden Horde. He asked for the continuation of peaceful relations with the sultan, and for inclusion in any treaty that Baybars might conclude with Abaqa, who had succeeded Hülegü as *ilkhan* in 663/1265. While accepting his overtures, Baybars informed Michael that he had no intention of making peace with Abaqa. The emperor had more success in securing peace with the Mongols through marriage alliances: one of his natural daughters was married to Abaqa, another to Nogay, the leading general of the Golden Horde and a kinsman of the khan.

On at least two occasions the emperor had sent Baybars a sworn undertaking as a means of maintaining good relations. Although the texts of these have not survived, a later undertaking with its counterpart sworn by the sultan is extant from the reign of Kalavun. After Kalavun had usurped the throne from the sons of Baybars in 678/1279, he found himself threatened by both internal and external enemies. Sungur al-

Ashqar in Damascus declared himself sultan, the Mongols of the ilkhanate were a continuing danger, while a more distant enemy, Charles of Anjou, was building up his power in the central and eastern Mediterranean, and claimed the Latin kingdom. In these circumstances Kalavun sent an embassy in Rabīʿ I 678/July 1280 to the Emperor Michael, who was also threatened by the ambitions of Charles of Anjou. Like Baybars's first embassy to Michael, it consisted of an amir and a Christian cleric – on this occasion the patriarch of Alexandria.

Michael was thus able to state his terms, which he did in an instrument sworn before Kalavun's ambassadors. He proposed a mutual undertaking to abstain from hostilities and a mutual guarantee of security for merchants. The sultan's ambassadors (sc. to the Golden Horde) were promised freedom of passage, as were merchants bringing out *mamlūks* and slave-girls. Other clauses safeguarded the emperor's special interests. Traffic in Christian *mamlūks* might be intercepted. The sultan was asked to allow emancipated Christian *mamlūks* to return to Byzantine territory, and to permit the redemption of Christian *mamlūks* by the emperor's subjects. The emperor also sought permission to buy horses in the Sultan's dominions. The instrument was sworn on 8 May 1281, and sent to Kalavun for acceptance at his discretion. The ambassadors reached Cairo on 30 Muḥarram 680/21 May 1281. The terms they brought from Constantinople had taken a long time in negotiation, and before Kalavun swore to a much amended counterpart to Michael's undertaking the situation changed to his advantage. A Mongol invasion of Syria was decisively defeated at the second battle of Ḥimṣ, to which Sungur al-Ashqar brought his forces in support of Kalavun (see above, p. 102). As the sultan was returning through Palestine after his victory, he was met by the envoys of Charles of Anjou, who wished to enter into negotiations.

The sultan was therefore able to reply to Michael from a position of strength. His reciprocal undertaking was sworn on 1 Ramaḍān 680/14 December 1281. The mutual abstention from hostilities and most of the other arrangements proposed by the emperor were confirmed, but notably absent from the sultan's undertaking was any reference to the traffic in Christian *mamlūks* or their redemption; nor was anything included about the purchase of horses by the Byzantines. Kalavun was clearly resolved to deny to Michael any standing in connection with the recruitment of *mamlūks* or any claim to be the protector of Christians under the sultan's jurisdiction. His reservation of the stock of horses for his own military needs is fully comprehensible. Nevertheless the agreement gave the emperor an unusual status since it was not a truce for a specified period embodied in a single instrument, as were the treaties with the Frankish states, but an exchange of sworn undertakings to maintain love and friendship (in the words of the documents) without limit of time. It is an irony of history that this status should be accorded to a Byzantine emperor, the successor of Heraclius, the most ancient Christian opponent of Islam.

Besides the political treaties concluded with the Frankish states and neighbouring Christian powers, the Muslim rulers of Egypt and Syria also made numerous commercial treaties with the maritime states of the West, especially the Italian republics and Aragon. In this respect, historical developments in Syria were at first somewhat different from those in Egypt. The contribution which the naval forces of the Italians had made to the establishment of the Frankish states had been rewarded by concessions of territory and privileges in the ports of the Levant. The Italian merchants thereby obtained secure bases in the Syro-Palestinian coastlands for the maintenance of their commerce. There is little evidence that they felt any need to assure it further by treaties with the Muslim rulers of the interior. Egypt, on the other hand, was never conquered by the Crusaders, and the colonies of Western merchants there were glad to secure their position by negotiation: there were, for example, close diplomatic relations between Pisa and Egypt in the late Fatimid period.

After Saladin's Holy War and the counter-offensive of the Third Crusade had spent themselves, relations between Franks and Muslims returned to the state of generally unfriendly coexistence which had characterized much of the previous century. But now both Egypt and Muslim Syria were dominated by the Ayyubids, the Frankish states were reduced to a narrow and interrupted strip of coastland, and the Western merchants became suppliants at the courts of the rulers of the hinterland. The Venetians, for example, negotiated a series of commercial treaties with the Ayyubids of Aleppo, who had become masters of much of the former territory of the principality of Antioch. The first of these was concluded with Saladin's son, al-Ẓāhir Ghāzī, in 604/1207–8; two were made with al-ʿAzīz Muḥammad in 1225 and 627/1229; and one with the last of the line, al-Nāṣir Yūsuf, in 1254.

In the same period, the Venetians were negotiating with the sultans of Egypt. An embassy to Saladin's brother, al-ʿĀdil Sayf al-Dīn, obtained a grant of privileges in 1208. In 636/1238 another embassy carried a letter from the doge which specified under thirty-two heads (*capitula* – whence the later term "capitulations" for Western treaties with the Ottomans) the requests of the merchants. The reigning sultan, al-ʿĀdil Abū Bakr, signified his assent, and the Venetian petition, thus transformed into a royal decree, was circulated to his officers and officials. Apart from giving a general guarantee of security to the persons, vessels and chattels of the Venetians, safeguarding them from new and extortionate dues, and enabling them to trade freely, the decree placed the two Venetian trading-factories under the jurisdiction of their own wardens, permitted the maintenance of a chapel and bath-house, and allowed the importation of wine for the merchants. Any dispute between a Venetian and another Christian was to be brought before the Venetian consul; any with a Muslim (*cum Saraceno*) was to be heard by the local (i.e. the *Sharīʿa*) court. No Venetian was to be taken as hostage if a Muslim merchant were captured by a corsair, nor was any to be arrested because of another's debt. The document shows in detail the conditions in which medieval Europeans lived and traded, not only in Egypt but generally in the eastern Mediterranean lands.

The establishment of the centralized Mamluk sultanate in Egypt and Syria in place of the constellation of Ayyubid principalities made no essential change in the position of European merchants in these lands. In 652/1254 (i.e. before the incorporation of Syria in the Mamluk sultanate), the Sultan al-Muʿizz Aybeg granted concessions to the Venetians which were very similar to those of al-ʿĀdil Abū Bakr sixteen years before, although somewhat more detailed. However, the substitution of the aggressive and militant Mamluks for the Ayyubids, the renewed threat to the remnants of the Frankish states, and the persisting Muslim fear of a crusade brought political as well as commercial considerations into view in negotiations later in the seventh/thirteenth century.

This appears in the developments which resulted in a treaty concluded between Kalavun and Genoa. When the sultan took Tripoli in Rabīʿ II 688/April 1289, the Genoese admiral, Benito Zaccaria, who had played a leading part in the last phase of the city's history, turned corsair and took an Alexandrian ship. On hearing of this the Genoese merchants in Egypt tried to flee but some of them were detained by the sultan. The authorities in Genoa forthwith disavowed Zaccaria, set free the captives he had taken, and sent an embassy to Egypt to negotiate a truce. The ambassador, Alberto Spinola, was made to await the sultan's pleasure, but Kalavun was well aware of the important contribution that the custom dues of Alexandria made to his revenue, and in Jumādā I 689/May 1290 the truce was concluded.

The surviving records are unique in two respects: first, both an Arabic and a Latin text of the truce are extant; secondly, the Arabic text is accompanied by four other documents which throw light on the procedure followed. It is, however, very noticeable that the Latin and Arabic texts are not in any strict sense counterparts. The Arabic text is essentially a sworn undertaking by Alberto Spinola on behalf of the

Genoese authorities, by which an assurance of security and protection is given to all Muslim travellers, the circumstances being very fully particularized. In form, therefore, this instrument resembles the sworn undertakings of the Emperor Michael VIII. It is supported by the text of the oath sworn by Spinola, the attestation of the oath by the Melkite bishop of Cairo who administered it, the attestation of Egyptian and Genoese witnesses, and the certification of the instrument by the bishop. The Latin text, on the other hand, is in the standard form of a truce negotiated bilaterally. The body of the instrument lists in detail the privileges of the Genoese merchants, which were very similar to those granted to the Venetians by Aybeg. Four appended clauses summarize the terms of Spinola's sworn undertaking.

The combination of political and commercial interests is evident in the dealings of the kingdom of Aragon with the Mamluk sultanate. The great trading-centre of the kingdom was the port of Barcelona in Catalonia – indeed the king is called by Arabic writers *al-Barshanūnī*, "the Barcelonan". Its prosperity increased with the growing initiative shown by Catalan merchants in the reign of King James I (1213–76), whose son and successor, Peter III (1276–85) married Constance of Hohenstaufen, the daughter of King Manfred of Sicily and granddaughter of the Emperor Frederick II. Manfred had been defeated and killed in 1266 by Charles of Anjou, who took his island kingdom. When in March 1282 Charles's supporters in Sicily were annihilated in the revolt known as the Sicilian Vespers, King Peter occupied and ruled the island in right of his wife. On his death, his eldest son, Alfonso III, succeeded him in Aragon, and his second son, James, in Sicily.

Alfonso entered upon negotiations with Kalavun, sending with his ambassadors seventy Muslim captives. The embassy included a Jewish physician, who possibly served as dragoman. A treaty was concluded in Rabīʿ II 689/April 1290, about three weeks before the treaty with Genoa. It is noteworthy that the ambassadors cited as a precedent the truce between the Ayyubid al-Kāmil and Alfonso's ancestor, the Emperor Frederick.

The terms agreed upon fall into three categories. First, in common with other treaties of the period, are the clauses in which the two rulers mutually guarantee the security of each other's territories – Kalavun's guarantee covering not only the kingdom of Aragon but also Sicily and the other possessions of Alfonso's family. Secondly, there is a group of clauses concerning merchants and other wayfarers, to which there are parallels in the various commercial treaties. Three of these call for special notice. One ensures the safety of the sultan's ambassadors and their retinue when crossing the king of Aragon's territory or if cast upon his coast. Another promises free access to Jerusalem for pilgrims bearing a passport sealed by the king. A third places commercial dealings in the sultan's dominions under the jurisdiction of the *Sharīʿa* courts. So far the provisions of the treaty have, except in detail, gone little beyond the content of other diplomatic instruments but the clauses in the third group are startling. The king and his brothers bind themselves in alliance with the sultan, undertaking to support him by land and sea in the event of any offensive against him by the pope, any Frankish ruler, Genoa, Venice, the Byzantines or the knightly orders. No assistance will be given to the Frankish states in the Levant if they commence hostilities against the sultan. The king will warn the sultan of any impending attack by the Christian rulers or the Mongols. Finally, the king will allow the export of metals and timber to Muslim ports. This clause must have seemed particularly scandalous to contemporaries, since the sale of war material to the Saracens had long been condemned by the Church, and as recently as 1274 King James I had forbidden the trade to his subjects in Barcelona. The other provisions in this group may have been intended by Kalavun to secure himself against European intervention during the final operations against the Latin kingdom, which he was contemplating after the capture of Tripoli.

Kalavun died a few months after the conclusion of this treaty, and Alfonso in the following year. His brother, the king of Sicily, succeeded him as James II of Aragon. Although the duration of the treaty of 689/1290 was not limited, and indeed it specifically provided that it should not be abrogated by the death of either party, a new agreement was negotiated by James II with Kalavun's successor, al-Ashraf Khalīl. This was virtually identical with the earlier treaty, including the military clauses. The friendly relations thus established continued into the third reign of al-Nāṣir Muḥammad: there are records of eight embassies sent from Aragon to Egypt between 699/1300 and 730/1330.

By the eighth/fourteenth century, the ideas of crusade and *jihād* played little part in the international relations of the Christians and Muslim states around the Mediterranean. The Mamluk sultanate, the Islamic great power in the region, maintained active commercial and diplomatic dealings with other rulers and states from Christian Aragon in the west to the still half-heathen Golden Horde in the east. The diplomatic procedures and usages of this period were in time to be inherited and developed by the Ottoman empire – in this as in some other respects the successor of the Mamluk sultanate.

CHAPTER NINETEEN

The Seljuk Sultanate of Rūm and its Successors

In some important respects the historical development of Anatolia between the fifth/eleventh century and the eighth/fourteenth century differed from that of the western Fertile Crescent and Egypt. The latter were old Islamic territories, originally conquered by the Arabs, and in them Arabic was the general mother-tongue and the language of learning and government. The coming of the Turks to these lands as Seljuk overlords, Mamluk warriors or nomadic herdsmen did not affect their fundamentally Arab culture. The case of Anatolia was very much different. To the Arabs it was *bilād al-Rūm*, "the land of the Romans" i.e. the Byzantine Greeks, who ruled what remained of the Eastern Roman empire. In the first century of Islam, the Arabs had twice unsuccessfully besieged Constantinople, and thereafter the conquest of the city was foreseen as an event of the Last Days. Warfare between Muslims and Byzantines was for the most part restricted to raids and campaigns in the march-lands between northern Syria and Anatolia. The transformation of *bilād al-Rūm* into Muslim Turkey (*Turchia*, as the peninsula came to be called by medieval Western writers) was a process in which the Arabs played no part, and the newly settled territories drew at first on the Persian Islamic culture of the Seljukid heartlands.

The history of Anatolia in this period from the beginning of the decline of Byzantine rule to the rise of the Ottomans is punctuated by three decisive battles of Manzikert (463/1071), Myriokephalon (572/1176) and Köse Dagh (641/1243) respectively. Each of them inaugurated a new stage in the transformation. Not long before the coming of the Turks, the Byzantines in the second half of the fourth/ninth century had been strong enough to take the offensive against their Muslim neighbours. Antioch was recaptured after over three centuries of Muslim rule in 358/969, and in 364/975 the Emperor John I Tzimisces invaded Syria, apparently with the intention of reconquering Jerusalem.

This he did not achieve, but his advance to Mount Tabor and return through the coastlands to Antioch, while achieving no permanent conquests, anticipated in a way the exploits of the First Crusade rather over 100 years later.

The force which was in the end to overthrow Byzantine rule in Anatolia manifested itself in the fifth/eleventh century as the Turcoman tribesmen led by the house of Seljuk migrated into the western provinces of Muslim Asia. From Azerbaijan they raided into Anatolia – not without encouragement from the Seljukid rulers, whose chieftaincy of a Turkish tribal confederation was becoming transformed into a settled Islamic sultanate (see above, pp. 10–11). Raids led to territorial conquests, but Byzantine military strength rendered these both precarious and temporary with the Turks returning to their safe bases in the east. The turning-point came with the first of the three great battles, that of Manzikert near Lake Van on the Muslim–Byzantine frontier. This encounter in Dhu'l-Qa'da 463/August 1071 did not result from Byzantine operations against the tribesmen but was a conflict between the field armies of the Emperor Romanus IV Diogenes and the Great Seljuk Sultan Alp-Arslan, who had broken off a campaign against Fatimid Egypt in order to secure his northern marches. The defeat and capture of the emperor followed by the breakdown of the settlement which Alp-Arslan had made with him (having no apparent desire to push further into *bilād al-Rūm*) resulted in the collapse of the Byzantine military frontier in the east.

Anatolia thus lay open to Turkish invasion and settlement. The invaders were of two kinds: nomadic Turcoman tribesmen seeking pasture for their flocks and herds, and march-warriors of a type which had long been familiar on the frontiers of Islam. These were the *gazis* (Arabic sing., *ghāzī*), the warriors for the Faith, bands of soldiers of fortune, who lived on the booty acquired in their raids on infidel territory. Their companies formed an intractable frontier society, distinct from the settled and orthodox Muslim population of the towns in the hinterland, which formed the channels by which the Perso-Arabic culture of western Asia was transmitted to Anatolia. In the march-territories, the *gazis* confronted their Byzantine counterparts, the *akritai*, themselves often Turkish mercenaries. The interrelationship of *gazis, akritai* and the local rural population, developed over many years in the marches, prepared the way for the absorption of these frontier regions into an Islamic world which was not wholly alien.

The Turcoman tribesmen and *gazi* war-bands flooded into the newly opened lands, and were little amenable to control by either the Great Seljuk sultan or the Byzantine emperor. Within a few years, however, a Seljukid prince, a kinsman of Malik-Shāh, had established his ascendancy over many of the Turks in Anatolia. This was a certain Süleymān, whose father, Kutlumush, had disputed the succession to the Great Seljuk sultanate with Alp-Arslan, and had lost his life in consequence. Exploiting factional struggles among the Byzantines and the support he received from the Turcomans, Süleymān carved out for himself an extensive kingdom in Anatolia. He acquired, however informally, the title of "sultan", and from his establishment of his capital at Iznik (Nicaea) in the far north-west of the peninsula may be dated the inception of the Seljuk sultanate of Rūm. With Byzantine power virtually extinct in Anatolia, Süleymān began to extend his dominions eastwards in the direction of the heartlands of the Great Seljuk sultanate. In 486/1073 he conquered Cilicia from an Armenian warlord, and in 477/1084 Antioch opened its gates to him, thus ending something over a century of Christian rule. This push to the east led to a clash with Tutush, who held Syria in appanage from his brother Malik-Shāh, and Süleymān was defeated and killed in 479/1086. Much of his newly acquired territory in Syria and the march-lands was lost to the Great Seljuks, and his son Kılıj-Arslan was sent to Malik-Shāh as a hostage. He returned to Iznik after Malik-Shāh's death in 485/1092, and began to restore the sultanate of Rūm after an interregnum.

In the meantime another Turkish power was coming to the fore in Anatolia. This was a *gazi* state founded by a certain Dānishmend – a Persian term signifying a learned man, not a personal name. His origin and deeds have been much obscured by later legend, and it is not even clear whether the early exploits of the family should be ascribed to him or to his son Gümüshtigin. Their territory was in the north and centre of Anatolia, while that of the Seljukids lay in the south and west. Although the rise of the Danishmendids coincided with that of the sultanate of Rūm, the two polities were essentially different. The Danishmendids were first and last heads of a *gazi* state, while the Seljukids quickly established an Islamic monarchy on the pattern of the Great Seljukid sultanate. The two dynasties were bound to be competitors and rivals for the hegemony in Rūm (where in the long term the advantage lay with the Seljukids), but they co-operated against the unexpected danger from the First Crusade at the battles of Dorylaeum and Heraclea in 490/1097. In these engagements the Turkish rulers were defeated, but in 493/1100 Gümüshtigin (or Dānishmend himself) captured Prince Bohemond of Antioch, and in alliance with Kılıj-Arslan he defeated two other crusading forces as they advanced across Anatolia in the summer of 494/1100.

With the restoration of Byzantine rule in Nicaea and the coastlands of western Anatolia, Kılıj-Arslan was pushed back into the interior, and transferred his capital to Konya (Iconium). Having made peace with the Emperor Alexius Comnenus, he turned towards the east, defeated the Danishmendid ruler, and established his suzerainty over eastern Anatolia. As with his father before him, this expansionist policy resulted in a clash with the Great Seljuks, and in 500/1107 he was defeated and killed in a battle on the Khābūr river, a tributary of the Euphrates in northern Mesopotamia. Another period of weakness ensued, during which the Byzantines strengthened their hold over the coastlands, and the Danishmendids theirs over the interior of Rūm. Kılıj-Arslan's eldest son, Shāhānshāh, ruled somewhat ineffectively from 504/1110 to 510/1116, when he was overthrown and succeeded by his brother Masʿūd, probably with Danishmendid support.

The Danishmendids were now the greatest power in Anatolia, and the Seljuk sultanate, reduced to the territory around Konya, was in effect their protectorate. The situation changed, however, with the death of the Danishmendid ruler (probably Gümüshtigin) in 529/1134, followed by that of his successor in 536/1142, and the break-up of the state. In these circumstances Sultan Masʿūd gained the ascendancy over the Danishmendids. During his reign the capture of Edessa by Zangī in 539/1144 led to the organization of the Second Crusade, and the arrival of the crusaders produced an agreement between the sultan and the Emperor Manuel Comnenus, the grandson of Alexius. The Turks attacked both the German contingent under Conrad III near Dorylaeum and the French under Louis VII on the River Menderes (Maeander) in 542/1147–8. From the point of view of the Muslim rulers in both Anatolia and Syria, the Crusade was a transient annoyance which achieved nothing (see above, pp. 43–4).

Towards the end of his reign, Masʿūd had completely restored the power of the Seljuk sultanate in Anatolia. The divided and quarrelsome Danishmendids were no longer serious rivals. The Byzantines were potentially a danger but matters here had not yet come to a head. Like his father and grandfather, Masʿūd had ambitions of expansion to the east, but here the situation had changed in the forty years since the battle on the Khābūr. The Great Seljuk sultanate had largely broken up into congeries of successor-states ruled by the *atabegs* (see above, p. 69). The *Atabeg* Zangī, lord of Mosul and Aleppo, and conqueror of Edessa, had become the sultan of Rūm's eastern neighbour, and on his death in 541/1146 he was succeeded in his Syrian possessions by Nūr al-Dīn, his equally vigorous son. Relations between the two rulers were tense, even hostile, and at this point the histories of Muslim Syria and Muslim Anatolia begin to be closely intertwined.

When Masʿūd died in 551/1155, he was succeeded by his son Kılıj-Arslan II, whose forceful action against the Danishmendids and his own malcontent brother resulted in their seeking aid from Nūr al-Dīn. In 568/1173 the Syrian ruler led a great army northwards, and captured Sivas (formerly a Danishmendid capital) and the important frontier fortress of Marʿash. But neither party was anxious to continue the struggle. Nūr al-Dīn in particular was at the end of a long line of communications in strange and difficult country, and he was anxious about Egypt, where Saladin was showing an inclination to independence (see above, pp. 51–2). In the circumstances an agreement was reached which did no substantial damage to Kılıj-Arslan's position.

The settlement with Nūr al-Dīn was followed by war on the sultan's western front. The Emperor Manuel Comnenus's growing mistrust of Kılıj-Arslan caused him to lead an expedition into the heart of the sultanate with the intention of taking Konya. While advancing towards the Seljukid capital, his army was ambushed and destroyed at the battle of Myriokephalon (Rabīʿ I 572/September 1176). It was as decisive a battle as Manzikert, just over 100 years before. Although Kılıj-Arslan granted lenient terms to Manuel, this was a turning-point after which there was no longer any possibility of a Byzantine reconquest of the lost Anatolian territories.

Saladin, like Nūr al-Dīn before him, presented Kılıj-Arslan with an acute problem as his power increased in the marches of northern Syria. In 574/1179 the Seljukid sultan attempted to regain Raʿbān, which Saladin's agents had occupied, but his forces were routed, and henceforward Saladin was able to take the offensive. In these borderlands the Artukid lordship of Ḥiṣn Kayfā was important as a buffer-state. A matrimonial question arising from the marriage of Nūr al-Dīn Muḥammad to a daughter of Kılıj-Arslan was the pretext for a diplomatic struggle between the two rulers to assert suzerainty over the principality. This ended with their meeting on the Gök Su (see above, p. 55), and again Saladin was successful (576/1180). The Third Crusade enabled Saladin to present himself as the champion of Islam in the Holy War in contrast to Kılıj-Arslan, who for years previously had been on good terms with the Emperor Frederick Barbarossa. Although Kılıj-Arslan sent letters to Saladin asking for help (586/1190), he would have been willing enough to allow the German Crusaders to pass through Rūm on their way to the Holy Land. But he was now virtually powerless, since in 582/1186 he had effectively abdicated by dividing his realm among his nine sons, his brother and his nephews. Conflicts arose between the Crusaders and the Turcomans and also Kılıj-Arslan's eldest son in Konya. The old sultan succeeded in patching up an agreement, and Frederick went on to Cilicia, where he met his death by drowning.

Kılıj-Arslan's partition of the sultanate, an act reminiscent of old Seljukid practice, had unfortunate results. Two years after it had taken place, his heirs began to quarrel among themselves. This period of weakness lasted until 593/1196, during which time the old sultan died (588/1192). The ultimate victor among the competing princes was Süleymān II, who took Konya in 593/1196. When he died in 600/1204, he was succeeded by his brother, Kay-Khusraw I, who had already reigned briefly during the preceding time of troubles. Under him and his two sons, Kay-Kāvūs I (608–16/1211–20) and Kay-Qubād I (616–34/1220–37), the Seljuk sultanate of Rūm attained its zenith of power and prosperity. In a period of increasing trade, Kay-Khusraw conquered the port of Antalya (Attaleia) on the southern coast of Anatolia in 603/1207, and Kay-Kāvūs the Black Sea port of Sinop (Sinope) in 611/1214. Sinop was strongly fortified as the base for the sultan's Black Sea fleet. Its counterpart on the Mediterranean was created by Kay-Qubād, who captured the maritime fortress of Kalonoros (617/1220–1), and renamed it 'Alā'iyye (now Alanya) from his own honorific of 'Alā' al-Dīn.

The capture of Constantinople by the Fourth Crusade and the establishment of the Latin empire (1204) paradoxically strengthened the Byzantines against the Seljukids. A Byzantine empire in exile was set up in the north-west of Anatolia with its capital at Nicaea, and Byzantine resources were concentrated in this region. The first emperor of Nicaea, Theodore Lascaris (1204–22), clashed with Kay-Khusraw, who was killed in battle on the Menderes. Otherwise the conflict had no significant outcome, and relations between the two powers were generally friendly. Another fragment of the Byzantine empire survived on the Anatolian coast of the Black Sea, the empire of Trebizond, under the descendants of the Emperor Alexius Comnenus, who styled themselves the Grand Comneni. It was from the empires of Nicaea and Trebizond respectively that the sultans took Antalya and Sinop.

In the seventh/thirteenth century, the descendants of Kılıj-Arslan II were to be threatened (like other rulers in western Asia) by a new danger from the east – the Mongols (see above, pp. 87–8). The Mongol pressure was at first felt as it were at one remove in 618/1220. In that year the Mongols conquered the realm of the Khwārazm-Shāhs, a successor-state to the Great Seljuks. The last Khwārazm-Shāh, Jalāl al-Dīn, passed his life as a fugitive before the Mongols. His career brought him to the eastern Anatolian marches, where in 627/1230 he captured the fortress-city of Akhlāṭ (Khilāṭ). The danger he represented was clear alike to Kay-Qubād I and to the Ayyubids. The Seljukid sultan hastily made an alliance with al-Ashraf Mūsā of Damascus, and together they inflicted a decisive defeat on Jalāl al-Dīn at Yasıchemen near Erzinjan (627/1230). Jalāl al-Dīn himself died a year later but his armed followers, known as the Khwarazmians, become masterless soldiers of fortune, remained for some time a turbulent element in the politics of the Near East (see above, pp. 65–6).

The devastating passage of Jalāl al-Dīn and the Khwarazmians served as a kind of prologue to the overwhelming advent of the Mongols themselves. Their approach set off a new immigration of Turcomans into Anatolia. The immigrants were not easy to control or to assimilate, and a messianic leader known as Baba Isḥāq or Baba Resūl headed a revolt against Kay-Qubād's successor, Kay-Khusraw II (634–44/1237–46), which was suppressed by force of arms in 638/1240. Three years later, the sultanate was invaded by a Mongol army under Bayju Noyan, the general of Batu, Chingiz Khan's grandson. The Seljukid forces gathered at Sivas, only to be routed at Köse Dagh in Muḥarram 641/June 1243. The sultan fled, while the Mongols advanced and sacked Kayseri. Henceforward the Seljuk sultanate of Rūm was a Mongol protectorate.

During the first phase of Mongol suzerainty, the leading roles on the Turkish side were played, not by the sultans but by a series of powerful ministers, who succeeded for over thirty years in preserving a measure of autonomy. The first of these was Kay-Khusraw's *vezīr*, Muhadhdhab al-Dīn, who personally undertook a mission to the Mongols when his master fled from the stricken field of Köse Dagh. This was followed by a formal embassy to Batu himself, from whom Kay-Khusraw received recognition as the vassal ruler of Rūm. The sultan died in 644/1246, two years after his *vezīr*, leaving three young sons by different mothers. Factional rivalry developed among the Turkish magnates in support of one or other of these princes, and a broad division appeared between those who sought to secure themselves by total submission to the Mongols, and those who tried to maintain some independence. The former group centred around the late sultan's second son, Rukn al-Dīn Kılıj-Arslan, and its principal figure was Muhadhdhab al-Dīn's son, Muʿīn al-Dīn Süleymān. The head (or figurehead of the latter group) was the eldest of the three princes, ʿIzz al-Dīn Kay-Kāvūs. His mother was a Greek woman, and he had as *atabeg* (following the old Seljukid practice) a Greek freedman named Karatay. It was to their Byzantine neighbours, first in Nicaea, then in Constantinople (after the restoration of the empire in 1261) that this group turned for help.

The following years were a time of instability as various arrangements were made to accommodate the ambitions of the princes and their partisans. At first the party of ʿIzz al-Dīn Kay-Kāvūs predominated, overcame a revolt of their opponents, and made an alliance with Nicaea. About this time Karatay died. In the meantime, a new Mongol push to the west had begun under Hülegü, to whom the control of Anatolia now passed. He required the territory for pasture for the Mongol herds and as a place of settlement for the tribesmen. The result was a resistance movement led by ʿIzz al-Dīn's supporters, and aided by Turcomans and by Christians from Nicaea. In a battle near Akseray in central Anatolia, Bayju won a second victory in 654/1256, and ʿIzz al-Dīn fled to Greek territory.

Muʿīn al-Dīn Süleymān now emerged as the leading Turkish statesman. Already viewed with favour by Bayju, he was appointed to the great offices under the sultanate of *ḥājib* and *pervāne*, by which latter title he is generally known. A settlement made in 655/1257 partitioned the sultanate between Kay-Kāvūs in the west and Kılıj-Arslan in the east, but this proved to be only a transient arrangement. Kay-Kāvūs fell foul of the Mongols, who were defeated in 658/1260 by the Mamluks of Egypt at the battle of ʿAyn Jālūt. As a doubtful vassal, he had to be eliminated, and he fled to the Emperor Michael VIII in Constantinople (659/1261). Rukn al-Dīn Kılıj-Arslan IV was now nominally ruler of the undivided sultanate, and its affairs were in the capable hands of the *Pervāne*. The fugitive ʿIzz al-Dīn opened negotiations with al-Ẓāhir Baybars, now sultan of Egypt, and an embassy which he sent to Cairo in 660/1262 placed half of his lost territories at Baybar's disposal, and empowered him to grant *iqṭāʿs* in Rūm to whomsoever he would. Another embassy in the following year announced that ʿIzz al-Dīn's enemies had fled, and that he was sending troops to besiege Konya. These unreal exercises in propaganda came to nothing (see above, pp. 96–7). ʿIzz al-Dīn was imprisoned by Michael VIII, and ultimately died in exile in the Crimea.

For seventeen years the *Pervāne* ruled the sultanate of Rūm. Until nearly the end of his career, he enjoyed the confidence of his Mongol overlords, the *Ilkhans* Hülegü and Abaqa. With their backing his authority was supreme. In 663/1265 he even disposed of his nominal sovereign, the sultan, whom he suspected of plotting against him, and installed Kılıj-Arslan's infant son, Kay-Khusraw III, as the puppet ruler. As time went on, however, he established contact with Baybars, the only ruler in the region who showed himself an equal in military capacity to the *ilkhans*. Communication began in 670/1272, and in the following years tension developed between the *Pervāne* and Ajay, Abaqa's brother and deputy in Anatolia. A conspiracy by some of the *Pervāne*'s associates came to a head prematurely, but in the next year (675/1277) Baybars led an expedition to Anatolia, defeated a Mongol army at Elbistan, and was enthroned as sultan of Rūm at Kayseri (Dhu'l-Qaʿda 675/April 1277). But the Turks did not rally to his support, the *Pervāne* wrote but did not arrive in person, and Abaqa was organizing another army. Baybars accordingly withdrew from Anatolia, and Abaqa arrived at Kayseri. In Rabīʿ I 676/August 1277 the *Pervāne* was put to death (see above, p. 97).

Thereafter Anatolia was directly administered by the Mongols. The sultanate of Rūm continued in name for about another thirty years, and then it faded out of history. A series of Mongol war-lords dominated the region. One of these was Sülemish, the grandson of Bayju Noyan. He revolted against the *Ilkhan* Ghazan in 698/1299, and was defeated at Akshehir, near Sivas. He fled to Syria, where he was welcomed, and provided with Mamluk reinforcements. On attempting to return to Anatolia, he was captured and put to death. Another notable Mongol rebel was Temür-Tash, whose father, Choban, was the all-powerful military chief in the reign of the *Ilkhan* Abū Saʿīd (717–36/1317–35). Temür-Tash, the viceroy of Rūm, proclaimed his independence in 722/1322. Çhoban went in person to recall his son to obedience, and Temür-Tash was pardoned and allowed to continue in office. In 721/1327, however, Abū Saʿīd decided to rid himself of the over-mighty Choban, who was put to death. Temür-Tash thereupon fled to Cairo, where he was received by al-Nāṣir Muḥammad. His death there in 728/1328 conveniently removed an obstacle to good relations between the Mamluk sultan and the *ilkhan*. The death of Abū Saʿīd was shortly followed by the fragmentation of the ilkhanate.

The passing of the sultanate of Rūm and the subsequent weakening of the *ilkhans'* hold over their Anatolian possessions, as shown by the revolts of Sülemish and Temür-Tash, were accompanied by a renewal of *gazi* warfare on the Byzantine frontier and the emergence of independent Turkish principalities throughout the peninsula. The early history of several of these is obscure, and not all of them will be mentioned here. The numbers and militancy of the *gazis* and Turcoman nomads had been increased by the arrival of fugitives as the Khwarazmians and Mongols moved westwards. The *gazis'* principal field of activity was in western Anatolia. There they steadily eroded the Byzantine provinces, which were neglected by the imperial government after the recapture of Constantinople in 1261. A chain of marcher-principalities was brought into being by *gazi* war-lords, who gave their names to the conquered territories. First of these was the principality (Turkish, *beylik*) of Menteshe in the south-west, which unusually was not conquered by land-warriors but by sea-pirates taking advantage of the dismantling of the Byzantine fleet in 1284. Its northern neighbour was Aydın, with whose *gazis* the sea-raiders from Menteshe joined forces. Still further north were Saruhan and Karası. To the east of Karası, the Ottoman *beylik*, which took its name from the war-lord ʿOsmān Gazi, was at first of minor importance.

To the east of this group were two other *beyliks* which had an earlier and different origin. Karaman, the founder of the first, was the leader of a war-band which seems to have been connected with the faction that supported ʿIzz al-Dīn Kay-Kāvūs against Rukn al-Dīn Kılıj-Arslan and the Mongols. The original capital of the principality was Larende in the western Taurus, a situation which enabled the Karamanids to fight as *gazis* against Lesser Armenia. After various attempts, the Karamanids finally captured the former Seljukid capital of Konya in 714/1314, and they increasingly represented themselves as the heirs of the sultans of Rūm. Later in the century, Karaman clashed with the rising power of the Ottomans, and the principality was annexed by Sultan Bāyezīd I in 800/1397. The second of the eastern principalities, Germiyan, developed from a group, probably of mixed Kurdish and Turkish origin, representing the pro-Mongol faction associated with Rukn al-Dīn. Their capital was at Kütahya, and as the Seljukid sultanate declined, Germiyan became an independent state. It was unlike its neighbours in that it did not bear the name of its founder, nor did it originate in a *gazi* war-band. It was, however, a nursery of *gazis*, three of whom, starting as vassals of Germiyan, founded the *beyliks* of Aydın, Saruhan and Karası, mentioned earlier.

Another principality, which was to play a part of some importance in later history, arose on the upper Euphrates. This was founded by the Turcoman dynasty of Dulkadır (arabicized as Dhu'l-Qadr) in the first half of the eighth/fourteenth century as the power of the ilkhanate crumbled. The capital was Elbistan, where Baybars had defeated the Mongols in the previous century. Lying as it did on the northern marches of Syria, the principality lay within the sphere of influence of the Mamluk sultanate, indeed the founder of the dynasty received formal recognition from al-Nāṣir Muḥammad as governor of Elbistan. In the following century, as will appear, Dulkadır was a buffer-state between the Mamluks and the Ottomans, who had become the dominant power in Anatolia.

A second Turcoman successor-state to the western region of the ilkhanate was established in north-eastern Anatolia by Eretna, a follower of Temür-Tash, who succeeded his master as the *ilkhan*'s representative in Rūm. After Abū Saʿīd's death, Eretna turned for support to the more effective power of al-Nāṣir Muḥammad. Since his dominions lay far beyond the marches of Syria, he remained independent, and assumed the title of sultan. His capital was first at Sivas, then at Kayseri. After his death in 753/1352, his successors were unable to control the powerful beys who were nominally their vassals, and in 781/1381–2 the sultanate was usurped by a judge named Burhān al-Dīn, who had been the *vezīr* He ruled vigorously for about eighteen years until he met a violent end in conflict with the rising Turcoman tribal confederacy of the Ak-Koyunlu. The principality was then annexed by Sultan Bāyezīd I.

By the end of the eighth/fourteenth century, the unification of Turkish Anatolia by the Ottoman sultanate was virtually complete. The Greeks retained a last foothold on the north coast in the so-called empire of Trebizond, which survived until 865/1461, eight years after the fall of Constantinople to the Turks. Karası was annexed by the Ottomans as early as 746/1345, but it was during the sultanate of Bāyezīd I (792–805/1389–1402) that the great acquisitions were made. The western *beyliks*, Menteshe, Aydın, Saruhan and Germiyan (much of which was already lost) were taken in 792/1389–90, Karaman and the former sultanate of Burhān al-Dīn a few years later. Dulkadır was to remain a thorn in the flesh to both Mamluks and Ottomans until it was annexed by Selīm the Grim in 928/1522. The invasion of Anatolia by Timur Leng, and his defeat of Bāyezīd at the battle of Ankara in 804/1402, placed the future of the Ottoman sultanate in jeopardy, and gave a new lease of life to the local rulers in the region. The respite was to be short. With the restoration of the united sultanate by Meḥmed I in 816/1413, the way was open to the recovery of the lost Anatolian provinces, and to further conquests in the Near East by Selīm the Grim in the next century.

CHAPTER TWENTY

The Mamluk Sultanate in Decline (1)

The Sons and Household of Barkuk 1399–1461

The Circassian Mamluk sultans, sometimes known from Kalavun's original recruitment of Circassians as the Burjiyya (see above, p. 139), formed a succession of 23 rulers from Barkuk's usurpation in 784/1382 to the Ottoman conquest in 922/1516–17. Barkuk's own sons and his military household provided the first series of his successors, who reigned from 801/1399 to 865/1461, and amongst whom the most important were al-Mu'ayyad Shaykh (815–24/1412–21) and al-Ashraf Barsbay (825–41/1422–38). The next series of sultans, in effect a second generation, sprang from the Mamluk households of Barkuk's first successors, and among them the most notable was al-Ashraf Kayitbay, who reigned from 872/1468 to 901/1496. All Kayitbay's successors came from his family or household, including al-Ashraf Kansawh al-Ghawrī (906–22/1501–16), who died in the battle of Marj Dābiq against Selīm the Grim.

Like al-Ẓāhir Baybars and Kalavun before him, Barkuk hoped to found a dynasty. He had endeavoured to establish his family in Egypt by bringing in his aged father Anaṣ (as has been mentioned, p. 127) and others of his kin. The day before he died, he convoked the Caliph al-Mutawakkil I, the judges, the amirs and the great officers to make a covenant for the succession of his eldest son Faraj (then ten years old) followed by the younger sons, ʿAbd al-ʿAzīz and Ibrāhīm. In the sultan's will, the *Atābak* Etmish al-Ẓāhirī, a member of Barkuk's Mamluk household, was appointed administrator of the kingdom, i.e. regent. There ensued a series of contests among the magnates for the control of the infant sultan. In Rabīʿ I 802/November 1399, Etmish and his supporters were ousted by a faction headed by Yashbeg al-Shaʿbānī, the sultan's tutor.

It was at this juncture that the long-threatened attack on the Mamluk sultanate by Timur Leng took place. Bāyezīd I, the Ottoman sultan, sought an alliance with Egypt but his proposals were rejected by the magnates, who commented, "Now he's become our friend. When our master Barkuk died, he invaded our country and took Malaṭya. He's no friend of ours. Let him fight for his country, and we'll fight for our country and our subjects." Preoccupied with the contest over the sultanate, they paid no heed to Timur, whose unremitting advance into eastern Anatolia and northern Syria was reported in the autumn of 803/1400. Aleppo fell in Rabīʿ I/October, and the invaders moved on towards Damascus. Military preparations were at last begun in Cairo, and on 8 Rabīʿ II/26 November the vanguard set out, followed by the main army and the boy-sultan. Faraj entered Damascus, but was soon forced to flee as the city was invested by Timur's forces. Early in 1401 Damascus fell; a participant in the events surrounding its capture was the Tunisian scholar Ibn Khaldūn, the greatest of the medieval Arabic historians.

It was not, however, Timur's intention to undertake the long and hazardous advance to Cairo – an operation which was to give pause to Selīm the Grim in the next century. His principal opponent in the west was the Ottoman sultan, and Timur turned against him, having secured his southern flank. At the battle of Ankara (27 Dhu'l-Ḥijja 804/28 July 1402), Bāyezīd was defeated and made captive, and the Ottoman state was to all appearances irretrievably ruined. Damascus and Syria as a whole had been ravaged by the invaders, but the Mamluk administration was quickly re-established, and the sultanate had still over a century of existence before it was overthrown by another invader from the north.

During the next decade, Syria was to play an important part in politics by serving as a base for ambitious malcontents as it had served Sanjar al-Ḥalabī and Sungur al-Ashqar in earlier times. Its significance in this respect appeared in late 807/summer 1405. The sultan was by now old enough to profit from the inveterate factional quarrels of the magnates, and in Ṣafar 807/August 1404 he had thrown his support, such as it was, against his old tutor Yashbeg, who held the great office of *dawādār*, and was effectively regent. A skirmish around the Citadel occurred. Yashbeg and his party were defeated and fled to Syria, where they were welcomed by the governor of Damascus, Shaykh al-Maḥmūdī, one of Barkuk's Mamluks. They were joined by another ex-regent, Jakam, who had captured Aleppo and thought of proclaiming himself sultan there – a project which he now deferred. In Dhu'l-Qa'da 807/May 1405 the triumvirate determined to advance on Egypt. Fighting with the sultan's forces took place below the Citadel, and the rebels suddenly lost heart. A number of their amirs submitted to the sultan, Yashbeg absconded in Cairo, while Shaykh and Jakam fled back to Syria. A new governor, Nawrūz al-Ḥāfiẓī (like Shaykh, one of Barkuk's Mamluks), was appointed to Damascus.

Al-Nāṣir Faraj now seemed fairly set to begin his effective reign. He carried out a reform of the treasury departments, and took as his adviser a young *'ālim* named Ibrāhīm Ibn Ghurāb, who had served his father as supervisor of the fisc. Yashbeg emerged from hiding, and on the intercession of the *Atābak* Baybars (a cousin of the sultan), he and Faraj were reconciled. But the sultan was growing weary of his position, and after a drunken spree he concluded that the magnates wanted to kill him. He made his escape secretly from the Citadel, and took refuge with Ibn Ghurāb. On the following day (26 Rabī' I 808/21 September 1405) he was deposed, and his half-brother 'Abd al-'Azīz was installed as sultan with the title of al-Malik al-Manṣūr.

The infant sultan was no more than a figurehead. The administration of the kingdom was undertaken by Ibn Ghurāb, who held the secretaryship, while the magnates struggled for power. They were split into two factions, one headed by the *Atābak* Baybars, who as a kinsman of Barkuk no doubt saw himself as sultan; the other by Yashbeg al-Sha'bānī, who worked with Ibn Ghurāb for the restoration of Faraj. At an appropriate moment, Faraj emerged from his hiding place. With a great and growing following he moved on the Citadel. The gate was thrown open to him, and Baybars fled with his supporters. He was captured and sent to Alexandria, while on 5 Jumādā II 808/28 November 1405 al-Nāṣir Faraj was restored to the sultanate. His allies were duly rewarded. Yashbeg al-Sha'bānī was invested as *atābak*, and an unusual honour was conferred on Ibrāhīm Ibn Ghurāb. Although an *'ālim* by training and a chancery official, he was made an honorary "man of the sword" by being given an amirate of the highest rank and appointed chief of the council, a body composed of the senior amirs. His brother succeeded him as secretary. Unfortunately for Faraj, Ibrāhīm Ibn Ghurāb died only a few months later. The deposed Sultan 'Abd al-'Azīz and his brother Ibrāhīm were sent to Alexandria, where they died in suspicious circumstances soon afterwards.

Syria continued to provide a base for powerful opponents of the sultan. In the kaleidoscope events of the next few years, three names continually recur. Jakam, foiled in his attempt with Shaykh to seize power in Egypt in 807/1405, declared himself sultan in Aleppo. Perhaps with a deliberate reminiscence of an earlier lord of Aleppo, Nūr al-Dīn b. Zangī, he took the title of al-Malik al-ʿĀdil. This was on 11 Shawwāl 809/21 March 1407, and he was recognized throughout Syria except in Ṣafad, where his former ally, Shaykh, was residing. The threat to the sultan was obvious: Jakam had indeed sent orders to the nomads and peasants of Egypt instructing them not to pay taxes to Faraj. However, Jakam decided first to secure Mesopotamia, and was killed in battle at Āmid (17 Dhu'l-Qaʿda 809/25 April 1407. There remained Shaykh and Nawrūz, each fighting for his own hand either separately or in combination, while the sultan endeavoured to play off one against the other.

In order to repress these magnates, who were virtually independent war-lords, al-Nāṣir Faraj made five expeditions in Syria between 809/1406 and 814/1412. It was a record like that of al-Ẓāhir Baybars over a similar period of years, not, however, to wage the *jihād* against infidel enemies but in civil warfare against overmighty subjects. During the expedition of 810/1407, the *Atābak* Yashbeg al-Shaʿbānī fell into disgrace and was arrested together with Shaykh. The two escaped, and captured Damascus as the sultan was on his way back to Egypt. Nawrūz, who after various vicissitudes had been reappointed governor of Damascus, defeated and killed Yashbeg at Baʿlabakk (13 Rabīʿ II 810/17 September 1407), while Shaykh fled. Three years later, Nawrūz and Shaykh were allies, and succeeded in bringing their forces to Cairo when the sultan was on campaign in Syria (Ramaḍān 813/January 1411). In the event they were dispersed by troops loyal to Faraj, and the leaders fled to al-Karak, where a reconciliation with the sultan was effected.

This produced no lasting settlement. In the following year, Shaykh and Nawrūz were again in rebellion. They drew their support from the Ẓāhiriyya, the veteran Mamluks of Barkuk, thus reproducing a pattern of political faction that went back to the time of al-Muʿaẓẓam Tūrān-Shāh (see above, p. 140). For a time Faraj was restrained from hasty action by his experienced father-in-law, the Amir Tangribirdi, whose son was the chronicler usually known as Ibn Taghrībirdī. But in Dhu'l-Qaʿda 813/March 1411, Tangribirdi was sent as governor to Damascus, where he died a year later. Freed from his influence, the sultan began to arrest and punish the Ẓāhiriyya in Egypt.

In Dhu'l-Ḥijja 814/March 1412, al-Nāṣir Faraj set out on his last expedition, accompanied as was usual by the caliph, now al-Mustaʿīn, the son of al-Mutawakkil I. A curious episode ensued. The sultan made an attack on the rebels and was defeated. His baggage and also the caliph fell into the rebels' hands. They decided to set up al-Mustaʿīn as sultan in order to checkmate Faraj, who was besieged in Damascus. Al-

Musta'īn, who was both fearful and reluctant, was tricked into accepting the sultanate. Faraj surrendered on 11 Ṣafar/23 May. He was put on trial before a commission of amirs, jurists and *'ulamā'*, and sentenced to death. There was deep division over the propriety of this since Faraj had surrendered on terms, but the caliph-sultan used his influence with the judges and jurists against his deposed predecessor.

On 2 Rabī' II/12 July, al-Musta'īn entered Cairo in the company of Shaykh, who completely dominated him. The caliph-sultan's attempts to obtain real power and even public recognition were frustrated. On 8 Rabī' II/18 July, he invested Shaykh as *atābak* in Egypt, and formally conferred plenary powers on him. Shaykh was in fact determined to obtain the sultanate, and al-Musta'īn's position is pathetically described by Ibn Taghrībirdī:

> The caliph became homesick for his kinsmen in the vast palaces of the Citadel; he was uneasy at the lack of visitors. In vain did he regret the position into which he had entered. To speak of his regret would not bring amirs or anyone else to his aid, so he kept silence about his distress.[1]

He was not to occupy the position for much longer. On 16 Jumādā I/24 August, the decree conferring plenary powers on Shaykh was published, and the *atābak* began to behave like a sultan. Three weeks later the last obstacle was removed from his path, when the death of his only serious rival in Cairo enabled him to canvass the other amirs for his own accession. He was installed by acclamation on 1 Sha'bān/6 November, and al-Musta'īn resigned the sultanate as he had accepted it six months before – unwillingly and under compulsion. Shaykh took the regnal title, previously unknown among the Mamluk sultans, of al-Malik al-Mu'ayyad, "the divinely-supported king".

Shaykh's accession ended his fragile alliance with Nawrūz, who had been appointed governor-general of the whole of Syria. Nawrūz refused to recognize him as sultan, and convoked an assembly of the Syrian governors in Damascus. At this he tried, although unsuccessfully, to obtain a legal opinion condemning Shaykh's usurpation and his imprisonment of the caliph. Thereupon Nawrūz set to work to recruit troops for war. In Muḥarram 817/March 1414, Shaykh moved out of Cairo against him. Nawrūz found himself confined within the citadel of Damascus, and sought to make terms with Shaykh. The losses on both sides had been heavy. Shaykh swore an apparently binding oath on the settlement but his secretary, who administered the oath, deliberately did so in faulty Arabic to render it invalid. The deception was not perceived by Nawrūz's ignorant Turkish jurists, and when he and his associates came out, confident of an amnesty, they were seized. Nawrūz was put to death (21 Rabīʿ II 817/10 July 1414). Al-Mu'ayyad Shaykh then made a royal progress as far as Malaṭya before returning to Egypt. The next year saw another revolt in Syria. Again the sultan led his troops from Cairo, and suppressed the rebels.

Al-Mu'ayyad Shaykh's third expedition to Syria had a different purpose. The Syrian provinces proper and their governors were now submissive to his rule, and the sultan's intention was to secure his hold over the autonomous principalities of the northern marches. The *beylik* of Karaman had been restored by Timur Leng, and its ruler had captured Tarsus in the reign of Faraj. There were also the two Turcoman principalities of Elbistan under the Dulkadırids (see above, p. 177), and Cilicia. This was formerly the territory of the kingdom of Lesser Armenia, which the Mamluks had brought to an end in 776/1375. Three years later a Turcoman governor named Ramazān (Arabic, Ramaḍān) was installed in its capital, Adana. His descendants ruled the province as vassals of the Mamluks and subsequently of the Ottomans.

The expedition was intended as an impressive demonstration of Shaykh's power. His son, al-Ṣārimī Ibrāhīm, who was about 20 years of age, commanded the vanguard. On 4 Ṣafar 820/23 March 1417 al-Mu'ayyad Shaykh left al-Raydāniyya, his base outside Cairo, accompanied by al-Mustaʿīn's successor as caliph, the four chief judges and several foreign ambassadors. Tarsus fell after siege. A force was sent under al-Ṣārimī Ibrāhīm to reduce Elbistan to submission. The outcome of the expedition was the checking of the power of Karaman, and the establishment of client rulers in the Ramazanid and Dulkadırid territories. On 15 Shawwāl/25 November the sultan made a state entry into Cairo with his son holding the royal parasol above his head and the Mamluks marching before him.

Another expedition by al-Ṣārimī Ibrāhīm in 822/1419 reached Kayseri, the capital of Karaman, and al-Mu'ayyad Shaykh was proclaimed sultan there. It was a triumph like that of al-Ẓāhir Baybars in 675/1277, and as impermanent. Al-Ṣārimī Ibrāhīm died in Cairo on 15 Jumādā II 823/27 June 1420. Al-Mu'ayyad Shaykh, elderly by medieval standards, was already a sick man. Deprived of a promising heir, he made what provision he could for the future of his family and his kingdom by convoking the caliph, the judges and the magnates for the designation of his son Aḥmad to succeed him. It was a desperate scheme. Aḥmad had been born on 2 Jumādā I 822/27 May 1419, and thus was not yet two years old when his father died on 9 Muḥarram 824/14 January 1421.

The arrangements which Shaykh had made for the government were quickly set aside. By a coup even before the old sultan was buried, full powers of regency were assumed by the Amir Ṭaṭar, another of Barkuk's veteran Mamluks. Having used his comrades, the Ẓāhiriyya, against Shaykh's younger Mamluks, the Mu'ayyadiyya, Ṭaṭar was strong enough to depose al-Muẓaffar Aḥmad on 29 Sha'bān 824/29 August 1421, and to usurp the sultanate. But his own reign was to be even shorter than Aḥmad's: he died on 4 Dhu'l-Ḥijja 824/30 November 1421. Like Shaykh, he solemnly designated his son as his heir, but al-Ṣāliḥ Muḥammad, aged about ten on his accession, suffered the same fate as al-Muẓaffar Aḥmad. After a nominal reign of five months he was deposed, and the magnates elected as sultan another of Barkuk's veterans, Barsbay al-Ẓāhirī, who had been al-Ṣāliḥ Muḥammad's regent (8 Rabī' II 825/31 March 1422).

The sixteen years of Barsbay's reign were the Indian summer of the Mamluk sultanate. He was the last successful leader of the *jihād* against the Franks, in which capacity he reduced the kingdom of Cyprus to tributary status. He imposed more effectively than his predecessors had done Mamluk suzerainty over the Holy Cities and the coastlands of the Red Sea, and he intervened to secure his interests in the marcher-principalities to the north of Syria. The link between the first two of these activities was his desire to protect Egyptian trade in the Mediterranean and Red Sea – a principal source of his revenue.

Although there had been no Frankish invasion of Mamluk territory since the brief occupation of Alexandria by King Peter I in 767/1365, the existence of a Christian state in Cyprus remained a constant threat to Muslim shipping. Frankish corsairs were the terror of the eastern Mediterranean. A few months after Barsbay's accession, they captured a Muslim vessel out of Alexandria carrying a valuable cargo. At the time the sultan was preoccupied with a revolt in Syria, but in the following year (826/1423) he sent a number of amirs to Alexandria and the coastlands to report on the movements of the Franks. Then in Rajab 827/June 1424 Barsbay learnt that two Muslim merchantmen had been taken off Damietta. He carried out immediate reprisals by sequestrating the property of Frankish traders in Syria, Alexandria and Damietta, and detaining the merchants themselves until restitution was made. It is notable that the sultan took this action against the advice of his treasury officials, who were no doubt conscious of the damage it would do to trading relations and the revenues of the state.

The sultan quickly learnt to distinguish between the Franks who were corsairs from Cyprus and the Franks who were merchants from western Europe. In Ramaḍān 827/August 1424 he sent out a number of galleys (to be reinforced by others from Syria) on an expedition to Cyprus, which was then ruled by King Janus of the house of Lusignan. They returned a few weeks later with booty and some prisoners, reporting that they had been well received by the governor of Famagusta (at this time a Genoese enclave), and had gone on to attack and loot Limassol. Encouraged by this success, Barsbay set in hand the building of warships at Būlāq, while to protect the coastal route from the eastern Delta, he constructed and garrisoned a fort at al-Ṭīna. A second expedition against Cyprus was launched in the summer of 828/1425. Sailing from Būlāq, the fleet again made a rendezvous at Tripoli to pick up the Syrian reinforcements, and then crossed to Famagusta. There they were welcomed by the Genoese governor, and told of the king's preparations to resist them. Raiding-parties were sent out, and the fleet sailed westwards along the coast. Two naval engagements and a hard-fought land-battle ensued. This was followed by some profitable raiding, but when the rumour spread that the king was bringing up a large army, the Mamluk commander thought it best to withdraw to Egypt.

The next summer (829/1426) Barsbay sent out his third expedition to Cyprus, disregarding the intercession of an embassy sent by John VIII Palaeologus, the Byzantine emperor. The fleet sailed down the Nile from Būlāq to Damietta; then along the Egyptian coast to Rosetta (where there was a skirmish with four Frankish ships) and Alexandria. The expedition made its landfall at Limassol, where the citadel was captured and destroyed on 26 Shaʿbān/3 July. Thereupon the land-army began its advance towards Nicosia, the capital. What happened is thus described by the contemporary chronicler, Ibn Taghrībirdī:

> Then the land-army proceeded in loose order. . . . They were not in battle-array but like travellers. Some of them were armed but most of them were unarmed because of the heat. Each one went forward on his own without waiting for another. They thought that the lord of Cyprus would only encounter them outside his capital. The amirs lingered with the rear-guard as is usual with military commanders, and the men were pushing ahead to get to Nicosia, where they would halt and rest their horses until the troops were assembled and the squadrons prepared for battle.
>
> While they were on the march, they were surprised by the ruler of Cyprus with his forces and troops, the Frankish rulers who had joined him, and others on every hand. The Muslims to whom the lord of Cyprus appeared were a very small detachment of the vanguard, mostly élite cavalry from the Royal Mamluks. When they saw one another, the Muslims could not wait for those following them to join them, but they seized the opportunity and devoted themselves to martyrdom, one saying to another, "This is the spoils of war!" Then, true of heart, they spurred their horses against the enemy, and made a mighty charge against the Franks, shouting "God is greatest!" They fought bitterly. Some of the company backed them up, others lagged behind – amongst them a leading man of the Privy Chamber, who stayed in the shadow of a tree there. . . . In spite of their fewness and small numbers, they remained steadfast until God gave the victory to Islam and abandoned the infidels to defeat. The

ruler of Cyprus was captured in spite of his many followers and innumerably great forces, and the small force of Muslims. There were fewer than 70 persons at the start of the battle. . . . When the forces of Islam came up, they rode after the Franks and put them to the sword, killing and capturing many. The rest of the Franks fled to the capital of Cyprus, Nicosia. . . . The Royal Mamluks and other fighters in the Holy War who made their way to Nicosia continued slaying and making captives as they went until they reached the city and entered the king's palace, which they looted.[2]

After this outstanding victory and the further defeat of the Franks in a naval battle, the expedition sailed for Egypt on 12 Ramaḍān/18 July. On 8 Shawwāl/13 August there was a triumphal procession of the warriors and their prisoners up to the Citadel, where the captive king of Cyprus was received in humiliating fashion by the sultan. The European consuls undertook to pay his ransom, and King Janus was allowed to return to his island as a vassal ruler subject to an annual tribute. When he died six years later, Barsbay sent a delegation to install his infant son as king, and to demand arrears of tribute. The new ruler, John II, duly swore fealty to Barsbay, and was invested with a robe of honour – in effect the sultan's livery (835–6/1432). One Frankish outpost in the eastern Mediterranean remained unconquered – the island of Rhodes in the hands of the Hospitallers. In Jumādā I 830/March 1427, after Barsbay's conquest of Cyprus, an ambassador from Rhodes came to avert the threat of an invasion.

As we have seen earlier (above, p. 96) the Mamluk sultans from the time of Baybars had regarded the Ḥijāz as a protectorate, but had been content to leave it under the autonomous rule of the dynasts of Mecca and Medina. Barsbay emphasized the claim to suzerainty over the Holy Cities, and the degree of administrative control increased: two developments resulting from both political and economic considerations. The special status of the sultan of Egypt was symbolized by the annual sending of the *kiswa* to cover the Kaʿba, a prerogative which Baybars had jealously maintained against the contemporary ruler of the Yemen (see above, p. 151). Barsbay, over a century and a half later, had a more formidable competitor in Shāh Rukh, the son of Timur Leng, who sought permission on several occasions to send a *kiswa* to the Kaʿba. The sultan's habitual response was to refuse the request and slight the messenger, but in 838/1434 he staged an ostentatious rejection of Shāh Rukh's claim. The ambassador, a man of distinction as a descendant of the Prophet, was received in full court held in *dār al-ʿadl* of the Citadel, where he delivered a letter stating that Shāh Rukh had made a vow to present the *kiswa*. Clearly a fine point of religious honour was involved, and the sultan convoked a session of the four chief judges to resolve the matter. The Ḥanafī judge declared the vow invalid, the other three kept silent. Armed with this decision, such as it was, Barsbay informed Shāh Rukh that the *kiswa* was an ancient, legal and inalienable prerogative of the rulers of Egypt. If Shāh Rukh wished, he might expiate his vow by selling the *kiswa* which he had had made and giving its price to feed the poor of Mecca. This, as will appear, by no means ended the tension between the two rulers, but it marked Barsbay's determination to prevent any extension of Shāh Rukh's influence to the Ḥijāz.

The sultan's interest in this region was not exclusively political. The commerce of the Red Sea was much disturbed at precisely this period. Ships bringing pepper, spices and other products of India and the Far East had hitherto made their landfall at Aden, to the considerable profit of the Rasulid rulers of the Yemen. But Barsbay's contemporary there, al-Nāṣir Aḥmad (803–27/1400–23), abandoned the sound policy of his predecessors, and drove the merchants away with his arbitrary exactions. Jedda, the port of Mecca, was well placed to take over the role of Aden, and ships from the East were already beginning to find their way there when in Rabīʿ I 828/January 1425 Barsbay sent out an expedition with the primary object of subduing the troublesome ruler of Mecca, the *Sharīf* Ḥasan b. ʿAjlān. Acting on the advice of a Mamluk amir long exiled in Mecca, the sultan sent with his troops a clerk to levy custom-dues on the Indian ships. Jedda was occupied, garrisoned and administered as a Mamluk enclave, although the question of a division of the customs revenue remained an issue between the sultan and the *sharīf*. The number of Indian vessels anchoring at Jedda increased rapidly, and in 835/1432 two Chinese junks discharged their cargo there. Barsbay's intention was to make Jedda the staple port, through which all Egyptian trade with the Red Sea had to pass.

Since Ayyubid times the commerce of the Indian Ocean and Red Sea, in which pepper and spices were the most important articles, had been controlled by a group of merchants called the Kārimīs, who had their commercial houses in Cairo, Aden and elsewhere. They were favoured by Barsbay's predecessors, and he himself at first employed a Kārimī as his agent in commercial transactions. Then he moved directly into the field by establishing a monopoly of pepper in 832/1438, and went on to fix the price for its sale to the Frankish merchants. This led to a long struggle with the Venetians who were compelled to buy the sultan's pepper at the sultan's price, and in the quantities he decreed. At the same time the royal monopoly led to the rapid eclipse of the Kārimīs. They and the other victims of Barsbay's commercial policy found a remote and ineffective advocate in Shāh Rukh, who in 838/1435 sent an angry letter to Cairo, reproaching the sultan for levying uncanonical dues on the merchants at Jedda and engaging in trade. But the sultan, we are told, paid no heed.

Barsbay's reign was comparatively undisturbed by internal revolts. At the start in 825/1422 there was a rising in Syria headed by the governor of Ṣafad, who was (or claimed to be) a partisan of the deposed al-Ṣāliḥ Muḥammad. Ṣafad was captured and the governor put to death. Another revolt, led by the governor of Damascus, ended in the defeat and execution of the rebel in Ṣafar 827/January 1424. Nevertheless until the last months of his life, Barsbay was never free from the fear of a yet more dangerous rival. This was the Amir Janibek al-Ṣūfī, whom al-Ẓāhir Ṭaṭar had nominated on his deathbed to be his son's regent, and who Barsbay had overthrown as a prelude to his own usurpation of the sultanate. Janibek, like Barsbay a Mamluk of al-Ẓāhir Barkuk's household, was imprisoned in Alexandria, but succeeded in making his escape in Shaʿbān 826/July 1423, after which he lay hidden in Cairo for some years. "Al-Ashraf [Barsbay's] life was troubled," says the chronicler, "from the day the news reached him. He was estranged from many of his amirs, arrested them and banished others".[3]

In course of time Janibek went on to Syria, then to Anatolia, where he made his appearance at Tokat in Shawwāl 838/May 1435. This was an alarming development for Barsbay in view of the unstable situation on the northern and north-eastern borders of the Mamluk sultanate. Something has already been said about the immediate neighbours of Mamluk Syria, Karaman and the marcher-principalities of the Ramazanids and Dulkadırids (above, p. 176). To the east were two Turcoman tribal confederations. The original homeland of the Shīʿī Kara-Koyunlu (i.e. the Black Sheep Turcomans) in eastern Anatolia had been increased by the addition of Azerbaijan, Iraq and some Persian territory. Their greatest chief, Kara-Yūsuf, died in 823/1420, and was succeeded by his son Iskandar. Their rivals, the Sunnī Ak-Koyunlu (i.e. the White Sheep Turcomans) had their centre in Diyār Bakr around Āmid, and their ruler was a certain ʿOsmān Bey, known as Kara-Yülük, "the Black Leech". Again further to the east was the rump of Timur Leng's vast but ephemeral empire, ruled at this time, as we have seen, by his son Shāh Rukh (807–50/1405–47).

The arrival of Janibek in Anatolia brought together the individuals and groups opposed to Barsbay and more generally to the Mamluk sultanate as such. Not less disturbing to Barsbay was a report he received in Ṣafar 839/August–September 1435 that the Ottoman sultan, the ruler of Karaman, Kara Yülük and the Dulkadırid Nāṣir al-Dīn Meḥmed had all accepted investiture as governors on behalf of Shāh Rukh. Nor did the ambition of the Timurid stop at this. In Rajab

839/January 1436 Barsbay received an embassy from Shāh Rukh offering him investiture as governor of Egypt. The sultan's rage at this revival of Timur Leng's pretensions to universal empire was unbounded. He tore to pieces the robe which Shāh Rukh had sent, and had the ambassador beaten and ducked in a horse-pond until he nearly died.

Meanwhile the threat from Janibek in the north continued. His followers included some of the Ak-Koyunlu under a son of Kara-Yülük, but these tribesmen were recalled on Shāh Rukh's orders to fight against Iskandar of the Kara-Koyunlu. It was a fatal encounter in which Kara-Yülük died (839/1435). Janibek went on to besiege Malaṭya, and there he was betrayed by a false friend, the son of Nāṣir al-Dīn Meḥmed, and taken a prisoner to Elbistan. Barsbay sent an embassy to obtain his surrender but it returned in Rajab 839/January 1436 without satisfaction. Nāṣir al-Dīn alleged that he could not honourably hand his prisoner over, and that he was under pressure from Shāh Rukh and other rulers not to do so. In fact Janibek was released and set about preparing fresh hostility to the sultan, who a few weeks later sent out an expeditionary force. This was joined by the Syrian governors with their contingents. After a raid into Elbistan, battle was joined near ʿAyntāb (25 Dhu'l-Ḥijja 839/10 July 1436). Janibek was defeated and fled. A year later, he and Nāṣir al-Dīn Meḥmed were raiding in the vicinity of Marʿash, but shortly afterwards the two confederates fell out and separated. Janibek made his way to the sons of Kara-Yülük, amongst whom the Ak-Koyunlu territories were now partitioned. They plotted to betray him to the governor of Aleppo. He died in captivity (26 Rabīʿ II 841/27 October 1437) and his head was sent to Cairo. There it was paraded through the streets, while a herald cried, "This is the reward of him who opposes kings and abandons his obedience."

So at last Barsbay was rid of the most dangerous of his enemies, but his own time was coming to an end. After six months' illness, he died on 13 Dhu'l-Ḥijja 841/7 June 1438, aged over 60. A few weeks before his death, he solemnly nominated his son Yūsuf as his heir in the presence of the caliph, the four chief judges and the magnates. Events soon showed that this device to secure the succession was to be as ineffective as in the past. Al-ʿAzīz Yūsuf was 14 years old and at his side stood one of the veterans of Barkuk's household, Chakmak al-Ẓāhirī. After three months of factional struggle, Chakmak usurped the throne on 19 Rabīʿ I 842/9 September 1438, and assumed the royal title of al-Malik al-Ẓāhir, rendered illustrious by Baybars and held by his own *ustādh*, Barkuk.

The principal importance of Chakmak's reign lay in his attempt to follow up Barsbay's establishment of suzerainty over Cyprus by the capture of Rhodes from the Hospitallers. Three expeditions were sent in 844/1440, 846/1442 and 848/1444 respectively. All of them failed in their object. Rhodes fell in the end to Süleymān the Magnificent, the Ottoman sultan, in 928/1522. From Chakmak the pertinacious Shāh Rukh at last obtained what Barsbay had steadfastly refused: an embassy in 848/1444 was permitted to present a *kiswa* to the Kaʿba. Chakmak was pleased to restore good relations with Shāh Rukh, but his complaisance deeply angered the amirs, and the ambassadors were attacked and robbed by a mob of Mamluks and townspeople as they returned to their lodgings from the Citadel.

Chakmak was an old man when he came to the throne, and he was over 80 when he died on 3 Ṣafar 857/13 February 1453. A few days earlier he had abdicated in favour of his son ʿUthmān, an 18-year-old who took the title of al-Malik al-Manṣūr. Less than two months passed before the usual history of usurpation repeated itself, and the young sultan was deposed by the *Atābak* Inal al-ʿAlāʾī, the last veteran of Barkuk's household to come to the throne. He was 73 years of age, and his short reign saw ominous developments in two directions. On 23 Shawwāl 857/27 October 1453 an embassy arrived from Sultan Meḥmed II of the Ottomans to congratulate Inal on his accession – and to announce the capture of Constantinople. At the news of this crowning mercy, the hope of Islam for eight centuries past, Cairo was illuminated and the people rejoiced. Yet more than any other single event it marked the emergence of the Ottomans as the greatest power in the Near East and the end of Mamluk hegemony. In consequence of this shift in the status of the two sultanates, their relations with the marcher-principalities on their common border became a major problem, as we shall see. There were also important developments in Cyprus. On the death of King John II in 1458, the succession was disputed between his daughter, Charlotte, and his illegitimate son, James, who sought and obtained Inal's support. This was the last significant Mamluk intervention in Cyprus. The sequel may be briefly summarized. James succeeded in his usurpation and reigned until 1473. He married a Venetian noblewoman, Catherine Cornaro, who followed him on the throne. But Cyprus in her reign was in effect a Venetian protectorate, and in 1489 Venice annexed the island, although tribute continued to be paid to the Mamluk sultan. This last shred of Frankish Outremer survived until it fell to the Ottomans in the reign of Sultan Selīm II in 979/1571, and was formally ceded by Venice in 980/1573.

Al-Ashraf Inal died on 15 Jumādā I 865/26 February 1461, aged about 80. In accordance with precedent he was succeeded by his son, al-Malik al-Muʾayyad Aḥmad. Equally in accordance with precedent, the throne was shortly afterwards usurped by the *Atābak* Khushqadam (19 Ramaḍān 865/28 June 1461). But Khushqadam came from the Mamluk household of al-Mu'ayyad Shaykh, and with him begins a new "generation" of sultans, the Mamluks of the Mamluks of Barkuk.

NOTES

1. Ibn Taghrībirdī, *al-Nujūm al-zāhira fī mulūk Miṣr wa'l-Qāhira*, XIII, [Cairo] 1390/1970, 204. English version P. M. Holt.
2. Ibn Taghrībirdī, *Nujūm*, XIV, [Cairo] 1391/1972, 292–5. English version P. M. Holt.
3. Ibn Taghrībirdī, *Nujūm*, XIV, 254. English version P. M. Holt.

CHAPTER TWENTY-ONE

The Mamluk Sultanate in Decline (2)

The Later Circassian Mamluk Sultans 1461–1517

The last period of the Mamluk sultanate, which opened with the usurpation of al-Ẓāhir Khushqadam in 865/1461 and ended with the Ottoman conquest by Selīm I, a little over half a century later, was a time of increasing political instability, military inefficiency and economic impoverishment. The two sultans who showed most capacity as rulers, al-Ashraf Kayitbay (872–901/1468–96) and al-Ashraf Kansawh al-Ghawrī (906–22/1501–16), could do little to avert the general decline.

One cause of the political disorder at the heart of the state was the multiplication of self-seeking political factions formed from the veterans of past royal households. Only 30 years elapsed between the death of Barsbay and the accession of Kayitbay, and at the end of this period there were still active groups of the Ashrafiyya Mamluks of Barsbay, the Ẓāhiriyya of Chakmak, the Ashrafiyya of Inal and the Ẓāhiriyya of Khushqadam, to say nothing of the *julbān*, the Mamluks whom Kayitbay had already recruited while an amir, and whose number he was to increase enormously as sultan. By the end of his reign, it is said, he had purchased 8,000 Mamluks, but there had been heavy losses among them from epidemics of plague.

It was a sinister feature of the period that the loyalty of the *julbān* to their *ustādh*, one of the two fundamental bonds of Mamluk society (see above, p. 138), could no longer be taken for granted. Insubordinate and mutinous, they contributed largely to the lack of public security in Cairo in this period. Their disorder had begun to show itself somewhat earlier. In 854/1450, during the reign of Chakmak, his *julbān* demonstrated their hostility to the sultan's finance minister by mobbing the magnates as they went down from the Citadel, and looting the minister's house. Shortly afterwards in order to mark their status as a military élite, they forbade the *'ulamā'* to ride on horseback – and the price of mules shot up in consequence. There were further hostile demonstrations by the *julbān* in Inal's reign, and in Dhu'l-Ḥijja 859/November 1455 the sultan dared not make the traditional public sacrifices at the annual feast for fear lest he be stoned by his own Mamluks. Under Kayitbay tumults of the *julbān* were a frequent occurrence, and it was not only the sultan who suffered at their hands – the traders of Cairo were victims of their shoplifting, and their depredations at the time of festivals made sacrificial beasts scarce and expensive.

As the insubordination of the Mamluks increased, their quality as soldiers declined. In earlier days the Mamluk warrior had been a superb horseman fighting with lance and bow, carefully trained, strictly disciplined, and slowly promoted in accordance with his merit and experience. By the mid-ninth/fifteenth century this was no longer the case. The great hippodromes constructed for cavalry training were allowed to fall into ruin, and no new ones were built from the time of al-Nāṣir Muḥammad to that of Kansawh al-Ghawrī, over a century and a half later. The traditional exercises were also increasingly neglected under the later Kalavunids and throughout the Circassian period, although again Kansawh al-Ghawrī made a late and anachronistic attempt to revive them. The eighth/fourteenth and ninth/fifteenth centuries had seen the development in Europe and the Near East of gunpowder and firearms, which were to dominate warfare for five hundred years to come. Cannon superseded the old mechanical artillery of the mangonels, hand-guns gradually mastered the bow and lance of the cavalry. Although cannon are mentioned in Egyptian sources as early as the 760s/1360s, they were used by the Mamluks only in siege-warfare and not on the battlefield. They employed the hand-gun even more reluctantly: at that date it was essentially a foot-soldier's weapon, and its use was relegated to second-rate troops, socially inferior to the Mamluk cavalrymen, such as *awlād al-nās* and Blacks. Here also Kansawh al-Ghawrī made a desperate effort to improve the defences of his kingdom by casting cannon and organizing a unit trained to fight with hand-guns. The contrast between the Mamluk attitude to firearms and that of the Ottomans is striking, and in the end Sultan Selīm's janissaries, foot-soldiers with firearms, were the chief military factor in his conquest of Syria and Egypt.

Underlying the political instability and military conservatism of the later Mamluk sultanate, and largely contributing to its decline, was a prolonged economic and financial crisis. The economic heyday of the sultanate had been from the middle of the seventh/thirteenth century, when Egypt escaped the Mongol flood that overwhelmed her neighbours, to the middle of the eighth/fourteenth century. A basic cause of the crisis lay in the heavy losses of population occasioned by successive epidemics of plague. The most serious of these was the Black Death. It struck the Mamluk dominions during the first reign of al-Nāṣir Ḥasan, reaching Aleppo in Jumādā I 748/August 1347, and spreading through Syria to Egypt, where it was at its height in 749/1348–9. The Arabic chroniclers like those of Europe have left horrifying accounts of its ravages. Medieval statistics are notoriously uncertain, but it has been estimated that Egypt and Syria lost a third of their population. Nor was this the only visitation: there were twelve severe epidemics between 819/1416 and 919/1513. While all classes and nationalities suffered, mortality was especially high among the Mamluks, who lacked the comparative immunity of the indigenous population. This must have necessitated very considerable expenditure by the sultans and amirs on their Mamluk households. Nevertheless there is evidence that Mamluk numbers fell in the Circassian period. Although the data are patchy and not always in agreement, it seems that the Royal Mamluks dropped in number from about 12,000 in the third reign of al-Nāṣir Muḥammad to less than half as many under the Circassian sultans.

It was, however, by its inroads upon the agrarian and industrial workers of Egypt that the plague inflicted its most severe and lasting damage upon the economy. Villages were deserted, irrigation works neglected, and cultivated land went back to waste. Landed revenue, which through the *iqṭāʿs* and the sultan's fisc supported the ruling and military establishment, steadily diminished: between 715/1215 and 923/1517 the land-tax of Egypt shrank from over nine million dinars to less than two million. Syria was even more impoverished than Egypt. Down to the end of the seventh/thirteenth century it had been the battleground of the Mamluks with the Franks and Mongols. It was subsequently the region in which Mamluk factional struggles were frequently fought out, and early in the ninth/fifteenth century it was once again devastated by the invasion of Timur Leng. The urban and industrial population of the sultanate also suffered, both directly and indirectly, from the effects of the plague – Alexandria, the centre of the textile industry (especially silk-weaving), was very badly hit by the Black Death, and its decline continued in the Circassian period.

The diminution of their revenues from land led the sultans and magnates to interfere in the commerce of the towns. A favoured device for raising money was the *ṭarḥ* or *rimāya* (both terms signifying a "throwing" of goods on the market), which was in effect a forced purchase of commodities at an enhanced price. There had been earlier but sporadic examples of this abuse, e.g. the operations of al-Nashw, al-Nāṣir Muḥammad's supervisor of the fisc (see above, p. 118). The supreme instance of this device was Barsbay's monopoly of pepper, described above (p. 187).

Al-Ẓāhir Khushqadam, whose reign from 865/1461 to 872/1467 inaugurated the final succession of Mamluk sultans, was not a Circassian but a Rūmī, meaning possibly an Anatolian Turcoman, possibly a Byzantine Greek. He was installed as a compromise candidate on the overthrow of al-Mu'ayyad Aḥmad, since it was assumed that he, not being a Circassian, could easily be ousted in due course. In fact he succeeded in getting rid of both his kingmaker and his rival, and died in his bed (Rabīʿ I 872/October 1467) after a troubled but undistinguished reign. An assembly of the magnates had already elected his successor, the *Atābak* Yalbay, who came from the household of al-Mu'ayyad Shaykh. He, however, was unable to overcome the factiousness of the Mamluk veterans, and was deposed two months later in favour of Temürbogha, an Albanian from the household of Chakmak. After an equally short period, he too was deposed in Rajab 872/January 1468, and gave place quite amicably to his *khushdāsh* Kayitbay, who in spite of the precarious and faction-ridden start of his reign was to hold on to power until his death in Dhu'l-Qaʿda 901/August 1496 at over 80 years of age.

Something has already been said about Kayitbay's persistent troubles with his *julbān*. The declining strength of the administration and the loss of public security were also demonstrated by the growing boldness of the nomadic tribesmen. In Lower Egypt, they infested the provinces that fringed the Delta; to the west the Buḥayra, and to the east the Sharqiyya – a critically important region through which ran the routes to Syria and the Ḥijāz. In 876/1472 tribesmen from the Sharqiyya looted the shops in the northern suburbs of Cairo for several hours, and a punitive expedition was mounted in response. But it was in Upper Egypt that the most serious tribal revolts occurred – serious not only because of their remoteness from the capital but also because Upper Egypt was the granary of Cairo. Here in the ninth/fifteenth century the dominant tribe was Hawwāra, Berber by origin but by this time thoroughly arabized (see above, p. 136). The Mamluk government endeavoured with mediocre success to control them by appointing and removing chiefs from their ruling clan, Banū ʿUmar, and by occasional punitive expeditions, which had no lasting effect. Kayitbay's principal minister in his dealings with Upper Egypt was the *dawādār*. In the early years of his reign, this office was held by a Mamluk of Chakmak (hence a *khushdāsh* of the sultan) named Yashbeg, who was sent in Muḥarram 874/July–August 1469 to collect corn in Upper Egypt. A dearth which ensued in Cairo during the following months was rumoured to be caused by the *dawādār*'s monopolization of the grain. He returned in Sha'bān 874/February–March 1470, bringing with him the booty of Upper Egypt which he presented to the sultan – gold coins, horses, camels, slaves, honey, sweetmeats and corn. With him came also tales of the atrocities he had committed:

> He perpetrated unheard-of oppressions in Upper Egypt, so that it is said that he roasted alive Maḥmūd, the shaykh of Banū 'Adī. Some of the Arabs were impaled, some flayed and some buried alive. Nobody before him had practised such kinds of torments on the Arabs. [1]

The sultan's kinsman Akbirdī, who became *dawādār* in Muḥarram 886/March 1481, was similarly responsible for maintaining Mamluk authority in Upper Egypt. An expedition in 892/1487 against the Aḥāmda tribe resulted in a victory. Women and children were sent as captives to the capital where in disregard of the *Sharī'a* they were sold, says Ibn Iyās, "like negro slaves". So as effective control over the remoter provinces lapsed, tribal disorder alternated with Mamluk frightfulness.

As well as these internal troubles, growing tension on the northern frontier marked Kayitbay's reign. Here the interests of three great powers intersected. Besides the Mamluks to the south and the Ottomans to the west, the Turcoman confederacy of the Ak-Koyunlu in northern Mesopotamia and eastern Anatolia was for a time at the height of its power. Its chief, Uzun Ḥasan, the grandson of Kara-Yülük (see above, p. 188), established his domination at the expense of the rival Kara-Koyunlu Turcomans and of the Timurids, but he came into conflict with the Ottomans, and was held and defeated by Meḥmed II at Bashkent on the upper Euphrates in 878/1473.

This left the Mamluks and the Ottomans as competitors for the overlordship of the marches. Of the three marcher-principalities (see above, pp. 176, 188), that of the Ramazanids in Cilicia played an insignificant part. Karaman fell to the Ottomans when it was annexed by Meḥmed II in 880/1475. Elbistan under the Dulkadırids remained the key to the frontier. Both the Ottomans and the Mamluks sought to assure their suzerainty by marriage-alliances and by backing rival claimants to the throne. The first crisis came in 870/1465 during the sultanate of Khushqadam, when the Mamluks succeeded in installing their candidate, Shāh Budak. He, however, was quickly driven out by his brother, the Ottoman nominee, Shāh Suvār. Khushqadam, shortly before his death, ordered an expedition to be sent against Shāh Suvār. It set out early in Kayitbay's reign (Shaʿbān 872/March 1468), and was decisively defeated a few weeks later. A second expedition in the following year met with no better success, but a third expedition defeated and captured Shāh Suvār. He was brought to Cairo and put to death (Rabīʿ I 877/August 1472), and Shāh Budak was duly reinstated as ruler of Elbistan. The Mamluk sultan thus reasserted his suzerainty, but not for long. In 884/1479 Shāh Budak was ousted by a third brother, ʿAlāʾ al-Dawla, whose daughter had married Meḥmed II's son, the future Sultan Bāyezīd II. ʿAlāʾ al-Dawla was to reign until he was overthrown, ironically enough, by his own grandson, Sultan Selīm the Grim, in 921/1515.

Relations between the Mamluk and the Ottoman sultan deteriorated sharply when Meḥmed the Conqueror died in 886/1481. Two of his sons, Bāyezīd and Jem, contended for the throne, and when the former won, Jem made his way to Cairo, where he was received by Kayitbay. After making the Pilgrimage, he sought permission to return to Turkey and fight his brother. After consulting his magnates, Kayitbay gave unwilling permission (Muḥarram 887/February–March 1482). The expedition was a failure, and Jem fled once more – this time to the protection of the Knights Hospitallers in Rhodes. The rest of his life was spent in exile, but until Jem's death in 900/1495 Bāyezīd II was never free of the fear that he would return with Frankish support to take the Ottoman throne.

It was in these circumstances that the first Ottoman–Mamluk war broke out with help sent by the Ottomans to ʿAlāʾ al-Dawla. The war was essentially a series of frontier-campaigns, not a fight to the death between two great powers. Bāyezīd, mindful of the potential threat from Jem, dared not commit his forces fully to operations against the Mamluks, while Kayitbay was hampered by the chronic financial weakness of his state, aggravated by the cost of the earlier campaigns against Shāh Suvār. At the start, Kayitbay made a curious and inept attempt at reconciliation by sending in 890/1485 an ambassador with a diploma from the caliph, in which Bāyezīd was appointed the Mamluk sultan's lieutenant in Anatolia and whatever subsequent conquests he might make. The fictitious grant of subordinate status by a puppet ʿAbbasid was unlikely to appeal to the son of the conqueror of Constantinople, and the ambassador returned to report an unsuccessful mission. During the war ʿAlāʾ al-Dawla played an equivocal part in regard to his son-in-law, Sultan Bāyezīd, who briefly replaced him by Shāh Budak. But when peace was negotiated in 896/1491 little had changed on the frontier. ʿAlāʾ al-Dawla was back in Elbistan and tolerably loyal to the Ottomans. Both great powers were exhausted by their efforts but the Mamluk sultanate was less able to recuperate than were the Ottomans.

Kayitbay died on 27 Dhu'l-Qaʿda 901/7 August 1496, and the next five years saw the succession of five sultans, of whom al-Nāṣir Muḥammad, the fourteen-year-old son of Kayitbay, was the first. His short and troubled reign was notable for his attempt to create a new military base for his authority in the shape of a force of black slaves with firearms. This experiment inevitably gave enormous offence to the Circassian Mamluk establishment, and the magnates from Kayitbay's household had their revenge on their *ustādh*'s son when the young sultan was assassinated near Giza on 15 Rabīʿ I 904/31 October 1498. His successor was his maternal uncle, a thirty-year-old Mamluk named Kansawh, who took the title of al-Malik al-Nāṣir. He was in fact the nominee of a certain Tumanbay, who had been a principal conspirator against al-Nāṣir Muḥammad. Tumanbay coveted the sultanate for himself but the time was not yet ripe, so he accepted appointment as *dawādār*, and like his recent predecessors in that office, he proceeded to make punitive expeditions against the insubordinate tribal Arabs. In Dhu'l-Qaʿda 905/June 1500 he felt strong enough to lead a faction to bombard the Citadel. Al-Ẓāhir Kansawh absconded in disguise, but once again Tumanbay was disappointed of the sultanate, which went to his senior *khushdāsh*, the *Atābak* Janpulat. Tumanbay shortly afterwards proclaimed himself sultan while on an expedition to Syria, and returned to drive his predecessor out of the Citadel (Jumādā II 906/January 1501).

Three months later al-ʿĀdil Tumanbay was himself overthrown, and al-Ashraf Kansawh al-Ghawrī unwillingly succeeded him at the behest of the magnates. They probably saw him as a stop-gap. He was about 60 years of age, and although he had held high office under Tumanbay, he had not played a leading part in the kaleidoscopic politics of the period. In fact he reigned for fifteen years and perished only in the death-agony of the Mamluk sultanate. These four successors of al-Nāṣir Muḥammad were all from Kayitbay's Mamluk household, so that the struggle for the sultanate from 904/1498 to 906/1501 was essentially a competition among *khushdāshiyya*.

Kansawh al-Ghawrī was beset throughout his reign by the same internal problems which had disturbed and sometimes destroyed his predecessors – overmighty and factious magnates, insubordinate *julbān*, ungovernable tribesmen, above all the perennial shortage of money with consequential extraordinary levies and extortion. Cash was needed not only to pacify the turbulent and rapacious Mamluks but also to finance the sultan's schemes for the defence of his realm. He followed the example of al-Nāṣir Muḥammad in raising a corps armed with hand-guns. Again the Mamluks would have nothing to do with it, and it was recruited from Turcomans, outlandish people, *awlād al-nās* and artisans. Kansawh also paid much attention to the casting of artillery, and often attended in person the testing of new cannon. These were not always happy occasions. Ibn Iyās describes one such trial in 916/1510:

> The sultan went down to the tomb of al-ʿĀdil at al-Raydāniyya, and they tested in his presence the cannon they had cast. When they fired the powder in them, they all exploded. Their bronze flew through the air, and not one of them was sound. There were about fifteen cannon. The sultan was increasingly upset on that day, and returned quickly to the Citadel. He had intended to give a feast to the amirs and spend the day rejoicing, but it was not to be.[2]

Another cause of expenditure was the need for warships to protect the Mediterranean coasts of Egypt and Syria from the raids of Frankish corsairs, and to counter the new threat to the Red Sea from the Portuguese. The Western European thrust to the east, of which the Crusades had been an earlier manifestation, had now found a new outlet as the Portuguese rounded the Cape of Good Hope in 1497, crossed the Indian Ocean, and established themselves on the East African coast and (in 1503) at Cochin in India. Their arrival in the Indian Ocean threatened to cut the great trade-route by which the products of India and the Far East came to Egypt – a branch of commerce which, as we have seen, Barsbay had monopolized for the benefit of his treasury. The Portuguese moreover deliberately attempted to exclude Muslim shipping from the Red Sea. Kansawh al-Ghawrī was not slow to respond. A naval expedition was sent in Jumādā II 911/November 1505 under the command of a certain Ḥusayn al-Kurdī (not a Mamluk) to assist the ruler of Gujarat against the Portuguese. On its way out it fortified Jedda. The combined Mamluk and Gujarati fleets defeated the Portuguese in Ramaḍān 913/January 1508, but after a Portuguese victory off Diu (Shawwāl 914/February 1509) the Mamluk expedition returned to Egypt.

The challenge to Muslim trade and security from a new and unexpected direction produced a degree of co-operation between the Ottoman and Mamluk sultans in this revival of the Holy War. Bāyezīd II sent timber, iron and gunpowder to Kansawh in 916/1511, and promised further supplies. Warships were under construction in the Gulf of Suez, and in 921/1515 a second naval expedition was ready to set out. To it the Ottomans contributed not only war materials but also a contingent of about 2,000 sailors under their own commander, Selmān Reʾīs, who shared the direction of the expedition with Ḥusayn al-Kurdī. It got no further than the Yemen, where it took Zabīd in Jumādā I 922/June 1516, and went on to make an unsuccessful attack on Aden. Although the expedition had only a limited success, it established a foothold in the Yemen which was soon to be exploited by the Ottomans, and the Muslim naval activity kept the Portuguese out of the Red Sea.

By an ironic coincidence, Mamluk–Ottoman co-operation in the Red Sea coincided with the second and final war between the two sultanates. The situation had changed considerably in the thirty years since the last major crisis. Bāyezīd II, whom circumstances and character had constrained to a generally cautious policy, had been succeeded in 918/1512 by his bellicose son, Selīm I. In the east the Ak-Koyunlu had sunk into impotence after the death of Uzun Ḥasan in 882/1478, but a new great power had come into existence. Shāh Ismāʿīl, the descendant of a Ṣūfī holy family which had its headquarters at Ardabīl in Azerbaijan, made himself the master of the whole of Persia and the eastern Fertile Crescent in the ten years from 906/1501. The Safavid state which he thus established set itself in deliberate opposition to the Ottomans: Shāh Ismāʿīl was champion of the Shīʿīs as the sultan was of the Sunnīs. The two powers competed for the allegiance of the Turcomans, and Kansawh al-Ghawrī was alarmed when the Safavids invaded Elbistan in 913/1507. The Mamluk sultanate (itself, of course, a Sunnī state) appeared increasingly inferior to its two powerful northern neighbours.

The final crisis began in 920/1514, when Sultan Selīm invaded Safavid territory and defeated Shāh Ismāʿīl at Chaldirān in Azerbaijan. Selīm's grandfather, ʿAlāʾ al-Dawla of Elbistan, who had refused help to the Ottomans when requested, was ruthlessly hunted down, and his principality passed finally under Ottoman domination. The Mamluk governors in Syria were alarmed at these developments, and in Rabīʿ II 922/May 1516 Kansawh, who was in touch with Shāh Ismāʿīl, left Cairo for Aleppo where he had already a numerous but disorderly field army. Selīm, who intended to make another campaign in the east against Shāh Ismāʿīl, decided not to leave this potentially hostile force on his flank. Negotiations broke down, and battle was joined at Marj Dābiq, north of Aleppo, on 25 Rajab 922/24 August 1516. The fate of the Mamluks was sealed when their left wing commanded by the governor of Aleppo, Khāʾir Bey, took to flight, probably by collusion with the Ottomans. The octogenarian Kansawh al-Ghawrī died of apoplexy during the battle. The Ottoman conquest of Syria rapidly ensued. Aleppo fell without a blow. Selīm marched south and entered Damascus on 13 Ramaḍān 922/10 October 1516.

When Kansawh left Cairo he appointed as his deputy his nephew, another Tumanbay, who had held office as *dawādār* since 913/1507, and like previous *dawādārs* had been active in the collection of revenue from

Upper Egypt and the repression of the tribesmen. When the news of his uncle's defeat and death became known, the Mamluk magnates in Egypt pressed him to accept the sultanate. Unwillingly he consented, and was installed on 14 Ramaḍān/11 October with maimed rites, since part of the regalia had been lost with the dead sultan in Syria, and the Caliph al-Mutawakkil III was a prisoner of war with the Ottomans. This second Sultan Tumanbay took the title of al-Malik al-Ashraf.

By his victory at Marj Dābiq and the occupation of Syria, the Ottoman sultan had safeguarded his flank in any further campaign against the Safavids. He seems not to have been anxious to go on and attempt a conquest of Egypt. An advance towards the Delta and Cairo would be hazardous in itself, and would dangerously prolong Selīm's lines of communication. But Selīm was urged by Mamluk collaborators (chief among them Khā'ir Bey, now a trusted adviser of the sultan) to continue the war, although it appears that he would have been willing to leave Tumanbay in Egypt as a vassal ruler. The difficult crossing of the Sinai desert was accomplished, and the Mamluks allowed the Ottomans to advance to al-Raydāniyya in the vicinity of Cairo before they made a stand. A brief battle ended in the rout of the Mamluks on 29 Dhu'l-Ḥijja 922/23 January 1517, and the next day Selīm's name replaced that of Tumanbay in the *khuṭba* in Cairo.

Tumanbay escaped from al-Raydāniyya, gathered a mixed force of Arabs and Mamluks at al-Bahnasā in Middle Egypt, and entered into negotiations with his Ottoman rival. But the negotiations were forcibly broken off by some of Tumanbay's Mamluk colleagues. There was another battle, this time at Giza on 10 Rabīʿ I 923/2 April 1517, and Tumanbay was again defeated. A few days later he was betrayed to the Ottomans, and the final scene in his life and in the history of the Mamluk sultanate is thus described by Ibn Iyās:

> When the Ottoman [i.e. Sultan Selīm] learnt that the people did not believe that Tumanbay had been taken, he was angered, and sent him across [to Cairo]. He went from Būlāq by way of al-Maqs, preceded by about 400 Ottomans and arquebusiers. He went by way of Sūq Marjūsh and passed through Cairo, greeting the people along the way until he arrived at the Zuwayla Gate, unaware of what would befall him. When he came to the Zuwayla Gate, they dismounted him and loosened his bonds, and the Ottomans surrounded him with drawn swords. When he realized that he was to be hanged, he stood up at the Zuwayla Gate and said to the people around him, "Say the *Fātiḥa*[3] three times for me." He spread out his hands and said the *Fātiḥa* three times, and the people said it with him. Then he said to the executioner, "Do your work." When they put the noose around his neck and raised the rope, it broke and he fell on the threshold of the Zuwayla Gate. It is said that the rope broke twice, and he fell to the ground. Then they hanged him .... When he died and his spirit went forth,

the people cried with a great cry, and there was much grief and sorrow for him.[4]

NOTES

1. Ibn Iyās, *Badā'i' al-zuhūr fī waqā'i' al-duhūr*, III, Cairo 1383/1963, 43. English version P. M. Holt.
2. Ibn Iyās, *Badā'i'*, IV, Cairo 1379/1960, 192. English version P. M. Holt.
3. *Sūrat al-Fātiḥa*, the opening chapter of the Qur'ān, is a characteristic part of Muslim devotions. Here it is used in effect as a prayer for Tumanbay's soul.
4. Ibn Iyās, *Badā'i'*, V, Cairo 1380/1961, 176. English version P. M. Holt.

Conclusion: Retrospect and Prospect

During the period of rather more than four hundred years surveyed in this book, one major theme in the political history of the eastern Mediterranean lands has been their progressive unification and ultimate consolidation under the administration of a single Muslim government. In the later fifth/eleventh century Syria was a debatable land between the Fatimid caliphate in the west and the Great Seljuk sultanate in the east. The movement towards the political unification of this territory was powerfully stimulated by the plantation of the Christian Frankish states on its periphery: the call to the Holy War sanctified the policies of the Muslim rulers and was a rallying-cry to their subjects. Although their territorial ambitions and political aims were by no means restricted to the *jihād* against the Franks and the redemption of the lost Islamic lands, Zangī, Nūr al-Dīn and Saladin can be seen in retrospect as the architects of the reconquest. The Syria which Saladin left to his kinsmen was not yet entirely free from Frankish domination, since the successors of the Crusaders still held fragments of their former possessions on the coast; nor was it yet administratively united, since the Ayyubid clan partitioned its provinces among themselves, wasting their strength in internecine struggles.

The territorial and political unification of the Ayyubid inheritance was achieved by their Turkish soldiery, the Mamluks, who in the middle years of the seventh/thirteenth century became the rulers of the lands of their former masters. The Mongol invasions were repulsed, the remnants of the Frankish states conquered, and under "the kings of the Turks" (as the chroniclers called them) Egypt and Syria were united. A militarized central and provincial administration was underpinned by a civil service of native-born, Arabic-speaking secretarial and financial officials. The Mamluk sultans were from one aspect Muslim autocrats, their authority legitimated by ʿAbbasid shadow-caliphs but with no institutional checks on their arbitrary will. Neither the Islamic judiciary nor the civil service developed an *esprit de corps* which would enable them to withstand the power of the sultan, nor were there precedents effective enough to channel his acts. From another aspect, the sultans were quasi-tribal chiefs of the Mamluks, the Turkish (and later the Circassian) immigrants into Egypt and Syria. In that quality they had to keep the Mamluk magnates who were their tribal peers in good humour with the booty of successful warfare, or with fat assignments of land-revenues, augmented as time went on with the profits of extortion and oppression. A sultan who failed to conciliate the magnates either through weakness or overweening strength was liable to encounter the sole real limitation on his power – deposition or regicide at their hands. Thus the politics of the Mamluk sultanate were largely the factional politics of a military aristocracy alien to the land in which it dwelt.

During these centuries another Holy War was being waged, although intermittently and with fluctuations of fortune, further to the north in Anatolia. Unlike the *jihād* in Syria, it was not in order to reconquer lands lost to the infidel, but to extend the bounds of Islam beyond the limits reached in the Arab conquests of the first/seventh century. In the long run it was successful, and Byzantine Anatolia became *Turchia*, Turkey. The first attempt to create a united Turkish kingdom in the new territories, the Seljuk sultanate of Rūm, had only limited success, and the Mongols wrecked it as they did not wreck the Mamluk sultanate. From the mosaic of Turkish *beyliks* which followed its dissolution emerged the last of the *gazi* states under the leadership of the house of ʿOsmān. Waging the Holy War not only against the last remains of Byzantine territory in Anatolia but also against the Christian states in Rumelia (i.e. south-eastern Europe), it had a foot in both continents. This enabled the Ottoman state to revive after the shock of defeat by Timur Leng, and to go on with renewed vigour to the conquest of Constantinople. Thereafter it was to confront the declining power of its rival, the Mamluk sultanate, ultimately defeating it and conquering Syria and Egypt. For four hundred years to come, the former territories of the Mamluk sultanate were to be provinces of the Ottoman empire.

Syria, detached from Egypt, was more or less effectively absorbed into the Ottoman administrative system. Egypt was, as always, something of a special case. With a long history of independence as a major power, an administrative and fiscal system adapted to its unique geographical conditions and elaborated over centuries, it received particular consideration from Selīm the Grim and his advisers, whose settlement of the country was remarkably conservative. Although the Mamluks who had fought against the Ottomans were proscribed, and many absconded or were killed, Selīm owed his new conquests very largely to Mamluk collaborators, notably Khā'ir Bey. These collaborators may have regarded Selīm less as an invader and conqueror than as a powerful outside supporter against their Mamluk rivals, Kansawh al-Ghawrī and Tumanbay – much as Mamluk malcontents at an earlier period had backed invasions of Syria by the *ilkhans*. However this may be, they had their reward. Khā'ir Bey was appointed viceroy of Egypt and reigned in the Citadel until he died, while another collaborator, Janbirdi al-Ghazālī, was appointed governor of Damascus.

The recruitment of Mamluks, mainly Circassians, went on until the early nineteenth century, and much of the old Mamluk system survived the Ottoman conquest. The Royal Mamluks disappeared with the sultanate, but Mamluk grandees continued to form their own military households. The existence of these is a notable feature from about the middle of the eleventh/seventeenth century, and as previously under the sultanate Egyptian politics were dominated by their factions. The Ottoman garrison in Egypt, originally a military counterpoise to the Mamluks, was increasingly drawn into the web of clientage and patronage which was the structure of neo-Mamluk society, to such an extent that in the twelfth/eighteenth century one of the great Mamluk households was founded by an Ottoman officer.

Although the establishment of Ottoman rule in Egypt was followed by a reorganization of the fiscal system (reminiscent of the *rawks* carried out by Saladin and al-Nāṣir Muḥammad to support their power), the neo-Mamluk grandees quickly secured a hold over a large share of the *iltizāms*, i.e. the tax-farms which fulfilled a role similar to that of the *iqṭā's* of the old regime. They also acquired a prescriptive right to three of the great offices of state; that of *amīr al-ḥājj*, the commander of the annual Pilgrimage-caravan (see above, p. 81), of *defterdār*, the head of the provincial fiscal administration, and of *qā'im maqām*, the acting viceroy who exercised supreme power when Egypt was awaiting the arrival of a new Ottoman viceroy. The leading Mamluk grandees held the Ottoman title of bey (in full, *sanjak beyi*) and were nominally 24 in number, which suggests that they were the institutional successors of the 24 amirs of the highest rank under the Mamluk sultanate (see above, p. 148). With such wealth and such power, it is hardly surprising that the neo-Mamluks of the Ottoman period occasionally dreamed of reviving the independent sultanate of Egypt. This was not to be, but these neo-Mamluks with all their political and personal failings helped to preserve the distinctiveness of Egypt under Ottoman rule. Muḥammad ʿAlī Pasha, the soldier from Macedonia who in 1811 finally eliminated the Mamluks as a political force, realized their aims when as viceroy of Egypt, he made himself all but independent of the Ottoman sultan.

Bibliographical Survey

ABBREVIATIONS

BSOAS: Bulletin of the School of Oriental and African Studies, London.
EHR: English Historical Review, London.

PRIMARY SOURCES

There are abundant Arabic sources, especially for the later part of the period from the late fifth/eleventh to the late eighth/fourteenth century. A fair number of them have been published or are in process of publication. This section surveys the main categories of sources, and describes a selection of the more important works and their authors.

The classical genre of Arabic historical writing was the chronicle, of which the model was *Ta'rīkh al-rusul wa'l-mulūk* (The history of the prophets and the kings), compiled by an author of an earlier period, Muḥammad b. Jarīr al-Ṭabarī (d. 310/923). It is significant that al-Ṭabarī was primarily a religious scholar, who also wrote a commentary on the Qur'ān and works on Islamic law. His vast compilation covers the course of history from pre-Islamic times to the ʿAbbasid caliphate as it presented itself to a pious and erudite Muslim. A more or less openly expressed religious and moral view of history informs the works of many of al-Ṭabarī's successors. In the period considered here, the compilation of universal chronicles continued, the most important being *al-Kāmil fi'l-ta'rīkh* (The complete chronicle) of ʿAlī b. Muḥammad Ibn al-Athīr (555–630/1160–1233). His home was in Mosul, where his father was an official in the service of the Zangids, and his own loyalty or partiality to this dynasty appears in his works. This bias does not affect the greater part of *al-Kāmil*, which is wide in its geographical range, and covers events from the Creation to 628/1230–1. Like al-Ṭabarī's chronicle, it is a many-volumed work. A later and much smaller universal chronicle is *al-Mukhtaṣar fī akhbār al-bashar* (A short history of mankind) by Ismāʿīl Abu'l-Fidā' (672–732/1273–1331), a member of the Ayyubid princely family of Ḥamāh, where he himself became sultan by grace of al-Nāṣir Muḥammad b. Kalavun (see above, p. 115). This chronicle brings the narrative of events down to 729/1328–9 with a later continuation. A great universal chronicle, left incomplete by its author, and extant only in a fragmentary state is *Ta'rīkh al-duwal wa'l-mulūk* (The history of the regimes and the kings) of Muḥammad b. ʿAbd al-Raḥīm Ibn al-Furāt (735–807/1334–1405), an Egyptian historian.

A contemporary of Abu'l-Fidā' was the author of a work which in form was a universal chronicle, but which in scope and outlook had some individual characteristics. This is *Kanz al-durar wa-jāmiʿ al-ghurar* (The treasure of pearls and gathering of choicest things) of Abū Bakr b. ʿAbdallāh b. Aybak al-Dawādārī, usually known as Ibn al-Dawādārī, who died after 736/1335, the date of completion of his work. He was of Mamluk descent. Of his nine volumes, the last four deal in increasing detail with the history of Egypt from the Fatimid caliphate to the reign of al-Nāṣir Muḥammad, which indeed occupies the whole of the final volume. Ibn al-Dawādārī's perspective implies that the whole of Egyptian history (or even human history) leads up to al-Nāṣir Muḥammad's sultanate. This is very different from al-Ṭabarī's theme of the providential history of the Muslim community, and indicates a new style of historical writing that became increasingly common from about the middle of the seventh/thirteenth century. Whereas the classical historiography had been an adjunct to the religious sciences, chronicles of the new type served primarily as literary entertainment – a development described by modern German scholars as *Literarisierung*.[1]

While Ibn al-Dawādārī's chronicle shrinks from a universal theme to a history of Egypt, other writers explicitly set out to record the annals of their local communities. One such chronicler at the beginning of the period was Ḥamza b. Asad Ibn al-Qalānisī, who died in 555/1160. He came of a good Damascene family, became head of the ruler's chancery and held office as *ra'īs* (see above, p. 71). His work is entitled *Dhayl ta'rīkh Dimashq* (The continuation of the chronicle of Damascus), and is ostensibly the supplement to an earlier universal chronicle. It is of great importance both because of the light it sheds on the internal politics of Damascus and Syria generally, and because it gives a contemporary account of the First and Second Crusades, and of the Muslim reaction.

At the end of the period are two local histories on a far greater scale –

chronicles of Muslim Egypt by al-Maqrīzī (766–845/1364–1442) and his younger contemporary Ibn Taghrībirdī (d. 874/1470). Taqī al-Dīn Aḥmad b. ʿAlī al-Maqrīzī, a scholar and teacher of the religious sciences in Cairo and Damascus, was a prolific writer. In his great chronicle, *Kitāb al-sulūk li-maʿrifat duwal al-mulūk* (The book of the ways to knowledge of the regimes of the kings), the author, after some introductory matter, deals with Saladin and the Ayyubids, but the bulk of the work treats of the Mamluk sultans down to 844/1440–1. Another of al-Maqrīzī's works, in form a topographical survey of Egypt, and particularly of Cairo, abounds in historical data of all kinds, including, for example, long excerpts from Ibn Sulaym al-Aswānī's account of his journey through Nubia in the later fourth/tenth century. The book's full title, *Kitāb al-mawāʿiẓ waʾl-iʿtibār bi-dhikr al-khiṭaṭ waʾl-āthār* (The book of exhortation and contemplation in the consideration of the districts and the antiquities) is usually abbreviated to *al-Khiṭaṭ*. Abuʾl-Maḥāsin Yūsuf Ibn Taghrībirdī, a pupil of al-Maqrīzī, came from a wholly different background from that of his teacher. His father was a Mamluk who attained high office under the Sultan al-Nāṣir Faraj b. Barkuk. Ibn Taghrībirdī himself was well educated, and his connection with the Mamluk military aristocracy gave him a particular insight into the politics of the regime. His chronicle, *al-Nujūm al-zāhira fī mulūk Miṣr waʾl-Qāhira* (The shining stars concerning the kings of Egypt and Cairo), covers the history of Muslim Egypt from the Arab conquest to 872/1467. The story of events is brought down to the Ottoman conquest and the years immediately following by Muḥammad b. Aḥmad b. Iyās, *Badāʾiʿ al-zuhūr fī waqāʾiʿ al-duhūr* (The marvellous flowers of the events of the times). Ibn Iyās (852–*c.* 930/1448–*c.* 1524) was of Mamluk descent. The major part of his chronicle deals in steadily increasing detail with the events of his own lifetime.

A type of historical writing which is well represented at two points in this period is the royal biography. There is a cluster of works of this kind around Saladin, and another around the early Mamluk sultans, al-Ẓāhir Baybars, Kalavun and al-Ashraf Khalīl. All the biographies were composed by men closely connected with the rulers about whom they wrote, and care must be taken in assessing the historical value of their work. Their possession of detailed inside knowledge must be balanced against their propensity to eulogize the ruler. Furthermore the authors wrote to a pattern, presenting their subject as conforming to the ideal of a Muslim ruler, even if he was (like Baybars or Kalavun) an immigrant of Turkish tribal origin and a recent convert to Islam. There is also a tendency by the later writers to magnify Baybars in comparison with Saladin, and Kalavun in comparison with Baybars. Inevitably those acts of the ruler which fit the pattern are presented and emphasized, and thereby a somewhat unrealistic portrait of a paragon and hero of Islam is set before an unwary reader.

Saladin's contemporary biographers set the tone (see above, pp. 38–9). They were men of his court, serving in his administration. Bahā' al-Dīn Ibn Shaddād (539–632/1145–1235) was his army-judge, ʿImād al-Dīn al-Iṣfahānī (519–97/1125–1201) was his secretary. The biography by the former is entitled *al-Nawādir al-sulṭāniyya wa'l-maḥāsin al-Yūsufiyya* (The rare virtues of Sultan Yūsuf [i.e. Saladin]). The latter wrote a chronicle of Saladin's life and times, *al-Barq al-Shāmī* (The Syrian thunderbolt) in seven volumes, only two of which are now extant. He also produced an elaborately rhetorical account of the last glorious phase of Saladin's career from the Ḥaṭṭīn campaign to his death, entitled *al-Fatḥ al-Qussī fi'l-fatḥ al-Qudsī*, which might be paraphrased "The eloquent exposition of the conquest of Jerusalem" – but the title contains two Arabic puns. It is perhaps significant that both of these writers had spent their earlier careers in the service of the Zangids, and the production of these encomia of the successful usurper may have been undertaken partly by way of self-justification.

The biographers of the early Mamluk sultans were also officials about the royal court. Muḥyī al-Dīn Ibn ʿAbd al-Ẓāhir (620–92/1223–92) and his maternal nephew, Shāfiʿ b. ʿAlī (649–730/1252–1330) both served in the Egyptian royal chancery, of which at one time Ibn ʿAbd al-Ẓāhir was the head. A third biographer, ʿIzz al-Dīn Ibn Shaddād (613–84/1217–85), apparently unrelated to Bahā' al-Dīn Ibn Shaddād, worked in the chancery of al-Nāṣir Yūsuf, the last Ayyubid ruler of Aleppo and Damascus, fled to Egypt when the Mongols invaded Syria, and entered the service of the Mamluk sultan. Ibn ʿAbd al-Ẓāhir wrote Baybars's court-biography, *al-Rawḍ al-zāhir fī sīrat al-Malik al-Ẓāhir* (The garden of flowers concerning the life of al-Malik al-Ẓāhir [Baybars]), probably modelled on *al-Nawādir*. An abridgement of this biography, entitled *Ḥusn al-manāqib al-sirriyya al-muntazaʿa min al-sīra al-Ẓāhiriyya* (The excellence of the mysterious virtues taken from the biography of al-Ẓāhir) was made by Shāfiʿ b. ʿAlī. In spite of the title, Shāfiʿ is at times openly critical both of Baybars and of his uncle as a biographer. His unusual plain-speaking is explained by the fact that he was writing under al-Nāṣir Muḥammad, when both Baybars and Ibn ʿAbd al-Ẓāhir were dead, and the Kalavunids had usurped the sultanate. Ibn Shaddād's biography of Baybars, which apparently had the same title as Ibn ʿAbd al-Ẓāhir's (although this has been denied)[2] occupies something of a middle position, showing the writer as one who had experienced the sultan's favour but was not his official biographer. In addition, Ibn ʿAbd al-Ẓāhir and Shāfiʿ b. ʿAlī both wrote biographies of Kalavun, and the former also one of al-Ashraf Khalīl.

Another genre of historical writing, the dynastic history, partakes of the characteristics of both the chronicle and the royal biography. Two important works of this kind are, first, a history of the Zangids by Ibn al-Athīr, *al-Taʾrīkh al-bāhir fiʾl-dawla al-atābakiyya* (The brilliant history of the regime of the *atabegs*); and, secondly, of the Ayyubids, *Mufarrij al-kurūb fī akhbār Banī Ayyūb* (The solace of troubles concerning the history of the Ayyubids) by Ibn Wāṣil. Muḥammad b. Sālim Ibn Wāṣil (604–97/1208–98) was a Syrian scholar who served the Ayyubids and the Mamluks, went as ambassador from Baybars to Manfred of Hohenstaufen, king of Sicily, and was tutor to Ismāʿīl Abuʾl-Fidāʾ. Ibn al-Athīr's history of the Zangids is a partisan work, which was apparently designed to state their case against the Ayyubids; it includes a long biography of Nūr al-Dīn b. Zangī, which may have been intended to serve as a retort to Bahāʾ al-Dīn Ibn Shaddād's *al-Nawādir* with its eulogistic presentation of Saladin. The rival historiographies of Saladin and the Zangids were reconciled by Abū Shāma (599–665/1203–68), a pious scholar of Damascus, who completed in 651/1253 his book, *Kitāb al-rawḍatayn fī akhbār al-dawlatayn al-Nūriyya waʾl-Ṣalāḥiyya* (The book of the two gardens concerning the two regimes of Nūr al-Dīn and Saladin).

Biographical materials are abundant in the sources of the period. Apart from the royal biographies, there are notices of important persons in some chronicles; Ibn Taghrībirdī, for example, provides under each regnal year obituaries of leading men of the religious and military institutions. There are also the biographical dictionaries, a genre which before modern times was practically unique to Islam. One such, a single-volume work compiled by a Christian official in Cairo, Faḍlallāh b. Abiʾl-Fakhr Ibn al-Ṣuqāʿī (d. 726/1328) is entitled *Tālī kitāb wafayāt al-aʿyān*, i.e. the continuation of *Wafayāt al-aʿyān* (The obituaries of notables), which was a great general biographical dictionary compiled by Ibn Khallikān (d. 681/1282). The *Tālī*, restricted to obituaries between 658/1259 and 725/1325, is a valuable source of information on leading men of the early Mamluk period. The manuscript of the *Tālī*, now in Paris, once belonged to another author of a biographical dictionary, Khalīl b. Aybak al-Ṣafadī (d. 764/1363), and was used by him in the compilation of his own many-volumed work, *al-Wāfī biʾl-wafayāt* (The complete obituaries). Al-Ṣafadī, the son of a Mamluk, served as a chancery official in Cairo and Syria, and was a prolific and highly esteemed writer.

Other types of works provide a good deal of historical information, especially on institutions and society. Officials of the elaborate and sophisticated Egyptian administration compiled manuals for the guidance of their subordinates and successors. Two of these, which throw light on the financial organization of the state, are *Kitāb al-minhāj fī ʿilm kharāj Miṣr* (The book of the easy road to knowledge of the taxation of Egypt), by ʿAlī b. ʿUthmān al-Makhzūmī, originally compiled in 565/1169–70, and revised in 581/1185–6; and *Kitāb qawānīn al-dawāwīn* (The book of regulations of the departments) by al-Asʿad Ibn Mammātī (d. 606/1209). Al-Makhzūmī, like his father a *qāḍī* by training, served in the financial departments of the Fatimids and Ayyubids. Ibn Mammātī came from a Coptic family with a similar record of service; his father was a convert to Islam. The most monumental of the chancery guides, a veritable encyclopaedia which draws largely on the works of preceding writers, is *Ṣubḥ al-aʿshā fī ṣināʿat al-inshā* (The dawn of the dim-sighted concerning the clerk's craft) of Aḥmad b. ʿAlī al-Qalqashandī (756–821/1355–1418), who after a legal training became a clerk of the bench (*kātib al-dast*; see above, p. 146) in 791/1389. His book covers the whole range of information needed by chancery clerks in the Mamluk sultanate. As well as data on the officials and procedures of Mamluk and earlier administrations, it preserves as models documents from lost archives, e.g. truces between the Mamluk sultans and the Frankish states.

Two travellers from the Muslim West, a century and a half apart, have left accounts of their experiences in the lands of the eastern Mediterranean. The earlier was Muḥammad b. Aḥmad Ibn Jubayr, born in Valencia in 540/1145, when it was still a Muslim city. An educated man and secretary to the governor of Granada, he made the Pilgrimage to Mecca in remorse at having drunk wine. His journey by way of Egypt and the Red Sea port of ʿAydhāb, and his return through Medina, Iraq, Muslim Syria and Frankish Acre, lasted for over two years (578–81/1183–5). It is described in his book, *al-Riḥla* (The journey). He died in Alexandria in 614/1217. His work was plagiarized by later writers, among them Ibn Juzayy, the amanuensis of Muḥammad b. ʿAbdallāh Ibn Baṭṭūṭa and editor of his travels. Ibn Baṭṭūṭa, who was born in Tangier in 703/1304, travelled far more widely than Ibn Jubayr. Between 725/1325 and 754/1353, he visited not only Egypt, the Holy Cities and the Fertile Crescent, as well as Anatolia, Constantinople, and the land of the Golden Horde, but also (or so he claims) he journeyed as far east as China and as far south as the Niger. He was, it appears, no great scholar, although he functioned as a *qāḍī* in India, and Ibn Juzayy provided literary embellishments for the memoirs he dictated. The work appeared in 757/1358 as *Tuḥfat al-nuẓẓār fī gharāʾib al-amṣār wa-ʿajāʾib al-asfār* (The spectators' rare gift being wonders of the cities and marvels of travel).

Although travel-writers such as Ibn Jubayr and Ibn Baṭṭūṭa tell us something of themselves in the course of their narratives, Muslim autobiographies as such are almost unknown before modern times. One of the few was written by an Arab aristocrat from Syria, Usāma b. Munqidh (488–584/1095–1188), whose family were lords of the castle of Shayzar on the River Orontes. Usāma's long lifetime spanned the years from the eve of the First Crusade to the eve of the Third. As a man of social standing and a warrior (although never a figure of much political significance) he moved as easily in the company of Muslim rulers as of Frankish knights, whom he describes with a somewhat contemptuous detachment. His autobiography was written late in life, when he was a pensioner of Saladin. Its title is *Kitab al-iʿtibār* (The book of learning by example) – an indication of its ostensibly didactic purpose. Another autobiography is concealed in the last part of the universal chronicle of Abu'l-Fidā' mentioned above. In his annal for 672/1273–4 he notes his own birth at a time when his family were refugees from the Mongols in Damascus. In 684/1285–6 he describes the siege of al-Marqab, the first military operation in which he himself participated, and from then until 729/1328–9 he records the events of his own life together with those in Syria and in the wider world. Although the later portions of many chronicles are accounts of contemporary affairs, it is unusual for the chronicler to set down what are in effect his personal memoirs as does Abu'l-Fidā'.

It is on literary sources that the modern historian of the Near East must chiefly depend. The archives of the pre-Ottoman Muslim states of the region have long since been dispersed and destroyed. Such state papers as have survived are mostly to be found in one or other of three places: the archives of the monastery of St Catherine on Mount Sinai, the archives of European states and the literary sources themselves. From the monastery of St Catherine come decrees of Fatimid, Ayyubid, and Mamluk rulers, mainly in response to petitions from the monks. They throw light on chancery procedure and on conditions in the Sinai region, but as they deal with the affairs of a marginal community in a remote area, they give little information of wide significance. Some of these documents have been published by S. M. Stern, *Fāṭimid decrees*, London [1964], with translations and a valuable commentary; others are in his articles, "Petitions from the Ayyūbid period", *BSOAS*, xxvii (1), 1964, 1–32, and "Two Ayyūbid decrees from Sinai" in S. M. Stern (ed.), *Documents from Islamic chanceries*, Oxford [1965], also with translations and commentary. Documents of the Mamluk period were published with German translations by Hans Ernst, *Die mamlukischen Sul-*

tansurkunden des Sinai-Klosters, Wiesbaden 1960, in connection with which should be read the review article by S. M. Stern, "Petitions from the Mamlūk period", *BSOAS*, xxix (2), 1966, 233–76.

The documents to be found in European archives are in the nature of the case mainly commercial treaties and related pieces. Latin and Italian versions of such instruments from the Venetian archives were published by G. L. Fr. Tafel and G. M. Thomas, *Urkunden zur älteren Handels- und Staatsgeschichte der Republik Venedigs*, 3 vols, Vienna 1856. The text and Spanish translation of Mamluk treaties with Aragon are found in M. A. Alarcón y Santón and R. García de Linares, *Los documentos árabes diplomáticos del Archivo de la Corona de Aragón*, Madrid and Granada 1940; see also Aziz Suryal Atiya, *Egypt and Aragon: embassies and diplomatic correspondence between 1300 and 1330 A.D.*, Leipzig 1938. Some pieces from Italian archives, relating to the period of the Circassian Mamluk sultans, are presented with translation and commentary in the following articles by John Wansbrough: "A Mamluk letter of 877/1473", *BSOAS*, xxiv (2), 1961, 200–13; "A Mamluk ambassador to Venice in 913/1507", *BSOAS*, xxvi (3), 1963, 503–30; "Venice and Florence in the Mamluk commercial privileges", *BSOAS*, xxviii (3), 1965, 483–523; "A Mamlūk commercial treaty concluded with the republic of Florence 894/1489" in Stern (ed.), *Documents from Islamic chanceries*, 39–79.

Among the texts of documents transmitted by al-Qalqashandī in *Ṣubḥ al-aʿshā* are four truces with the Frankish states and one with the king of Aragon, while other pieces are given by Ibn ʿAbd al-Ẓāhir in *Tashrīf al-ayyām wa'l-ʿuṣūr fī sīrat al-Malik al-Manṣūr*, ed. Murād Kāmil [Cairo 1961], and Shāfiʿ b. ʿAlī in *al-Faḍl al-ma'thūr min sīrat al-sulṭān al-Malik al-Manṣūr* (Bodleian MS Marsh 424), their respective biographies of Kalavun. On these see the relevant articles by P. M. Holt, "Qalāwūn's treaty with Acre in 1283", *EHR*, XCI, CCCLXI, 1976, 802–12; "Qalawun's treaty with Genoa in 1290", *Der Islam*, 57 (1), 1980, 101–8; "The treaties of the early Mamluk sultans with the Frankish states", *BSOAS*, xliii (1), 1980, 67–76. Documents from the archives of a ruling family in Syria, the Buhturid amirs of the Gharb in Lebanon, are preserved in the family history written by one of its members, Ṣāliḥ b. Yaḥyā (d. 1436), and edited by Francis Hours and Kamal Salibi, *Tārīḫ Bayrūt*, Beirut 1969.

The text and French translation of some of these sources (either as extracts or in full) are printed in *Recueil des historiens des Croisades: Historiens orientaux*, 5 vols, Paris 1872–1906. This is a useful collection, although the standard of editing and translation is not consistent. A much smaller anthology of translated passages is Francesco Gabrieli,

Arab historians of the Crusades, London [1969]. The English edition of this work is itself a translation (by E. J. Costello) from the Italian.

There are various translations of the whole or part of individual works. Selections from Ibn al-Furāt, *Ta'rīkh al-duwal wa'l-mulūk*, have been published with translations by U. and M. C. Lyons, *Ayyubids, Mamlukes and Crusaders*, 2 vols, Cambridge 1971. The chronological range of the passages selected is from 641/1243–44 to 676/1277–8. A historical introduction and notes are provided by J. S. C. Riley-Smith. A large portion of Ibn al-Qalānisī, *Dhayl ta'rīkh Dimashq*, was translated by H. A. R. Gibb, *The Damascus Chronicle of the Crusades*, London 1932. This covers the years 490/1096–7 to 555/1160, and has a valuable introduction. An annotated translation of the early part of al-Maqrīzī, *Kitāb al-sulūk*, from 648/1250 to 708/1309 was made by the great French orientalist, E. Quatremère, *Histoire des sultans mamlouks de l'Égypte*, 2 vols (4 pts), Paris 1837–45. The appendices give the text and translation of a number of documents. The later volumes of Ibn Taghrībirdī, al-*Nujūm*, dealing with the Circassian Mamluk sultans, were translated by William Popper, *History of Egypt 1382–1469 A.D.*, Berkeley and Los Angeles 1954–60. The latter part of Ibn Iyās, *Badā'i' al-zuhūr*, which records contemporary events, has been translated by Gaston Wiet in three volumes: *Histoire des Mamlouks circassiens: Tome II* [sic] *(872–906)*, Cairo, 1945; *Journal d'un bourgeois du Caire*, [Paris, 1955]; *Journal d'un bourgeois du Caire: Tome II*, [Paris], 1960. *Al-Fatḥ al-Qussī* of 'Imād al-Dīn al-Iṣfahānī was translated by Henri Massé, *Conquête de la Syrie et de la Palestine par Saladin*, Paris 1972. Ibn 'Abd al-Ẓāhir's life of Baybars, *al-Rawḍ al-zāhir*, has been partially translated from a fragmentary MS by Syedah Fatima Sadeque, *Baybars I of Egypt*, Dacca 1956. The text and a French translation of Ibn al-Ṣuqā'ī, *Tālī Kitāb wafayāt al-a'yān*, Damascus 1974, were published by Jacqueline Sublet. The portions of al-Qalqashandī, *Ṣubḥ al-a'shā*, dealing with Syria were translated with a comprehensive introduction and notes by [Maurice] Gaudefroy-Demombynes, *La Syrie à l'époque des Mamelouks*, Paris 1923. An English translation of Ibn Jubayr, *Riḥla*, was made by R. Broadhurst, *The travels of Ibn Jubayr*, London 1952; and a French translation by Maurice Gaudefroy-Demombynes as Ibn Jobair, *Voyages*, 4 vols, Paris 1949–65. The earlier part of Ibn Baṭṭūṭa, *Tuḥfat al-nuẓẓār*, describing his travels in (among other lands) Egypt and the countries of the eastern Mediterranean, was translated by H. A. R. Gibb, *The travels of Ibn Battuta A.D. 1325–1354*, I, II, Cambridge, 1958, 1962. A translation of Usāma b. Munqidh, *Kitāb al-i'tibār*, was published by Philip K. Hitti, *An Arab-Syrian gentleman and warrior in the period of the Crusades*, New York 1929. The autobiography of Ismā'īl Abu'l-Fidā' in the last part of his *al-*

Mukhtaṣar has been translated by P. M. Holt, *The memoirs of a Syrian prince*, Wiesbaden 1983.

An appraisal of the sources for this period is given in the following articles in Bernard Lewis and P. M. Holt (eds) *Historians of the Middle East*, London 1962: Claude Cahen, "The historiography of the Seljukid period"; M. Hilmy M. Ahmad, "Some notes on Arabic historiography during the Zengid and Ayyubid periods (521/1127–648/1250)"; Francesco Gabrieli, "The Arabic historiography of the Crusades"; Sami Dahan, "The origin and development of the local histories of Syria". The sources for the early Mamluk sultanate have been investigated by Ulrich Haarmann, *Quellenstudien zur frühen Mamlukenzeit*, Freiburg im Breisgau 1970; and Donald Presgrave Little, *An introduction to Mamlūk historiography*, Wiesbaden 1970. Royal biographies are discussed in three articles, by P. M. Holt, "The virtuous ruler in thirteenth-century Mamluk royal biographies", *Nottingham Medieval Studies*, xxiv, 1980, 27–35; "Saladin and his admirers: a biographical reassessment", *BSOAS*, xlvi (2), 1983, 235–9; and "Three biographies of al-Ẓāhir Baybars", in D. O. Morgan (ed.), *Medieval historical writing in the Christian and Islamic worlds*, London 1982. The same volume has also an article on Ibn al-Athīr by D. S. Richards, "Ibn al-Athīr and the later part of the *Kāmil*: a study of aims and methods".

MODERN WORKS

Works of reference

The encyclopaedia of Islam, 1st edn, Leiden 1918–38; 2nd edn, 1960– (in progress), should be consulted in connection with the principal persons, places, institutions and other topics of this period. Among the longer articles in the second edition, two by Claude Cahen may be noted: "AYYŪBIDS" and "CRUSADES".

The two principal bibliographical guides to the period are Claude Cahen (reviser), *Jean Sauvaget's Introduction to the history of the Muslim East*, Berkeley and Los Angles 1965 (earlier editions in French, *Introduction à l'histoire de l'Orient musulman: éléments de bibliographie*, Paris 1943, 1961); and for articles in periodicals and Festschriften, J. D. Pearson, *Index islamicus 1906–1955*, Cambridge [1958], with its numerous *Supplements* from 1962 onwards.

The choice of historical atlases is very limited. Ranging very widely both geographically and chronologically is William C. Brice (ed.), *An historical atlas of Islam*, Leiden 1981. There are useful sketch-maps and related materials in William Popper, *Egypt and Syria under the Circassian sultans 1382–1468 A.D. Systematic notes to Ibn Taghrī Birdī's Chronicles of Egypt*, Berkeley and Los Angeles 1955 (the first of two volumes so entitled). C. F. Beckingham (introd.), *Atlas of the Arab world and the Middle East*, London 1960, although concerned with present-day political geography, is nevertheless useful for earlier periods.

General historical works

There are relevant chapters in *The Cambridge history of Islam*, 2 vols, Cambridge, 1970; *The Cambridge history of Iran*, v, Cambridge 1968; and *The Cambridge medieval history*, IV, pt 1, Cambridge 1966. Kenneth M. Setton (gen. ed.), *A history of the Crusades*, I, II, 2nd edn, Madison 1969, contains valuable chapters by H. A. R. Gibb, "The caliphate and the Arab states", "Zengi and the fall of Edessa", "The career of Nūr-ad-Dīn", "The rise of Saladin 1169–1189", "The Aiyūbids"; Bernard Lewis, "The Ismā'īlites and the Assassins"; Claude Cahen, "The Turkish invasion: the Selchükids", "The Turks in Iran and Anatolia before the Mongol invasions", "The Mongols and the Near East"; and Mustafa M. Ziada, "The Mamluk sultans to 1293". General histories of Egypt covering this period are Stanley Lane-Poole, *A history of Egypt in the Middle Ages*, London 1901; and Gaston Wiet, *L'Égypte arabe*, Paris 1937 (vol. IV in G. Hanotaux (ed.), *Histoire de la nation égyptienne*). Economic history is dealt with in two works of wider scope, W. Heyd, *Histoire du commerce du Levant au moyen-âge*, 2 vols, Leipzig 1885–6; and E. Ashtor, *A social and economic history of the Near East in the Middle Ages*, London 1976; to which may be added a useful collection of articles by Ashtor, *The medieval Near East: social and economic history*, London 1978. A very full study of judicial institutions is provided by Émile Tyan, *Histoire de l'organisation judiciaire en pays d'Islam*, Leiden 1960. The history and organization of Sufism are surveyed in J. Spencer Trimingham, *The Sufi orders in Islam*, Oxford 1971.

The Crusades

As well as the Setton *History of the Crusades* mentioned in the previous section, two further histories of the Crusading period, based mainly on European sources, are Hans Eberhard Mayer, *The Crusades* (tr. John Gillingham), Oxford 1972; and Steven Runciman, *A history of the Crusades*, 3 vols, Cambridge 1951–4. W. E. Stevenson, *The Crusaders in the East*, Cambridge 1907, draws largely on the Arabic sources. A very wide range of materials is exploited by Claude Cahen, *La Syrie du nord à l'époque des croisades et la principauté franque d'Antioche*, Paris 1940; and several of the same author's articles on the Latin East and the Turks are reprinted in his *Turcobyzantina et Oriens christianus*, London 1974. An authoritative account of the Latin kingdom is given by J. Prawer, *Histoire du royaume latin de Jérusalem*. 2 vols, 2nd edn, Paris 1975. The same historian's *The Latin kingdom of Jerusalem*, London [1972], examines the political, military and social structure and institutions of the kingdom. Particular attention is given to the government and constitution of the kingdom by Jonathan Riley-Smith, *The feudal nobility and the kingdom of Jerusalem 1174–1277* [London 1973]. R. C. Smail, *Crusading warfare (1097–1193)* Cambridge 1956, examines the structure and tactics of the Christian and Muslim armies. The Muslim response to the Crusades is the subject of a detailed investigation by Emmanuel Sivan, *L'Islam et la croisade*, Paris 1968.

Zangids and Ayyubids

The Zangid period is the subject of a detailed study by Nikita Elisséeff, *Nūr ad-Dīn: un grand prince musulman de Syrie au temps des croisades (511–569 AH./1118–1174)*, 3 vols, Damascus 1967.

The personality and career of Saladin have occupied biographers to the almost total exclusion of the other Ayyubids. The detailed account of his career given by Stanley Lane-Poole, *Saladin and the fall of the kingdom of Jerusalem*, London 1898, is still useful. Of later biographers, Hamilton [A. R.] Gibb, *The life of Saladin*, Oxford 1973, presents a favourable interpretation. This book, published posthumously, expands the chapter (noted above) in Setton, *A history of the Crusades*. Two important articles, "The armies of Saladin" and "The achievement of Saladin", are reprinted in Hamilton A. R. Gibb, *Studies on the civilization of Islam*, Boston [Mass. 1962]. An unfavourable view is given by Andrew S. Ehrenkreutz, *Saladin*, Albany 1972; while a full and judicious study is offered by Malcolm Cameron Lyons and D. E. P. Jackson, *Saladin: the politics of the Holy War*, Cambridge [1982]. The final stage of Saladin's career is the subject of a monograph which utilizes European, Byzantine and Arabic source-materials: Hannes Möhring, *Saladin und der Dritte Kreuzzug*, Wiesbaden 1980.

Two other Ayyubids have been the subject of monographs. Saladin's brother is studied in Franz-Josef Dahlmanns, *Al-Malik al-ʿĀdil. Ägypten und der Vordere Orient in den Jahren 589/1193 bis 615/1218* [Giessen] 1975; and al-ʿĀdil's son in Hans L. Gottschalk, *Al-Malik al-Kāmil von Egypten und seine Zeit*, Wiesbaden 1958.

An excellent history of Ayyubid Syria (which also to some extent compensates for the lack of an equivalent work on Egypt) is R. Stephen Humphreys, *From Saladin to the Mongols: the Ayyubids of Damascus, 1193–1260*, Albany 1977. Humphreys is also the author of an important article which traces continuity and development between the Ayyubid and Mamluk sultanates, "The emergence of the Mamluk army", *Studia Islamica*, xlv, 1977, 67–99; xlvi, 1977, 147–82. The history of fiscal institutions in the Ayyubid and Mamluk periods is investigated by Hassanein Rabie, *The financial system of Egypt A. H. 564–741/A.D. 1169–1341*, London 1972. Also spanning both periods (and covering the whole history of the movement) is Bernard Lewis, *The Assassins: a radical sect in Islam*, London 1967. Some articles relevant to this subject are reprinted in his *Studies in classical and Ottoman Islam (7th–16th centuries)*, London 1976.

The Mamluk sultanate

There is no good general history. W. Muir, *The Mameluke or slave dynasty of Egypt*, London 1896, is outdated and superficial. Problems concerning Shajar al-Durr and the transition from the Ayyubid to the Mamluk sultanate are discussed by Götz Schregle, *Die Sultanin von Ägypten*, Wiesbaden 1961. The data for the career of al-Ẓāhir Baybars, largely drawn from Ibn ʿAbd al-Ẓāhir, are succinctly presented by Abdul-Aziz Khowaiter, *Baibars the First: his endeavours and achievements*, London 1978. A detailed and systematic study by Aḥmad A. Darrag, *L'Égypte sous le règne de Barsbay: 825–841/1422–1438*, Damascus 1961, is a valuable contribution to the history of the Circassian Mamluk sultanate. The importance of Upper Egypt in this period is brought out in a monograph by Jean-Claude Carcin, *Un centre musulman de la Haute-Égypte médiévale: Qūṣ*, Cairo [1976]. Studies of institutions are comparatively abundant. The pioneer work of A. N. Poliak, *Feudalism in Egypt, Syria, Palestine, and the Lebanon, 1250–1900*, London 1939, should be used with caution. The articles of David Ayalon, many assembled in his two collections, *Studies on the Mamlūks of Egypt (1250–1517)*, London 1977; and *The Mamlūk military society*, London 1979, are models of meticulous scholarship. A factor in the decline of the Mamluk sultanate is examined in his book, *Gunpowder and firearms in the Mamluk kingdom: a challenge to a mediaeval society*, London 1956. Ira Marvin Lapidus, *Muslim cities in the later Middle Ages*, Cambridge, Mass. 1967, is a study of urban society history and institutions (particularly in Syria) in the Mamluk period. Two articles by P. M. Holt deal with the central government: "The position and power of the Mamluk sultan", *BSOAS*, xxxviii (2),

1975, 237–49; and "The structure of government in the Mamluk sultanate", in P. M. Holt (ed.), *The eastern Mediterranean lands in the period of the Crusades*, Warminster [1977].

Nubia

A full treatment of the history of Christian Nubia is given by Ugo Monneret de Villard, *Storia della Nubia cristiana*, Rome 1938. For a summary account, see J. Spencer Trimingham, *Islam in the Sudan*, London 1949. A more recent study is by Giovanni Vantini, *Christianity in the Sudan* [Bologna] 1981. The Arab migration into Nubia and its historical background are examined by Yūsuf Faḍl Ḥasan, *The Arabs and the Sudan*, Edinburgh [1967].

Anatolia

The standard work in English on the Seljukids in Anatolia is Claude Cahen, *Pre-Ottoman Turkey*, London [1968], which has a full bibliography. Important articles by the same author are reprinted in his *Turcobyzantina et Oriens christianus*, London 1974. The process of turcification is investigated in detail by Speros Vryonis, *The decline of medieval Hellenism in Asia Minor and the process of islamization from the eleventh through the fifteenth century*, Berkeley 1971.

NOTES

1. Ulrich Haarmann, *Quellenstudien zur frühen Mamlukenzeit*, Freiburg im Breisgau 1970, 159–83.
2. Cf. P. M. Holt, "Three biographies of al-Ẓāhir Baybars", in D. O. Morgan, *Medieval historical writing in the Christian and Islamic worlds*, London 1982, at p. 24 and n. 16.

Glossary

Most of the terms in the following glossary are Arabic, a few Turkish and Persian.

It should be noted that the terms are defined according to their meaning in the Near East during the period covered by this volume. In other parts of the Islamic world, and at other times, some of them were used in other senses.

Aḥdāth The urban militia of some Syrian towns.
Ajlāb, julbān The *mamlūks* bought, trained and emancipated by a reigning sultan in the Circassian Mamluk period.
Ajnād Territorial cavalry forming reserve troops.
Amīr In general a military commander; more specifically a military office-holder, e.g. *a. silāḥ* (sword-bearer), *a. ākhūr* (constable). *A. al-ḥājj*, the commander of a Pilgrimage caravan to Mecca. *A. al-ʿarab*, an official title denoting paramountcy over nomadic Arab tribes.
Arbāb al-aqlām "Men of the Pens"; civilian administrative officials, civil servants.
Arbāb al-suyūf "Men of the Swords"; military officers, some holding court or administrative offices.
ʿAskar The guard (in effect the standing army) of a ruler. *ʿAskarī*, a member of an *ʿaskar*.
Atabeg Originally the guardian of a Seljukid prince and the regent of his appanage; subsequently the ruler of a successor-state to the Seljukids. In Egypt at the beginning of the Mamluk period *atābak al-ʿasākir* meant a commander-in-chief deputizing for a sultan who could not command in person, but by the late eighth/fourteenth century it was merely a title held by the senior amir (*al-amīr al-kabīr*).
Awlād al-nās "The sons of the People"; the descendants of Mamluks.
Baqṭ An arrangement for barter-trade between Muslim Egypt and

Christian Nubia, represented in Arabic sources as tribute imposed by treaty.

Barīd The system of royal post-horses (also carrier-pigeons) organized to link the provinces with the capital. *Ṣāḥib al-barīd*, the postmaster-general, i.e. chief intelligence officer.

Bay'a The oath of allegiance performed to the caliph or (sometimes) the sultan.

Bayt al-māl "House of wealth"; the original treasury of Islamic states.

Beylik A Turkish principality in Anatolia.

Bid'a An innovation in religion, equivalent to heresy.

Caliph (Ar. *khalīfa*) The member of the 'Abbasid (or alternatively the Fatimid) family recognized by his followers as the legitimate head of the universal Muslim community.

Dā'ī al-du'āt The Fatimid chief missionary.

Dār al-'adl "House of justice"; an edifice for the sessions of a ruler for the hearing of complaints and petitions (see *Maẓālim*).

Dār al-ḥarb "House of war"; in Islamic international law, all territories not under Muslim jurisdiction.

Dār al-islām "House of Islam"; in Islamic international law, all Muslim territories.

Dawādār "The bearer of the inkwell"; under the Mamluk sultanate a great officer who formed the channel of communication between the sultan and the royal chancery.

Dhimmī A non-Muslim belonging to one of the monotheistic communities (here Christians, Jews and Samaritans) who had a recognized and tolerated but subordinate status in an Islamic polity.

Dīwān A department of government e.g. *d. al-inshā'* (the chancery), *d. al-jaysh* (the army department).

Faqīh (pl., fuqahā') An Islamic jurist.

Futuwwa Originally a young men's organization; reformed by the Caliph al-Nāṣir, and subsequently revived by al-Ẓāhir Baybars as a quasi-order of chivalry.

Gazi (Ar. *ghāzī*) A fighter in the Holy War, especially a warrior on the Turkish–Byzantine frontier.

Ḥājib Chamberlain; a great officer with military functions.

Ḥajj The annual Pilgrimage to Mecca.

Ḥalqa Originally the bodyguard of an Ayyubid ruler; in the Mamluk period an obsolescent military unit recruited increasingly among *awlād al-nās* (q.v.).

Ḥilf A covenant of loyalty made with a new Mamluk sultan by his supporters.

Hudna A treaty between a Muslim and a non-Muslim power; in Islamic international law, technically a truce for a limited and specified period.
Ilkhan The ruler of the Mongol kingdom in Persia and Iraq.
Imām (a) A leader in communal prayer; (b) the divinely guided legitimate head of the universal Muslim community according to Shīʿī doctrine, i.e. ʿAlī b. Abī Ṭālib and his descendants.
Iqṭāʿ, *i. al-istighlāl* Sometimes misleadingly translated "fief"; an assignment of (usually landed) revenue, sometimes accompanied by a grant of administrative functions.
Jāmakiyya The salary of a Mamluk trooper.
Jāmiʿ A congregational mosque for the Friday prayer.
Jihād In Islamic law, the Holy War against unbelievers.
Jizya In Islamic law, the poll-tax payable by a *dhimmī* (q.v.).
Kātib (pl., *kuttāb*) A clerk, e.g. *k. al-sirr* (the secretary of the Mamluk sultan), *k. al-darj* (clerk of the roll), *k. al-dast* (clerk of the bench).
Khānaqāh A convent for Ṣūfis (q.v.). Cf. *Ribāṭ*.
Khāṣṣ The fisc; the treasury of the Mamluk sultan which superseded *Bayt al-māl* (q.v.) as the principal state treasury.
Khāṣṣakiyya The Mamluk sultan's immediate personal entourage, in effect the Mamluks of the Privy Chamber.
Khushdāsh A Mamluk's comrade, i.e. a fellow-member of a military household. *Khushdāshiyya* serves both as the collective and to signify the loyalty among Mamluk comrades.
Khuṭba The Friday sermon, pronounced by the *khaṭīb*, which includes a prayer. Mention of the ruler's name in this prayer was a prerogative of Islamic sovereignty.
Kiswa The veil or outer covering of the Kaʿba.
Madhhab Often translated "rite" or "school of law". One of the four systems of Islamic law regarded as equally orthodox by the Sunnīs. They are named after their founders as respectively the Shāfiʿī, Ḥanafī, Mālikī and Ḥanbalī *madhhab*.
Madrasa A school of higher Islamic learning.
Maḥmil An empty litter sent annually with the Pilgrimage caravan from Egypt in token of sovereignty.
Malik A ruling member of the Seljukid house subordinate to the sultan.
Mamlūk A slave imported into Islamic territory, usually from Central Asia or the Black Sea region, for military purposes.
Maẓālim Literally "oppressions"; a jurisdiction supplementary to that of the *qāḍī* (q.v.), exercised by Muslim rulers to deal with the grievances and petitions of their subjects.

Miḥrāb The niche in a mosque indicating the direction of Mecca (*qibla*).

Muḥtasib An official whose jurisdiction (*ḥisba*) was to maintain the proprieties according to Islamic law, and to act as a market-inspector. The latter function was discharged in the Latin kingdom by an official known as the *mathesep*.

Munāṣafāt Condominia; districts on the frontiers of the Frankish states where the revenues and some administrative functions were shared with the neighbouring Muslim ruler.

Muqṭaʿ The assignee of an *iqṭāʿ* (q.v.).

Nā'ib Literally "deputy" [of the sultan]; a Mamluk governor. *N. al-salṭana bi-Miṣr*, the sultan's vicegerent in Egypt.

Nāẓir The supervisor or controller of a government department, e.g. *n. al-jaysh* (supervisor of the army department).

Qāḍī An Islamic judge; *q. al-quḍāt*, the chief judge.

Qarāniṣ, *qarāniṣa* The veteran Mamluks of previous sultans in the Circassian Mamluk period. Cf. *Ajlāb*.

Quriltai The Mongol tribal assembly.

Ra'īs (pl., *ru'asā'*) Sometimes misleadingly translated "mayor"; a civilian urban leader.

Rawk A cadastral survey (especially of Egypt) followed by a redistribution of *iqṭāʿs* (q.v.).

Ribāṭ A convent for Ṣūfīs (q.v.). Cf. *Khānaqāh*.

Ṣāḥib The title of some heads of government departments, e.g. *ṣāḥib al-shurṭa* (chief of police).

Shaḥna Often given as *shiḥna*; a military governor.

Sharīʿa The Holy Law of Islam.

Sharīf An honorific given to descendants of the Prophet; especially applied as a title to the ruler of Mecca.

Shīʿa, Shīʿīs Muslims who do not recognize the legitimacy of the historical caliphate but regard ʿAlī b. Abī Ṭālib and his descendants as the divinely guided *imāms* and heads of the Islamic community. The majority of the Shīʿa recognize a succession of twelve *imāms*, the Ismāʿīlīs of seven.

Shurṭa The police force.

Ṣūfīs Islamic mystics.

Sultan (Ar. *sulṭān*, originally meaning "power") A title of Seljukid and subsequent rulers, theoretically delegates of the ʿAbbasid caliph. The title was also held by the later Fatimid *wazīrs* (q.v.).

Sunnīs Muslims who recognize the historical caliphate as legitimate.

Ṭarīqa An order of Ṣūfīs following the teaching and ritual of a given mystical guide.

'Ulamā' (sing., *'ālim*) Scholars in the Islamic religious sciences.
Umma The universal Islamic community.
Ustādār (from *ustādh al-dār*, "master of the household") The high steward at the court of the Mamluk sultan. The office acquired financial functions.
Ustādh The master of a *mamlūk*; the head of a military household.
Waqf An endowment (usually of land) for religious or charitable purposes.
Wazīr (Turkish, *vezīr*) Originally an omnicompetent minister. During the Mamluk sultanate the position lost its importance.

Genealogical Tables

1 The Royal House of Jerusalem to 1192

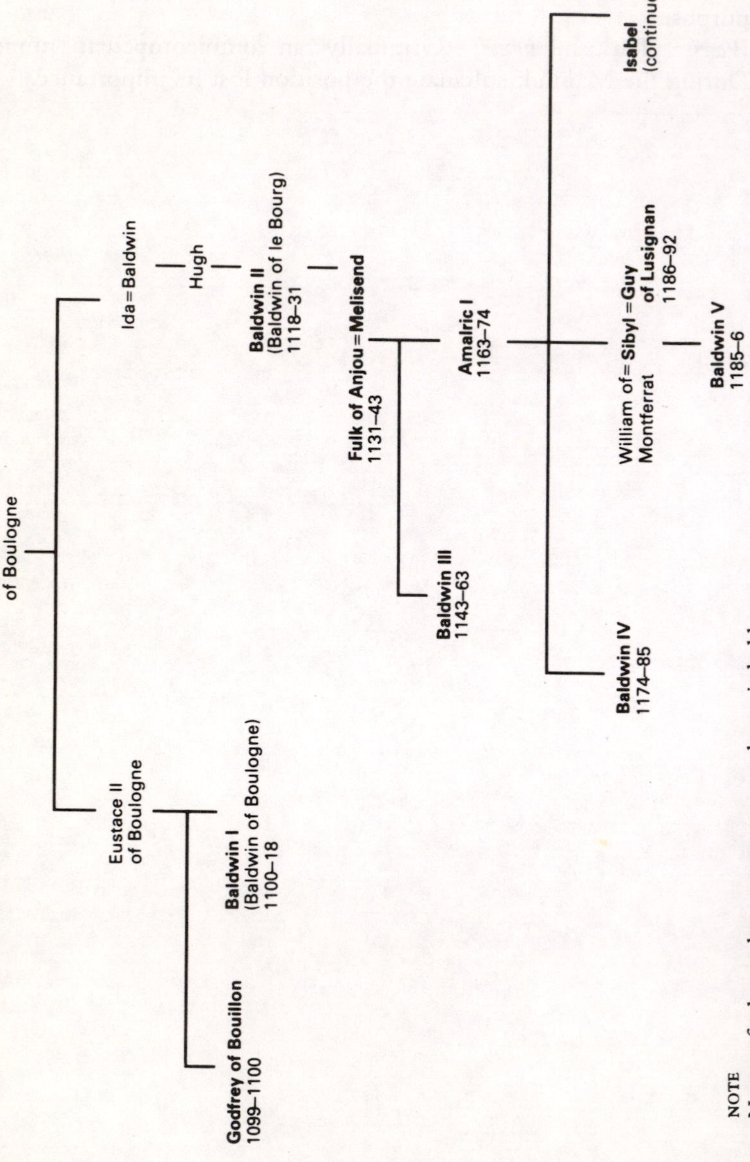

NOTE
Names of rulers and queens regnant are shown in bold type.

2 The Royal House of Jerusalem, 1192–1291

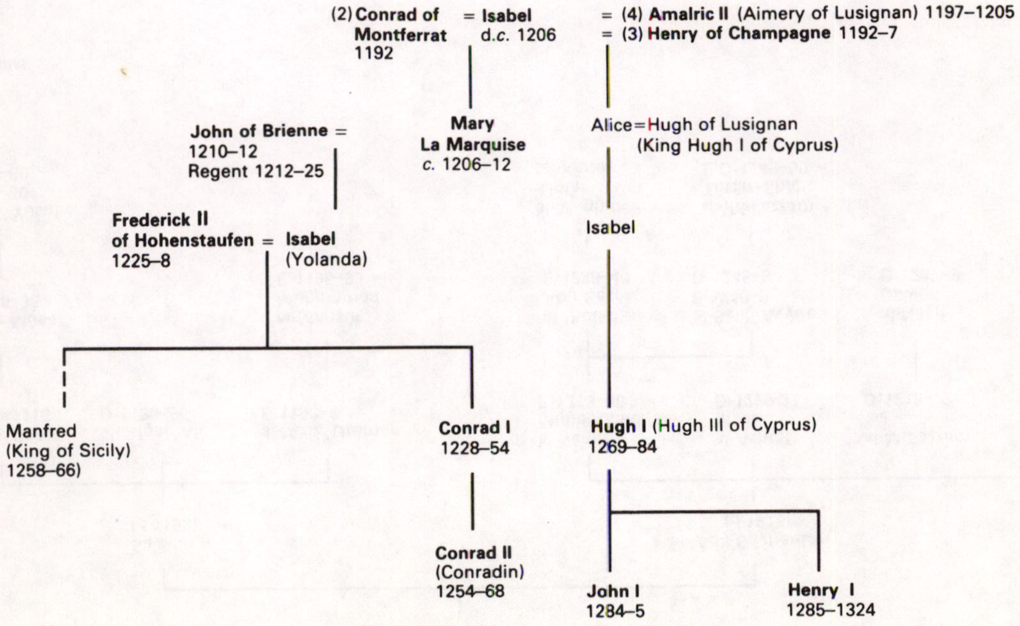

NOTE
Names of rulers and queens regnant are shown in bold type.

3 The Ayyubids of Egypt, Damascus and Aleppo

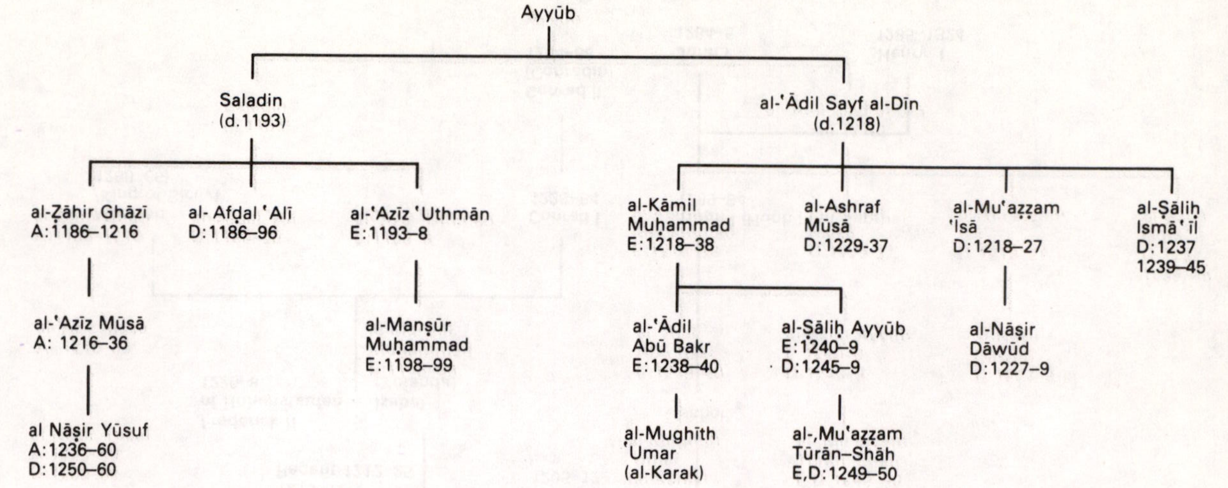

Key:
A:Aleppo
D:Damascus
E:Egypt

4 Al-Ṣāliḥ Ayyūb and the Early Mamluk Sultans

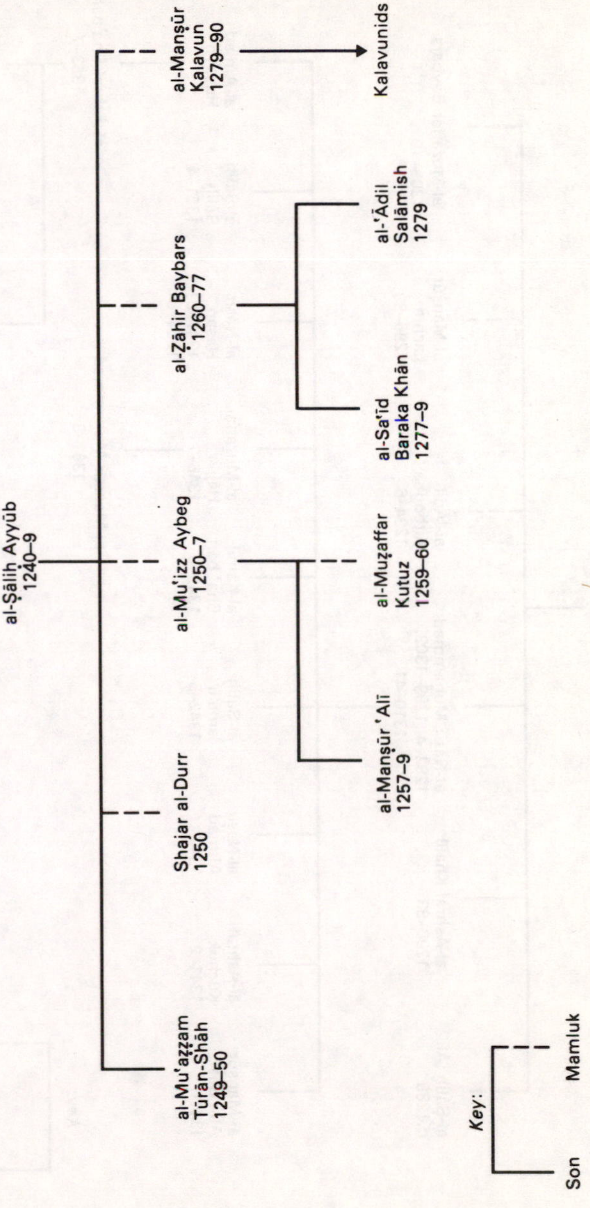

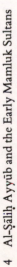

5 The House of Kalavun

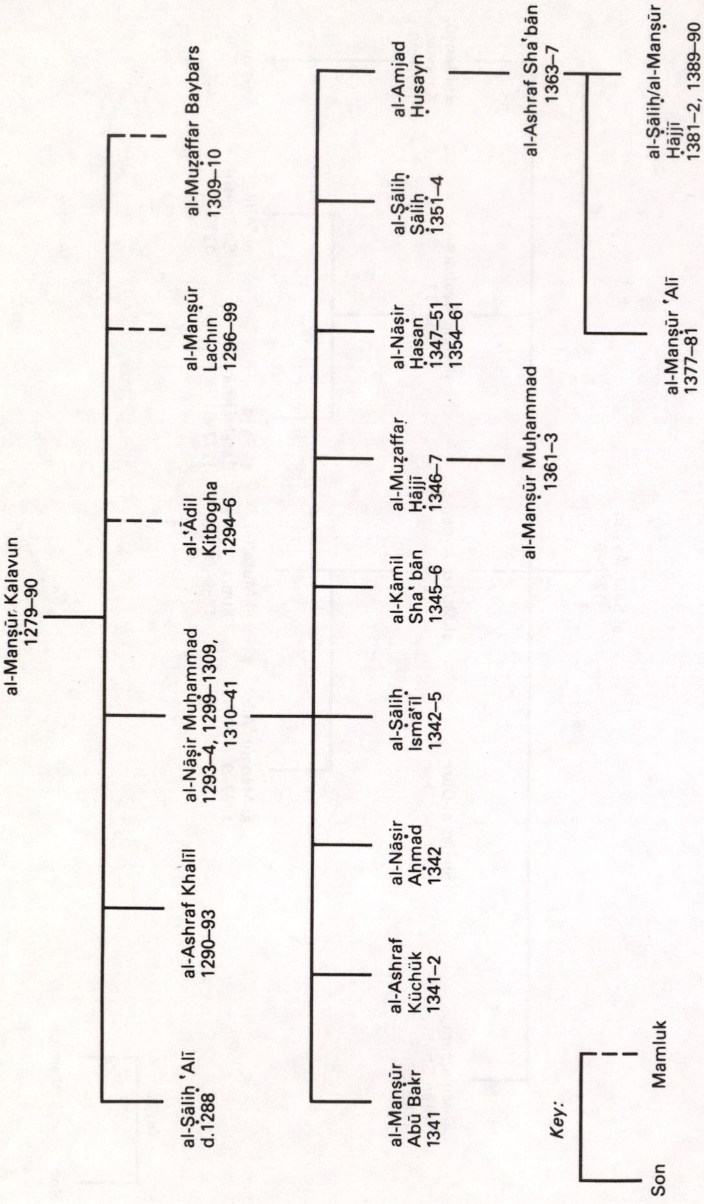

6 The Circassian Mamluk Sultans

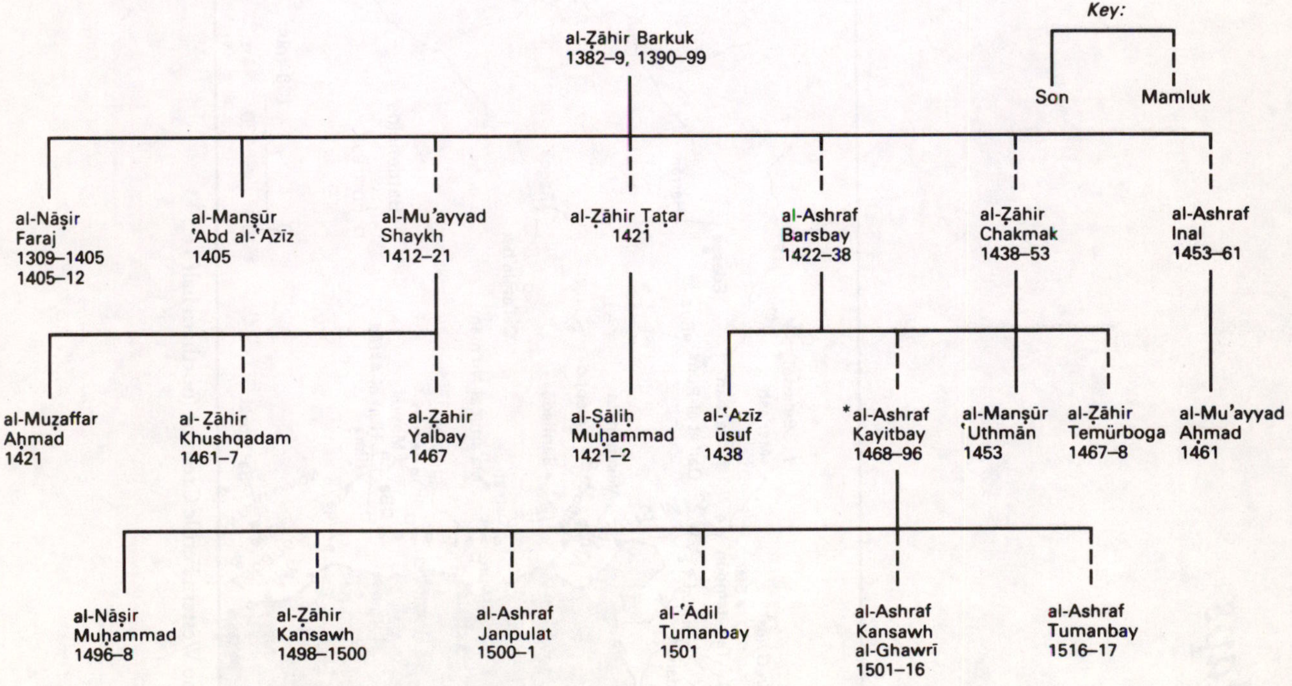

*Kayitbay was originally in the household of Barsbay, later in that of Chakmak.

Maps

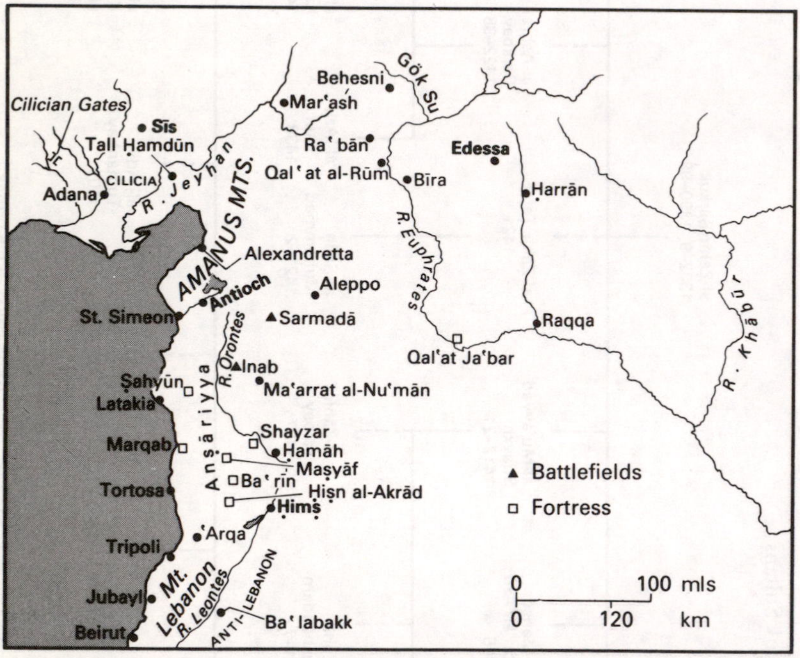

1 The Western Fertile Crescent (northern half)

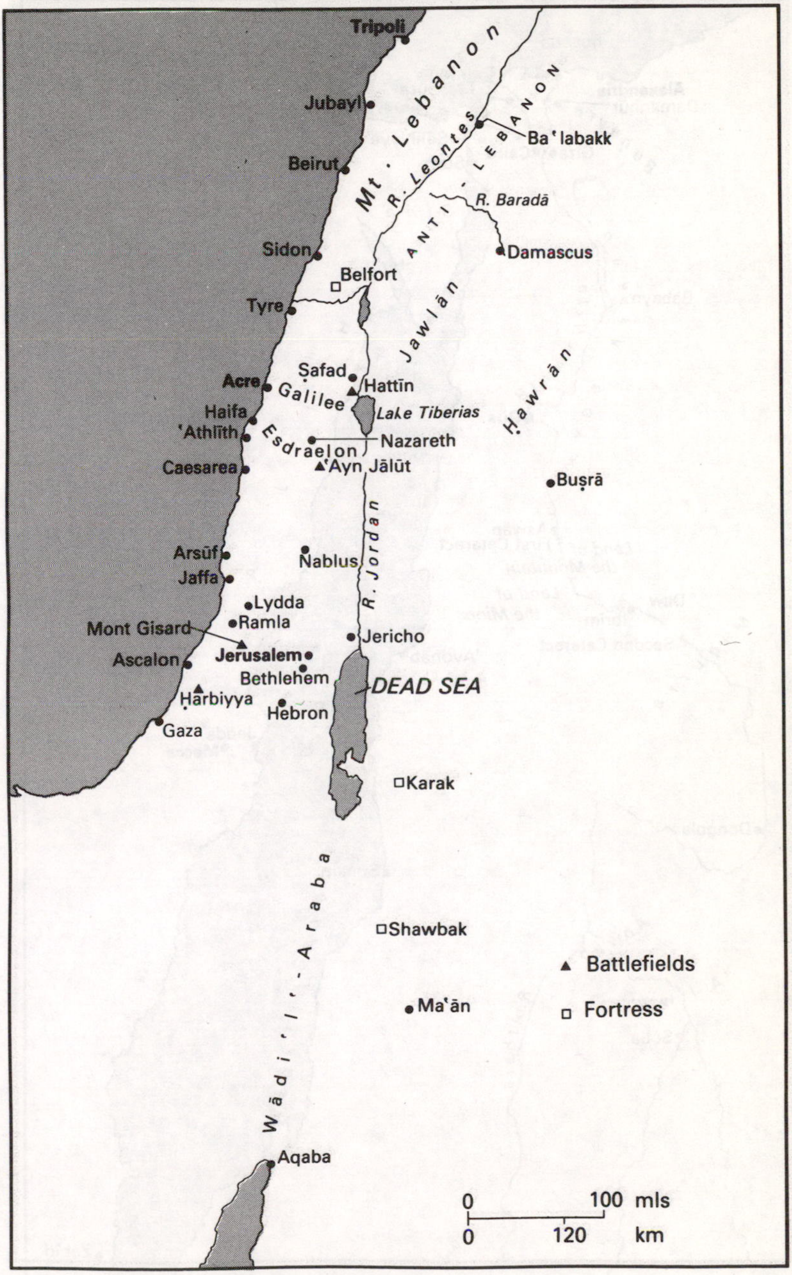

2 The Western Fertile Crescent (southern half)

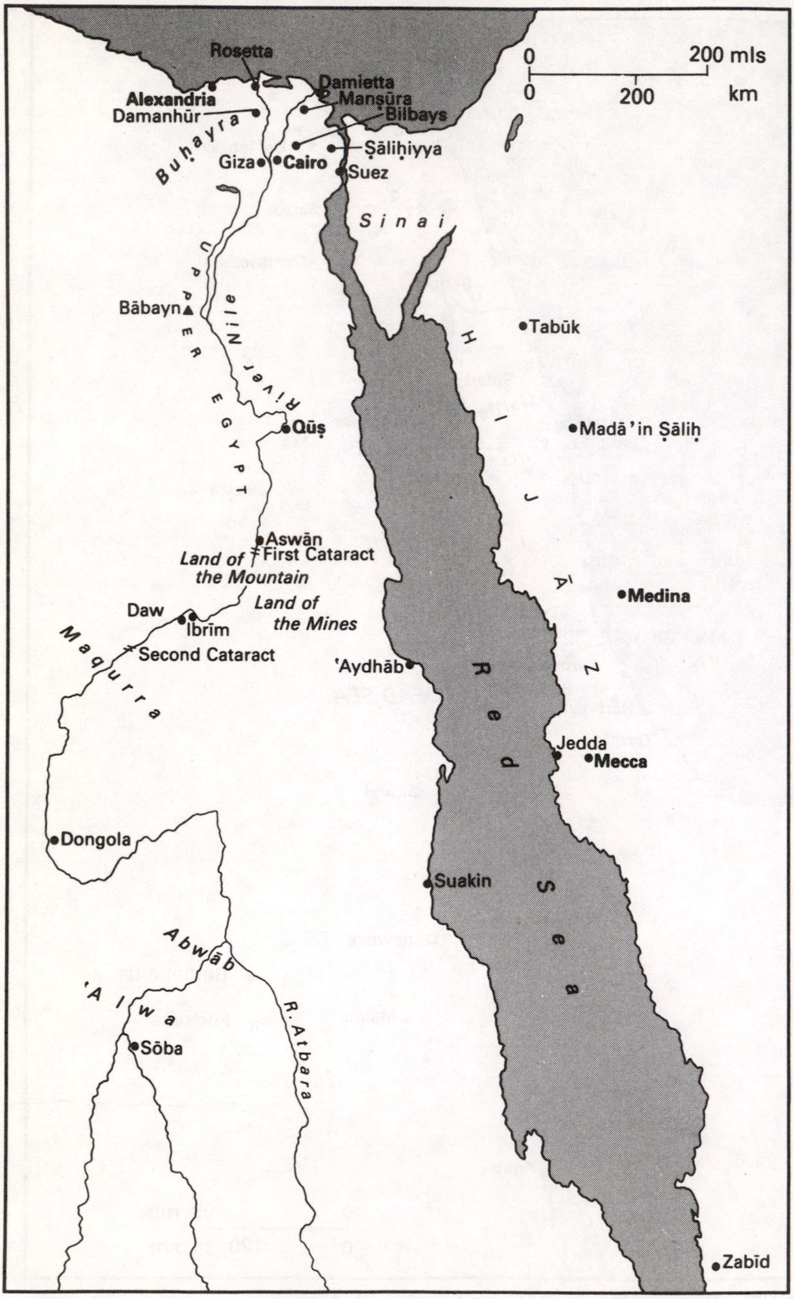

3 The Nile Valley and Red Sea

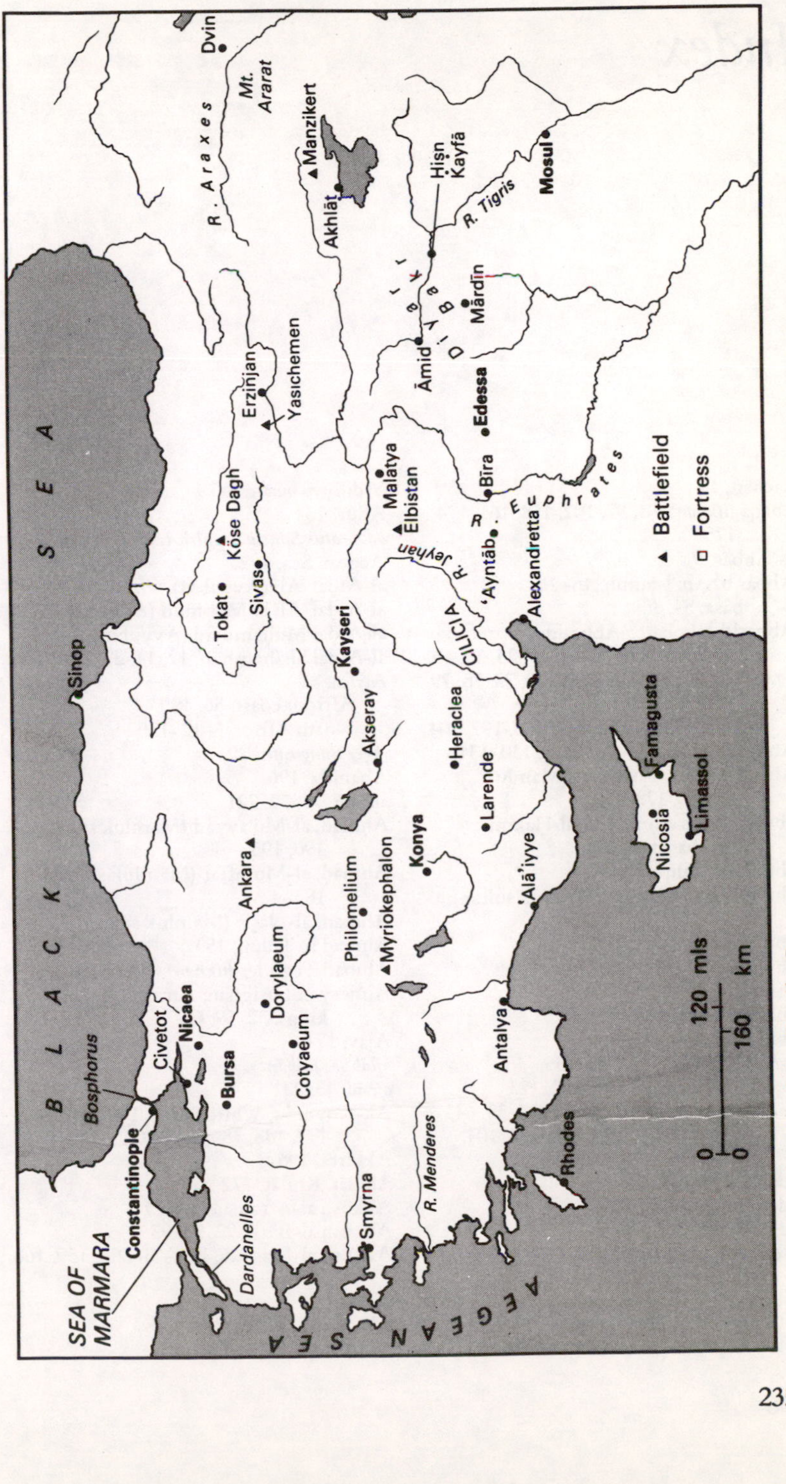

4 Anatolia and the Northern Fertile Crescent

Index